**BLACK LEGACY PRESS™**
WWW.BLACKLEGACYPRESS.ORG

# SLAVE NARRATIVES

VOLUME IV
GEORGIA NARRATIVES
PART 1

By
United States.
Work Projects Administration

Copyright © 2024 by BLACKLEGACYPRESS.ORG

All rights reserved. No part of this publication may be reproduced or transmitted in any form or by any means electronic or mechanical, including information storage and retrieval systems without permission in writing from the publisher, except for student research using the appropriate citations.

ISBN: 978-1-63652-213-5

# SLAVE NARRATIVES

A Folk History of Slavery in the United States.
From Interviews with Former Slaves

**UNITED STATES.
WORK PROJECTS ADMINISTRATION**

TYPEWRITTEN RECORDS PREPARED BY
THE FEDERAL WRITERS' PROJECT
1936-1938
ASSEMBLED BY
THE LIBRARY OF CONGRESS PROJECT
WORK PROJECTS ADMINISTRATION
FOR THE DISTRICT OF COLUMBIA
SPONSORED BY THE LIBRARY OF
CONGRESS

WASHINGTON 1941

# VOLUME IV
## GEORGIA NARRATIVES
## PART 1

Prepared by
The Federal Writers' Project of
The Works Progress Administration
For the State of Georgia

# CONTENTS

RACHEL ADAMS ... 1

WASHINGTON ALLEN ... 9

ALLEN REV. W.B ... 11

JACK ATKINSON ... 17

HANNAH AUSTIN ... 19

CELESTIA AVERY ... 23

MRS. CELESTIA AVERY ... 31

MRS. EMMALINE HEARD ... 37

GEORGIA BAKER ... 45

ALICE BATTLE ... 63

JASPER BATTLE ... 65

ARRIE BINNS ... 77

HENRY BLAND ... 85

RIAS BODY ... 93

JAMES BOLTON ... 97

ALEC BOSTWICK ... 111

NANCY BOUDRY ... 119

ALICE BRADLEY ... 125

KIZZIE COLQUITT ... 131

| | |
|---|---:|
| **DELLA BRISCOE** | 133 |
| **GEORGE BROOKS** | 141 |
| **EASTER BROWN** | 143 |
| **JULIA BROWN** | 149 |
| **JULIA BUNCH** | 163 |
| **MARSHAL BUTLER** | 169 |
| **MRS. SARAH BYRD** | 177 |
| **MRS. MARIAH CALLAWAY** | 183 |
| **SUSAN CASTLE** | 191 |
| **ELLEN CLAIBOURN** | 199 |
| **BERRY CLAY** | 205 |
| **PIERCE CODY** | 211 |
| **WILLIS COFER** | 219 |
| **MARY COLBERT** | 229 |
| **JOHN COLE** | 241 |
| **JULIA COLE** | 247 |
| **MARTHA COLQUITT** | 253 |
| **MINNIE DAVIS** | 267 |
| **MOSE DAVIS** | 279 |
| **IKE DERRICOTTE** | 287 |
| **BENNY DILLARD** | 299 |
| **GEORGE EASON** | 311 |

| | |
|---|---|
| **CALLIE ELDER** | 319 |
| **MARTHA EVERETTE** | 329 |
| **LEWIS FAVOR** | 331 |
| **MARY FERGUSON** | 339 |
| **CARRIE NANCY FRYER** | 345 |
| **ANDERSON FURR** | 359 |

PLANTATION LIFE

RACHEL ADAMS, Age 78
300 Odd Street
Athens, Georgia

Written by:
Sadie B. Hornsby [HW: (White)]
Athens

Edited by:
Sarah H. Hall
Athens

and
John N. Booth
District Supervisor
Federal Writers' Project
Residencies 6 & 7
Augusta, Georgia

# RACHEL ADAMS

Rachel Adams' two-room, frame house is perched on the side of a steep hill where peach trees and bamboo form dense shade. Stalks of corn at the rear of the dwelling reach almost to the roof ridge and a portion of the front yard is enclosed for a chicken yard. Stepping gingerly around the amazing number of nondescript articles scattered about the small veranda, the visitor rapped several times on the front door, but received no response. A neighbor said the old woman might be found at her son's store, but she was finally located at the home of a daughter.

Rachel came to the front door with a sandwich of hoecake and cheese in one hand and a glass of water in the other. "Dis here's Rachel Adams," she declared. "Have a seat on de porch." Rachel is tall, thin, very black, and wears glasses. Her faded pink outing wrapper was partly covered by an apron made of a heavy meal sack. Tennis shoes, worn without hose, and a man's black hat completed her outfit.

Rachel began her story by saying: "Miss, dats been sich a long time back dat I has most forgot how things went. Anyhow I was borned in Putman County 'bout two miles from Eatonton, Georgia. My Ma and Pa was 'Melia and Iaaac Little and, far as I knows, dey was borned and bred in dat same county. Pa, he was sold away from Ma when I was still a baby. Ma's job was to weave all de cloth for de white folks. I have wore many a dress made out of de homespun what she wove. Dere was 17 of us chillun, and I can't 'member de names of but two of 'em now—dey was John and Sarah. John was Ma's onliest son; all de rest of de other 16 of us was gals.

"Us lived in mud-daubed log cabins what had old stack chimblies made out of sticks and mud. Our old home-made beds didn't have no slats or metal springs neither. Dey used stout cords for springs. De cloth what dey made the ticks of dem old hay mattresses and pillows out of was so coarse dat it scratched us little chillun most to death, it seemed lak to us dem days. I kin still feel dem old hay mattresses under me now. Evvy time I moved at night it sounded lak de wind blowin' through dem peach trees and bamboos 'round de front of de house whar I lives now.

"Grandma Anna was 115 years old when she died. She

had done wore herself out in slavery time. Grandpa, he was sold off somewhar. Both of 'em was field hands.

"Potlicker and cornbread was fed to us chillun, out of big old wooden bowls. Two or three chillun et out of de same bowl. Grown folks had meat, greens, syrup, cornbread, 'taters and de lak. 'Possums! I should say so. Dey cotch plenty of 'em and atter dey was kilt ma would scald 'em and rub 'em in hot ashes and dat clean't 'em jus' as pretty and white. OO-o-o but dey was good. Lord, Yessum! Dey used to go fishin' and rabbit huntin' too. Us jus' fotched in game galore den, for it was de style dem days. Dere warn't no market meat in slavery days. Seemed lak to me in dem days dat ash-roasted 'taters and groundpeas was de best somepin t'eat what anybody could want. 'Course dey had a gyarden, and it had somepin of jus' about evvything what us knowed anything 'bout in de way of gyarden sass growin' in it. All de cookin' was done in dem big old open fireplaces what was fixed up special for de pots and ovens. Ashcake was most as good as 'taters cooked in de ashes, but not quite.

"Summertime, us jus' wore homespun dresses made lak de slips dey use for underwear now. De coats what us wore over our wool dresses in winter was knowed as 'sacques' den, 'cause dey was so loose fittin'. Dey was heavy and had wool in 'em too. Marse Lewis, he had a plenty of sheep, 'cause dey was bound to have lots of warm winter clothes, and den too, dey lakked mutton to eat. Oh! dem old brogan shoes was coarse and rough. When Marse Lewis had a cow kilt dey put de hide in de tannin' vat. When de hides was ready, Uncle Ben made up de shoes, and sometimes dey let Uncle Jasper holp him if dere was many to be made all at one time. Us wore de same sort of clothes on Sunday as evvyday, only dey had to be clean and fresh when dey was put on Sunday mornin'.

"Marse Lewis Little and his wife, Miss Sallie, owned us, and Old Miss, she died long 'fore de surrender. Marse Lewis, he was right good to all his slaves; but dat overseer, he would beat us down in a minute if us didn't do to suit him. When dey give slaves tasks to do and dey warn't done in a certain time, dat old overseer would whup 'em 'bout dat. Marster never had to take none of his Niggers to court or put 'em in jails neither; him and de overseer sot 'em right. Long as Miss Sallie lived de carriage driver driv her and Marse Lewis around lots, but atter she died dere warn't so much use of de carriage. He jus' driv for Marse Lewis and piddled 'round de yard den.

"Some slaves larnt to read and write. If dey went to meetin' dey had to go wid deir white folks 'cause dey didn't have no sep'rate churches for de Niggers 'til atter de war. On our Marster's place, slaves didn't go off to meetin' a t'all. Dey jus' went 'round to one another's houses and sung songs. Some of 'em read de Bible by heart. Once I heared a man preach what didn't know how to read one word in de Bible, and he didn't even have no Bible yit.

"De fust baptizin' I ever seed was atter I was nigh 'bout grown. If a slave from our place ever jined up wid a church 'fore de war was over, I never heared tell nothin' 'bout it.

"Lordy, Miss! I didn't know nothin' 'bout what a funeral was dem days. If a Nigger died dis mornin', dey sho' didn't waste no time a-puttin' him right on down in de ground dat same day. Dem coffins never had no shape to 'em; dey was jus' squar-aidged pine boxes. Now warn't dat turrible?

"Slaves never went nowhar widout dem patterollers beatin' 'em up if dey didn't have no pass.

"Dere was hunderds of acres in dat dere plantation. Marse Lewis had a heap of slaves. De overseer, he had a bugle what he blowed to wake up de slaves. He blowed it long 'fore day so dat dey could eat breakfast and be out dere in de fields waitin' for de sun to rise so dey could see how to wuk, and dey stayed out dar and wukked 'til black dark. When a rainy spell come and de grass got to growin' fast, dey wukked dem slaves at night, even when de moon warn't shinin'. On dem dark nights one set of slaves helt lanterns for de others to see how to chop de weeds out of de cotton and corn. Wuk was sho' tight dem days. Evvy slave had a task to do atter dey got back to dem cabins at night. Dey each one hed to spin deir stint same as de 'omans, evvy night.

"Young and old washed deir clothes Sadday nights. Dey hardly knowed what Sunday was. Dey didn't have but one day in de Christmas, and de only diff'unce dey seed dat day was dat dey give 'em some biscuits on Christmas day. New Year's Day was rail-splittin' day. Dey was told how many rails was to be cut, and dem Niggers better split dat many or somebody was gwine to git beat up.

"I don't 'member much 'bout what us played, 'cept de way us run 'round in a ring. Us chillun was allus skeered to play in de thicket nigh de house 'cause Raw Head and Bloody Bones lived der. Dey used to skeer us out 'bout red 'taters. Dey was fine 'taters, red on de outside and pretty and white on de inside, but white folks called 'em 'nigger-killers.' Dat was one of deir tricks to keep us from stealin' dem 'taters. Dere wern't nothin' wrong wid dem 'taters; dey was jus' as good and healthy as any other 'taters. Aunt Lucy, she was de cook, and she told me dat slaves was skeered of dem 'nigger-killer' 'taters and never bothered 'em much den lak dey does de yam patches dese days. I used to think I seed ha'nts at night, but it allus turned out to be somebody dat was tryin' to skeer me.

"'Bout de most fun slaves had was at dem cornshuckin's. De general would git high on top of de corn pile and whoop and holler down leadin' dat cornshuckin' song 'til all de corn was done shucked. Den come de big eats, de likker, and de dancin'. Cotton pickin's was big fun too, and when dey got through pickin' de cotton dey et and drunk and danced 'til dey couldn't dance no more.

"Miss, white folks jus' had to be good to sick slaves, 'cause slaves was property. For Old Marster to lose a slave, was losin' money. Dere warn't so many doctors dem days and home-made medicines was all de go. Oil and turpentine, camphor, assfiddy (asafetida), cherry bark, sweetgum bark; all dem things was used to make teas for grown folks to take for deir ailments. Red oak bark tea was give to chillun for stomach mis'ries.

"All I can ricollect 'bout de comin' of freedom was Old Marster tellin' us dat us was free as jack-rabbits and dat from den on Niggers would have to git deir own somepin t'eat. It warn't long atter dat when dem yankees, wid pretty blue clothes on come through our place and dey stole most evvything our Marster had. Dey kilt his chickens, hogs, and cows and tuk his hosses off and sold 'em. Dat didn't look right, did it?

"My aunt give us a big weddin' feast when I married Tom Adams, and she sho' did pile up dat table wid heaps of good eatments. My weddin' dress was blue, trimmed in white. Us had six chillun, nine grandchillun, and 19 great-grandchillun. One of my grandchillun is done been blind since he was three weeks old. I sont him off to de blind school and now he kin git around 'most as good as I kin. He has made his home wid me ever since his Mammy died.

"'Cordin' to my way of thinkin', Abraham Lincoln done a good thing when he sot us free. Jeff Davis, he was all right too, 'cause if him and Lincoln hadn't got to fightin' us would have been slaves to dis very day. It's mighty good to do jus' as you please, and bread and water is heaps better dan dat somepin t'eat us had to slave for.

"I jined up wid de church 'cause I wanted to go to Heben when I dies, and if folks lives right dey sho' is gwine to have a good restin' place in de next world. Yes Mam, I sho b'lieves in 'ligion, dat I does. Now, Miss, if you ain't got nothin' else to ax me, I'se gwine home and give dat blind boy his somepin t'eat."

United States. Work Projects Administration

[HW: Dist. 6
Ex-Slv. #4]

WASHINGTON ALLEN, EX-SLAVE
Born: December --, 1854
Place of birth: "Some where" in South Carolina
Present Residence: 1932-Fifth Avenue, Columbus, Georgia
Interviewed: December 18, 1936
[MAY 8 1937]

*[TR: Original index refers to "Allen, Rev. W.B. (Uncle Wash)"; however, this informant is different from the next informant, Rev. W.B. Allen.]*

# WASHINGTON ALLEN

The story of "Uncle Wash", as he is familiarly known, is condensed as follows:

He was born on the plantation of a Mr. Washington Allen of South Carolina, for whom he was named. This Mr. Allen had several sons and daughters, and of these, one son—George Allen—who, during the 1850's left his South Carolina home and settled near LaFayette, Alabama. About 1858, Mr. Washington Allen died and the next year, when "Wash" was "a five-year old shaver", the Allen estate in South Carolina was divided—all except the Allen Negro slaves. These, at the instance and insistence of Mr. George Allen, were taken to LaFayette, Alabama, to be sold. All were put on the block and auctioned off, Mr. George Allen buying every Negro, so that not a single slave family was divided up.

"Uncle Wash" does not remember what he "fetched at de sale", but he does distinctly remember that as he stepped up on the block to be sold, the auctioneer ran his hand "over my head and said: Genilmens, dis boy is as fine as split silk". Then when Mr. George Allen had bought all the Allen slaves, it dawned upon them, and they appreciated, why he had insisted on their being sold in Alabama, rather than in South Carolina.

Before he was six years of age, little "Wash" lost his mother and, from then until freedom, he was personally cared for and looked after by Mrs. George Allen; and the old man wept every time he mentioned her name.

During the '60's, "Uncle Wash's" father drove a mail and passenger stage between Cusseta and LaFayette, Alabama—and, finally died and was buried at LaFayette by the side of his wife. "Uncle Wash" "drifted over" to Columbus about fifty years ago and is now living with his two surviving children.

He has been married four times, all his wives dying "nachul" deaths. He has also "buried four chillun".

He was taught to read and write by the sons and daughters of Mr. George Allen, and attended church where a one-eyed white preacher—named Mr. Terrentine—preached to the slaves each Sunday "evenin'" (afternoon). The salary of this preacher was paid by Mr. George Allen.

When asked what this preacher usually preached about, "Uncle Wash" answered: "He was a one-eyed man an' couldn' see good; so, he mout a'made some mistakes, but he sho tole us plenty 'bout hell fire 'n brimstone."

"Uncle Wash" is a literal worshipper of the memory of his "old time white fokes."

J.R. Jones

REV. W.B. ALLEN, EX-SLAVE
425-Second Ave
Columbus, Georgia
(June 29, 1937)
[JUL 28 1937]

*[TR: Original index refers to "Allen, Rev. W.B. (Uncle Wash)"; however, this informant is different from the previous informant, Washington Allen, interviewed on Dec. 18, 1936. The previous interview for Rev. Allen that is mentioned below is not found in this volume.]*

# ALLEN REV. W.B

In a second interview, the submission of which was voluntarily sought by himself, this very interesting specimen of a rapidly vanishing type expressed a desire to amend his previous interview (of May 10, 1937) to incorporate the following facts:

"For a number of years before freedom, my father bought his time from his master and traveled about over Russell County (Alabama) as a journeyman blacksmith, doing work for various planters and making good money—as money went in those days—on the side. At the close of the war, however, though he had a trunk full of Confederate money, all of his good money was gone.

Father could neither read nor write, but had a good head for figures and was very pious. His life had a wonderful influence upon me, though I was originally worldly—that is, I drank and cussed, but haven't touched a drop of spirits in forty years and quit cussing before I entered the ministry in 1879.

I learned to pray when very young and kept it up even in my unsaved days. My white master's folks knew me to be a praying boy, and asked me—in 1865—when the South was about whipped and General Wilson was headed our way—to pray to God to hold the Yankees back. Of course, I didn't have any love for any Yankees—and haven't now, for that matter—but I told my white folks straight-from-the-shoulder that I could not pray along those lines. I told them flat-footedly that, while I loved them and would do any reasonable praying for them, I could not pray against my conscience: that I not only wanted to be free, but that I wanted to see all the Negroes freed!

I then told them that God was using the Yankees to scourge the slave-holders just as He had, centuries before, used heathens and outcasts to chastise His chosen people—the Children of Israel."

(Here it is to be noted that, for a slave boy of between approximately 15 and 17 years of age, remarkable familiarity with the Old Testament was displayed.)

The Parson then entered into a mild tirade against Yankees, saying:

"The only time the Northern people ever helped the Nigger was when they freed him. They are not friends of the Negro and many a time, from my pulpit, have I warned Niggers about going North. No, sir, the colored man doesn't belong in the North—-has no business up there, and you may tell the world that the Reverend W.B.

Allen makes no bones about saying that! He also says that, if it wasn't for the influence of the white race in the South, the Negro race would revert to savagery within a year! Why, if they knew for dead certain that there was not a policeman or officer of the law in Columbus tonight, the good Lord only knows what they'd do tonight"!

When the good Parson had delivered himself as quoted, he was asked a few questions, the answers to which—as shall follow—disclose their nature.

"The lowest down Whites of slavery days were the average overseers. A few were gentlemen, one must admit, but the regular run of them were trash—commoner than the 'poor white trash'—and, if possible, their children were worse than their daddies. The name, 'overseer', was a synonym for 'slave driver', 'cruelty', 'brutishness'. No, sir, a Nigger may be humble and refuse to talk outside of his race—because he's afraid to, but you can't fool him about a white man!

And you couldn't fool him when he was a slave! He knows a white man for what he is, and he knew him the same way in slavery times."

Concerning the punishment of slaves, the Reverend said:

"I never heard or knew of a slave being tried in court for any thing. I never knew of a slave being guilty of any crime more serious than taking something or violating plantation rules. And the only punishment that I ever heard or knew of being administered slaves was whipping.

I have personally known a few slaves that were beaten to death for one or more of the following offenses:

Leaving home without a pass,

Talking back to—'sassing'—a white person,

Hitting another Negro,

Fussing, fighting, and rukkussing in the quarters,

Lying,

Loitering on their work,

Taking things—the Whites called it stealing.

Plantation rules forbade a slave to:

Own a firearm,

Leave home without a pass,

Sell or buy anything without his master's consent,

Marry without his owner's consent,

Have a light in his cabin after a certain hour at night,

Attend any secret meeting,

Harbor or [HW: in] any manner assist a runaway slave,

Abuse a farm animal,

Mistreat a member of his family, and do

A great many other things."

When asked if he had ever heard slaves plot an insurrection, the Parson answered in the negative.

When asked if he had personal knowledge of an instance of a slave offering resistance to corporal punishment, the Reverend shook his head, but said:

"Sometimes a stripped Nigger would say some hard things to the white man with the strap in his hand, though he knew that he (the Negro) would pay for it dearly, for when a slave showed spirit that way the master or overseer laid the lash on all the harder."

When asked how the women took their whippings, he said:

"They usually screamed and prayed, though a few never made a sound."

The Parson has had two wives and five children. Both wives and three of his children are dead. He is also now superannuated, but occasionally does a "little preaching", having only recently been down to Montezuma, Georgia, on a special call to deliver a message to the Methodist flock there.

United States. Work Projects Administration

[HW: Dist. 6
Ex-Slave #2]
Henrietta Carlisle

JACK ATKINSON—EX-SLAVE
Rt. D
Griffin, Georgia
Interviewed August 21, 1936
[MAY 8 1937]

# JACK ATKINSON

"Onct a man, twice a child," quoted Jack Atkinson, grey haired darkey, when being interviewed, "and I done started in my second childhood. I useter be active as a cat, but I ain't, no mo."

Jack acquired his surname from his white master, a Mr. Atkinson, who owned this Negro family prior to the War Between the States. He was a little boy during the war but remembers "refugeeing" to Griffin from Butts County, Georgia, with the Atkinsons when Sherman passed by their home on his march to the sea.

Jack's father, Tom, the body-servant of Mr. Atkinson, "tuck care of him" [HW: during] the four years they were away at war. "Many's the time I done heard my daddy tell 'bout biting his hands he wuz so hongry, and him and Marster drinking water outer the ruts of the road, they wuz so thirsty, during the war."

"Boss Man (Mr. Atkinson), wuz as fine a man as ever broke bread", according to Jack.

When asked how he got married he stated that he "broke off a love vine and threw it over the fence and if it growed" he would get married. The vine "just growed and growed" and it wasn't long before he and Lucy married.

"A hootin' owl is a sho sign of rain, and a screech owl means a death, for a fact."

"A tree frog's holler is a true sign of rain."

Jack maintains that he has received "a second blessing from the Lord" and "no conjurer can bother him."

Whitley
1-25-37
[HW: Dis #5
Unedited]
Minnie B. Ross

EX TOWN SLAVE HANNAH AUSTIN
[HW: about 75-85]
[APR 8 1937]

# HANNAH AUSTIN

When the writer was presented to Mrs. Hannah Austin she was immediately impressed with her alert youthful appearance. Mrs. Austin is well preserved for her age and speaks clearly and with much intelligence. The interview was a brief but interesting one. This was due partly to the fact that Mrs. Austin was a small child when The Civil War ended and too because her family was classed as "town slaves" so classed because of their superior intelligence.

Mrs. Austin was a child of ten or twelve years when the war ended. She doesn't know her exact age but estimated it to be between seventy and seventy five years. She was born the oldest child of Liza and George Hall. Their master Mr. Frank Hall was very kind to them and considerate in his treatment of them.

Briefly Mrs. Austin gave the following account of slavery as she knew it. "My family lived in a two room well built house which had many windows and a nice large porch. Our master, Mr. Hall was a merchant and operated a clothing store. Because Mr. Hall lived in town he did not need but a few slaves. My family which included my mother, father, sister, and myself were his only servants. Originally Mr. Hall did not own any slaves, however after marrying Mrs. Hall we were given to her by her father as a part of her inheritance.

My mother nursed Mrs. Hall from a baby, consequently the Hall family was very fond of her and often made the statement that they would not part with her for anything in the world, besides working as the cook for the Hall family my mother was also a fine seamstress and made clothing for the master's family and for our family. We were allowed an ample amount of good clothing which Mr. Hall selected from the stock in his store. My father worked as a porter in the store and did other jobs around the house. I did not have to work and spent most of my time playing with the Hall children. We were considered the better class of slaves and did not know the meaning of a hard time.

Other slave owners whipped their slaves severely and often, but I have never known our master to whip any one of my family. If any one in the family became ill the family doctor was called in as often as he was needed.

We did not have churches of our own but were allowed to attend the white churches in the afternoon. The White families attended in the forenoon. We seldom heard a true religious sermon; but were constantly preached the doctrine of obedience to our masters and mistresses. We were required to attend church every Sunday.

Marriages were conducted in much the same manner as they are today. After the usual courtship a minister was called in by the master and the marriage ceremony would then take place. In my opinion people of today are more lax in their attitude toward marriage than they were in those days. Following the marriage of a slave couple a celebration would take place often the master and his family would take part in the celebration.

I remember hearing my mother and father discuss the war; but was too young to know just the effect the war would have on the slave. One day I remember Mr. Hall coming to my mother telling her we were free. His exact words were quote—"Liza you don't belong to me any longer you belong to yourself. If you are hired now I will have to pay you. I do not want you to leave as you have a home here as long as you live." I watched my mother to see the effect his words would have on her and I saw her eyes fill with tears. Mr. Hall's eyes filled with tears also.

Soon after this incident a Yankee Army appeared in our village one day. They practically destroyed Mr. Hall's store by throwing all clothes and other merchandise into the streets. Seeing my sister and I they turned to us saying, "Little Negroes you are free there are no more masters and mistresses, here help yourselves to these clothes take them home with you." Not knowing any better we carried stockings, socks, dresses, underwear and many other pieces home. After this they opened the smoke house door and told us to go in and take all of the meat we wanted.

On another occasion the mistress called me asking that I come in the yard to play with the children". Here Mrs. Austin began to laugh and remarked "I did not go but politely told her I was free and didn't belong to any one but my mama and papa. As I spoke these words my mistress began to cry.

My mother and father continued to live with the Halls even after freedom and until their deaths. Although not impoverished most of the Hall's fortune was wiped out with the war".

Mrs. Austin married at the age of 16 years; and was the mother of four children, all of whom are dead. She was very ambitious and was determined to get an education if such was possible. After the war Northern white people came south and set up schools for the education of Negroes. She remembers the organization of the old Storrs School from which one of the present Negroes Colleges originated.

Mrs. Austin proudly spoke of her old blue back speller, which she still possesses; and of the days when she attended Storrs School.

As the writer made ready to depart Mrs. Austin smilingly informed her that she had told her all that she knew about slavery; and every word spoken was the truth.

[HW: Dist. 5
Ex Slave #1
Ross]

"A FEW FACTS OF SLAVERY"
As Told by CELESTIA AVERY—EX-SLAVE
[MAY 8 1937]

# CELESTIA AVERY

Mrs. Celestia Avery is a small mulatto woman about 5 ft. in height. She has a remarkably clear memory in view of the fact that she is about 75 years of age. Before the interview began she reminded the writer that the facts to be related were either told to her by her grandmother, Sylvia Heard, or were facts which she remembered herself.

Mrs. Avery was born 75 years ago in Troupe County, LaGrange, Ga. the eighth oldest child of Lenora and Silas Heard. There were 10 other children beside herself. She and her family were owned by Mr. & Mrs. Peter Heard. In those days the slaves carried the surname of their master; this accounted for all slaves having the same name whether they were kin or not.

The owner Mr. Heard had a plantation of about 500 acres and was considered wealthy by all who knew him. Mrs. Avery was unable to give the exact number of slaves on the plantation, but knew he owned a large number. Cotton, corn, peas, potatoes, (etc.) were the main crops raised.

The homes provided for the slaves were two room log cabins which had one door and one window. These homes were not built in a group together but were more or less scattered over the plantation. Slave homes were very simple and only contained a home made table, chair and bed which were made of the same type of wood and could easily be cleaned by scouring with sand every Saturday. The beds were bottomed with rope which was run backward and forward from one rail to the other. On this framework was placed a mattress of wheat straw. Each spring the mattresses were emptied and refilled with fresh wheat straw.

Slaves were required to prepare their own meals three times a day. This was done in a big open fire place which was filled with hot coals. The master did not give them much of a variety of food, but allowed each family to raise their own vegetables. Each family was given a hand out of bacon and meal on Saturdays and through the week corn ash cakes and meat; which had been broiled on the hot coals was the usual diet found in each home. The diet did not vary even at Christmas only a little fruit was added.

Each family was provided with a loom and in Mrs. Avery's family, her grandmother, Sylvia Heard, did most of the carding and spinning of the thread into cloth. The most common cloth for women clothes was homespun, and calico. This same cloth was dyed and used to make men shirts and pants. Dye was prepared by taking a berry known as the shumake berry and boiling them with walnut peelings. Spring and fall were the seasons for masters to give shoes and clothing to their slaves. Both men and women wore brogan shoes, the only difference being the piece in the side of the womens.

One woman was required to do the work around the house there was also one slave man required to work around the house doing odd jobs. Other than these two every one else was required to do the heavy work in the fields. Work began at "sun up" and lasted until "sun down". In the middle of the day the big bell was rung to summon the workers from the field, for their mid-day lunch. After work hours slaves were then free to do work around their own cabins, such as sewing, cooking (etc.)

"Once a week Mr. Heard allowed his slaves to have a frolic and folks would get broke down from so much dancing" Mrs. Avery remarked. The music was furnished with fiddles. When asked how the slaves came to own fiddles she replied, "They bought them with money they earned selling chickens." At night slaves would steal off from the Heard plantation, go to LaGrange, Ga. and sell chickens which they had raised. Of course the masters always required half of every thing raised by each slave and it was not permissible for any slave to sell anything. Another form of entertainment was the quilting party. Every one would go together to different person's home on each separate night of the week and finish that person's quilts. Each night this was repeated until every one had a sufficient amount of covering for the winter. Any slave from another plantation, desiring to attend these frolics, could do so after securing a pass from their master.

Mrs. Avery related the occasion when her Uncle William was caught off the Heard plantation without a pass, and was whipped almost to death by the "Pader Rollers." He stole off to the depths of the woods here he built a cave large enough to live in. A few nights later he came back to the plantation unobserved and carried his wife and two children back to this cave where they lived until after freedom. When found years later his wife had given birth to two children. No one was ever able to find his hiding place and if he saw any one in the woods he would run like a lion.

Mr. Heard was a very mean master and was not liked by any one of his slaves. Secretly each one hated him. He whipped unmercifully and in most cases unnecessarily. However, he sometimes found it hard to subdue some slaves who happened to have very high tempers. In the event this was the case he would set a pack of hounds on him. Mrs. Avery related to the writer the story told to her of Mr. Heard's cruelty by her grandmother. The facts were as follows: "Every morning my grandmother would pray, and old man Heard despised to hear any one pray saying they were only doing so that they might become free niggers. Just as sure as the sun would rise, she would get a whipping; but this did not stop her prayers every morning before day. This particular time grandmother Sylvia was in "family way" and that morning she began to pray as usual. The master heard her and became so angry he came to her cabin seized and pulled her clothes from her body and tied her to a young sapling. He whipped her so brutally that her body was raw all over. When darkness fell her husband cut her down from the tree, during the day he was afraid to go near her. Rather than go back to the cabin she crawled on her knees to the woods and her husband brought grease for her to grease her raw body. For two weeks the master hunted but could not find her; however, when he finally did, she had given birth to twins. The only thing that saved her was the fact that she was a mid-wife and always carried a small pin knife which she used to cut the navel cord of the babies.

After doing this she tore her petticoat into two pieces and wrapped each baby. Grandmother Sylvia lived to get 115 years old.

Not only was Mr. Henderson cruel but it seemed that every one he hired in the capacity of overseer was just as cruel. For instance, Mrs. Henderson's grandmother Sylvia, was told to take her clothes off when she reached the end of a row. She was to be whipped because she had not completed the required amount of hoeing for the day. Grandmother continued hoeing until she came to a fence; as the overseer reached out to grab her she snatched a fence railing and broke it across his arms. On another occasion grandmother Sylvia ran all the way to town to tell the master that an overseer was beating her husband to death. The master immediately jumped on his horse and started for home; and reaching the plantation he ordered the overseer to stop whipping the old man. Mrs. Avery received one whipping, with a hair brush, for disobedience; this was given to her by the mistress.

Slaves were given separate churches, but the minister, who conducted the services, was white. Very seldom did the text vary from the usual one of obedience to the master and mistress, and the necessity for good behavior. Every one was required to attend church, however, the only self expression they could indulge in without conflict with the master was that of singing. Any one heard praying was given a good whipping; for most masters thought their prayers no good since freedom was the uppermost thought in every one's head.

On the Heard plantation as on a number of others, marriages were made by the masters of the parties concerned. Marriage licenses were unheard of. If both masters mutually consented, the marriage ceremony was considered over with. After that the husband was given a pass to visit his wife once a week. In the event children were born the naming of them was left entirely to the master. Parents were not allowed to name them.

Health of slaves was very important to every slave owner for loss of life meant loss of money to them. Consequently they would call in their family doctor, if a slave became seriously ill. In minor cases of illness home remedies were used. "In fact," Mrs. Avery smilingly remarked, "We used every thing for medicine that grew in the ground." One particular home remedy was known as "Cow foot oil" which was made by boiling cow's feet in water. Other medicines used were hoarhound tea, catnip tea, and castor oil. Very often medicines and doctors failed to save life; and whenever a slave died he was buried the same day. Mrs. Avery remarked, "If he died before dinner the funeral and burial usually took place immediately after dinner."

Although a very young child, Mrs. Avery remembers the frantic attempt slave owners made to hide their money when the war broke out. The following is a story related concerning the Heard family. "Mr. Heard, our master, went to the swamp, dug a hole, and hid his money, then he and his wife left for town on their horses. My oldest brother, Percy, saw their hiding place; and when the Yanks came looking for the money, he carried them straight to the swamps and showed than where the money was hidden." Although the Yeard [TR: typo "Heard"] farm was in the country the highway was very near and Mrs. Avery told of the long army of soldiers marching to La Grange singing the following song: "Rally around the flag boys, rally around the flag, joy, joy, for freedom." When the war ended Mr. Heard visited every slave home and broke the news to each family that they were free people and if they so desired could remain on his plantation. Mrs. Avery's family moved away, in fact most slave families did, for old man Heard had been such a cruel master everyone was anxious to get away from him. However, one year later he sold his plantation to Mr George Traylor and some of the families moved back, Mrs. Avery's family included.

Mrs. Avery married at the age of 16; and was the mother of 14 children, three of whom are still living. Although she has had quite a bit of illness during her life, at present she is quite well and active in spite of her old age. She assured the writer that the story of slavery, which she had given her, was a true one and sincerely hoped it would do some good in this world.

United States. Work Projects Administration

FOLKLORE (Negro)
Minnie B. Ross

[MRS. CELESTIA AVERY]

# MRS. CELESTIA AVERY

In a small house at 173 Phoenix Alley, N.E. lives a little old woman about 5 ft. 2 in. in height, who is an ex-slave. She greeted the writer with a bright smile and bade her enter and have a seat by the small fire in the poorly lighted room. The writer vividly recalled the interview she gave on slavery previously and wondered if any facts concerning superstitions, conjure, signs, etc. could be obtained from her. After a short conversation pertaining to everyday occurrences, the subject of superstition was broached to Mrs. Avery. The idea amused her and she gave the writer the following facts: As far as possible the stories are given in her exact words. The interview required two days, November 30 and December 2, 1936.

"When you see a dog lay on his stomach and slide it is a true sign of death. This is sho true cause it happened to me. Years ago when I lived on Pine Street I was sitting on my steps playing with my nine-months old baby. A friend uv mine came by and sat down; and as we set there a dog that followed her began to slide on his stomach. It scared me; and I said to her, did you see that dog? Yes, I sho did. That night my baby died and it wuzn't sick at all that day. That's the truth and a sho sign of death. Anudder sign of death is ter dream of a new-born baby. One night not so long ago I dreamt about a new-born baby and you know I went ter the door and called Miss Mary next door and told her I dreamed about a new-born baby, and she said, Oh! that's a sho sign of death. The same week that gal's baby over there died. It didn't surprise me when I heard it cause I knowed somebody round here wuz go die." She continued:

"Listen, child! If ebber you clean your bed, don't you never sweep off your springs with a broom. Always wipe 'em with a rag, or use a brush. Jest as sho as you do you see or experience death around you. I took my bed down and swept off my springs, and I jest happened to tell old Mrs. Smith; and she jumped up and said, 'Child, you ought not done that cause it's a sign of death.' Sho nuff the same night I lost another child that wuz eight years old. The child had heart trouble, I think."

Mrs. Avery believes in luck to a certain extent. The following are examples of how you may obtain luck:

"I believe you can change your luck by throwing a teaspoonful of sulphur in the fire at zackly 12 o'clock in the day. I know last week I was sitting here without a bit of fire, but I wuzn't thinking bout doing that till a 'oman came by and told me ter scrape up a stick fire and put a spoonful of sulphur on it; and sho nuff in a hour's time a coal man came by and gave me a tub uv coal. Long time ago I used ter work fer some white women and every day at 12 o'clock I wuz told ter put a teaspoonful of sulphur in the fire."

"Another thing, I sho ain't going ter let a 'oman come in my house on Monday morning unless a man done come in there fust. No, surree, if it seem lak one ain't coming soon, I'll call one of the boy chilluns, jest so it is a male. The reason fer this is cause women is bad luck."

The following are a few of the luck charms as described by Mrs. Avery:

"Black cat bone is taken from a cat. First, the cat is killed and boiled, after which the meat is scraped from the bones. The bones are then taken to the creek and thrown in. The bone that goes up stream is the lucky bone and is the one that should be kept." "There is a boy in this neighborhood that sells liquor and I know they done locked him up ten or twelve times but he always git out. They say he carries a black cat bone," related Mrs. Avery.

"The Devil's shoe string looks jest like a fern with a lot of roots. My mother used to grow them in the corner of our garden. They are lucky.

"Majres (?) are always carried tied in the corner of a handkerchief. I don't know how they make 'em.

"I bought a lucky stick from a man onct. It looked jest lak a candle, only it wuz small; but he did have some sticks as large as candles and he called them lucky sticks, too, but you had to burn them all night in your room. He also had some that looked jest lak buttons, small and round."

The following are two stories of conjure told by Mrs. Avery:

"I knowed a man onct long ago and he stayed sick all der time. He had the headache from morning till night. One day he went to a old man that wuz called a conjurer; this old man told him that somebody had stole the sweat-band out of his cap and less he got it back, something terrible would happen. They say this man had been going with a 'oman and she had stole his sweat-band. Well, he never did get it, so he died.

"I had a cousin named Alec Heard, and he had a wife named Anna Heard. Anna stayed sick all der time almost; fer two years she complained. One day a old conjurer came to der house and told Alec that Anna wuz poisoned, but if he would give him $5.00 he would come back Sunday morning and find the conjure. Alec wuz wise, so he bored a hole in the kitchen floor so that he could jest peep through there to der back steps. Sho nuff Sunday morning the nigger come back and as Alec watched him he dug down in the gound a piece, then he took a ground puppy, threw it in the hole and covered it up. All right, he started digging again and all at onct he jumped up and cried: 'Here 'tis! I got it.' 'Got what?' Alec said, running to the door with a piece of board. 'I got the ground puppy dat wuz buried fer her.' Alec wuz so mad he jumped on that man and beat him most to death. They say he did that all the time and kept a lot of ground puppies fer that purpose." Continuing, she explained that a ground puppy was a worm with two small horns. They are dug up out of the ground, and there is a belief that you will die if one barks at you.

Mrs. Avery related two ways in which you can keep from being conjured by anyone.

"One thing I do every morning is ter sprinkle chamber-lye [HW: (urine)] with salt and then throw it all around my door. They sho can't fix you if you do this. Anudder thing, if you wear a silver dime around your leg they can't fix you. The 'oman live next door says she done wore two silver dimes around her leg for 18 years."

Next is a story of the Jack O'Lantern.

"Onct when I wuz a little girl a lot of us chillun used to slip off and take walnuts from a old man. We picked a rainy night so nobody would see us, but do you know it looked like a thousand Jack ma' Lanterns got in behind us. They wuz all around us. I never will ferget my brother telling me ter get out in the path and turn my pocket wrong side out. I told him I didn't have no pocket but the one in my apron; he said, 'well, turn that one wrong side out.' Sho nuff we did and they scattered then."

Closing the interview, Mrs. Avery remarked: "That's bout all I know; but come back some time and maybe I'll think of something else."

MRS. EMMALINE HEARD

[TR: This interview, which was attached to the interview with Mrs. Celestia Avery, is also included in the second volume of the Georgia Narratives.]

# MRS. EMMALINE HEARD

On December 3 and 4, 1936, Mrs. Emmaline Heard was interviewed at her home, 239 Cain Street. The writer had visited Mrs. Heard previously, and it was at her own request that another visit was made. This visit was supposed to be one to obtain information and stories on the practice of conjure. On two previous occasions Mrs. Heard's stories had proved very interesting, and I knew as I sat there waiting for her to begin that she had something very good to tell me. She began:

"Chile, this story wuz told ter me by my father and I know he sho wouldn't lie. Every word of it is the trufe; fact, everything I ebber told you wuz the trufe. Now, my pa had a brother, old Uncle Martin, and his wife wuz name Julianne. Aunt Julianne used ter have spells and fight and kick all the time. They had doctor after doctor but none did her any good. Somebody told Uncle Martin to go ter a old conjurer and let the doctors go cause they wan't doing nothing fer her anyway. Sho nuff he got one ter come see her and give her some medicine. This old man said she had bugs in her head, and after giving her the medicine he started rubbing her head. While he rubbed her head he said: 'Dar's a bug in her head; it looks jest like a big black roach. Now, he's coming out of her head through her ear; whatever you do, don't let him get away cause I want him. Whatever you do, catch him; he's going ter run, but when he hits the pillow, grab 'em. I'm go take him and turn it back on the one who is trying ter send you ter the grave.' Sho nuff that bug drap out her ear and flew; she hollered, and old Uncle Martin ran in the room, snatched the bed clothes off but they never did find him. Aunt Julianne never did get better and soon she died. The conjurer said if they had a caught the bug she would a lived."

The next story is a true story. The facts as told by Mrs. Heard were also witnessed by her; as it deals with the conjuring of one of her sons. It is related in her exact words as nearly as possible.

"I got a son named Albert Heard. He is living and well; but chile, there wuz a time when he wuz almost ter his grave. I wuz living in town then, and Albert and his wife wuz living in the country with their two chillun. Well, Albert got down sick and he would go ter doctors, and go ter doctors, but they didn't do him any good. I wuz worried ter death cause I had ter run backards and for'ards and it wuz a strain on me. He wuz suffering with a knot on his right side and he couldn't even fasten his shoes cause it pained him so, and it wuz so bad he couldn't even button up his pants. A 'oman teached school out there by the name of Mrs. Yancy; she's dead now but she lived right here on Randolph Street years ago. Well, one day when I wuz leaving Albert's house I met her on the way from her school. 'Good evening, Mrs. Heard,' she says. 'How is Mr. Albert?' I don't hardly know, I says, cause he don't get no better. She looked at me kinda funny and said, don't you believe he's hurt?' Yes mam, I said, I sho do. 'Well,' says she, 'I been wanting to say something to you concerning this but I didn't know how you would take it. If I tell you somewhere ter go will you go, and tell them I sent you?' Yes mam, I will do anything if Albert can get better. 'All right then', she says. 'Catch the Federal Prison car and get off at Butler St.' In them days that car came down Forrest Ave. 'When you get to Butler St.', she says, 'walk up to Clifton St. and go to such and such a number. Knock on the door and a 'oman by the name of Mrs. Hirshpath will come ter the door. Fore she let you in she go ask who sent you there; when you tell 'er, she'll let you in. Now lemme tell you she keeps two quarts of whisky all the time and you have ter drink a little with her; sides that she cusses nearly every word she speaks; but don't let that scare you; she will sho get your son up if it kin be done.' Sho nuff that old 'oman did jest lak Mrs. Yancy said she would do. She had a harsh voice and she spoke right snappy. When she let me in she said, sit down. You lak whisky?' I said, well, I take a little dram sometimes. 'Well, here take some of this', she said. I poured a little bit and drank it kinda lak I wuz afraid. She cursed and said 'I ain't go conjure you. Drink it.' She got the cards and told me to cut 'em, so I did. Looking at the cards, she said: 'You lak ter wait too long; they got him marching to the cemetery. The poor thing! I'll fix those devils. (A profane word was used instead of devils). He got a knot on his side, ain't he?' Yes, Mam, I said. That 'oman told me everything that was wrong with Albert and zackly how he acted. All at once she said; 'If them d----d things had hatched in him it would a been too late. If you do zackly lak I tell you I'll get him up from there.' I sho will, I told her. 'Well, there's a stable sets east of his house. His house got three rooms and a path go straight to the stable. I see it there where he hangs his harness. Yes, I see it all, the devils! Have you got any money?' Yes, mam, a little, I said. 'All right then,' she said. 'Go to the drug store and get 5¢ worth of blue stone; 5¢ wheat bran; and go ter a fish market and ask 'em ter give you a little fish brine; then go in the woods and get some poke-root berries. Now, there's two kinds of poke-root berries, the red skin and the white skin berry. Put all this in a pot, mix with it the guts from a green gourd and 9 parts of red pepper. Make a poultice and put to his side on that knot. Now, listen, your son will be afraid and think you are trying ter do something ter him but be gentle and persuade him that its fer his good.' Child, he sho did act funny when I told him I wanted to treat his side. I had ter tell him I wuz carrying out doctors orders so he could get well. He reared and fussed and said he didn't want that mess on him. I told him the doctor says you do very well till you go ter the horse lot then you go blind and you can't see. He looked at me. 'Sho nuff, Ma, he said, 'that sho is the trufe. I have ter always call one of the chillun when I go there cause I can't see how ter get back ter the house.' Well, that convinced him and he let me fix the medicine for him. I put him ter bed and made the poultice, then I put it ter his side. Now this 'oman said no one wuz ter take it off the next morning but me. I wuz suppose ter fix three, one each night, and after taking each one off ter bury it lak dead folks is buried, east and west, and ter make a real grave out of each one. Well, when I told him not ter move it the next morning, but let me move it, he got funny again and wanted to know why. Do you know I had ter play lak I could move it without messing up my bed clothes and if he moved it he might waste it all. Finally he said he would call me the next morning. Sho nuff, the next morning he called me, ma! ma! come take it off. I went in the room and he wuz smiling. I slept all night long he said, and I feel so much better. I'm so glad, I said, and do you know he could reach down and fasten up his shoe and it had been a long time since he could do that. Later that day I slipped out and made my first grave under the fig bush in the garden. I even put up head boards, too. That night Albert said, 'Mama, fix another one. I feel so much better.' I sho will, I said. Thank God you're better; so fer three nights I fixed poultices and put ter his side and each morning he would tell me how much better he felt. Then the last morning I wuz fixing breakfast and he sat in the next room. After while Albert jumped up and hollered, Ma! Ma!' What is it,' I said. 'Mama, that knot is gone. It dropped down in my pants.' What! I cried. Where is it? Chile, we looked but we didn't find anything, but the knot had sho gone. Der 'oman had told me ter come back when the knot moved and she would tell me what else ter do. That same day I went ter see her and when I told her she just shouted, 'I fixed 'em, The devils! Now, says she, do you [TR: know?] where you can get a few leaves off a yellow peachtree. It must be a yellow peach tree, though. Yes, mam, I says to her. I have a yellow peachtree right there in my yard. Well, she says, get a handful of leaves, then take a knife and scrape the bark up, then make a tea and give him so it will heal up the poison from that knot in his side, also mix a few jimson weeds with it. I come home and told him I wanted ter give him a tea. He got scared and said, what fer, Ma? I had ter tell him I wuz still carrying out the doctor's orders. Well, he let me give him the tea and that boy got well. I went back to Mrs. Hirshpath and told her my son was well and I wanted to pay her. Go on, she said, keep the dollar and send your chillun ter school. This sho happened ter me and I know people kin fix you. Yes sir."

The next story was told to Mrs. Heard by Mrs. Hirshpath, the woman who cured her son.

I used to go see that 'oman quite a bit and even sent some of my friends ter her. One day while I wuz there she told me about this piece of work she did.

"There was a young man and his wife and they worked fer some white folks. They had jest married and wuz trying ter save some money ter buy a home with. All at onct the young man went blind and it almost run him and his wife crazy cause they didn't know what in the world ter do. Well, somebody told him and her about Mrs. Hirshpath, so they went ter see her. One day, says Mrs. Hirshpath, a big fine carriage drew up in front of her door and the coachman helped him to her door. She asked him who sent him and he told her. She only charged 50¢ for giving advice and after you wuz cured it wuz up ter you to give her what you wanted to. Well, this man gave her 50¢ and she talked ter him. She says, boy, you go home and don't you put that cap on no more. What cap? he says. That cap you wears ter clean up the stables with, cause somebody done dressed that cap fer you, and every time you perspire and it run down ter your eyes it makes you blind. You jest get that cap and bring it ter me. I'll fix 'em; they's trying ter make you blind, but I go let you see. The boy was overjoyed, and sho nuff he went back and brought her that cap, and it wuzn't long fore he could see good as you and me. He brought that 'oman $50, but she wouldn't take but $25 and give the other $25 back ter him.

"What I done told you is the trufe, every word of it; I know some other things that happened but you come back anudder day fer that."

United States. Work Projects Administration

PLANTATION LIFE

GEORGIA BAKER, Age 87
369 Meigs Street
Athens, Georgia

Written by:
Mrs. Sadie B. Hornsby [HW: (White)]
Athens

Edited by:
Mrs. Sarah H. Hall
Athens

and
John N. Booth
Dist. Supvr.
Federal Writers' Project
Residencies 6 & 7
Augusta, Ga.

August 4, 1938

# GEORGIA BAKER

Georgia's address proved to be the home of her daughter, Ida Baker. The clean-swept walks of the small yard were brightened by borders of gay colored zinnias and marigolds in front of the drab looking two-story, frame house. "Come in," answered Ida, in response to a knock at the front door. "Yessum, Mammy's here. Go right in dat dere room and you'll find her."

Standing by the fireplace of the next room was a thin, very black woman engaged in lighting her pipe. A green checked gingham apron partially covered her faded blue frock over which she wore a black shirtwaist fastened together with "safety first" pins. A white cloth, tied turban fashion about her head, and gray cotton hose worn with black and white slippers that were run down at the heels, completed her costume.

"Good mornin'. Yessum, dis here's Georgia," was her greeting. "Let's go in dar whar Ida is so us can set down. I don't know what you come for, but I guess I'll soon find out."

Georgia was eager to talk but her articulation had been impaired by a paralytic stroke and at times it was difficult to understand her jumble of words. After observance of the amenities; comments on the weather, health and such subjects, she began:

"Whar was I born? Why I was born on de plantation of a great man. It was Marse Alec Stephens' plantation 'bout a mile and a half from Crawfordville, in Taliaferro County. Mary and Grandison Tilly was my Ma and Pa. Ma was cook up at de big house and she died when I was jus' a little gal. Pa was a field hand, and he belonged to Marse Britt Tilly.

"Dere was four of us chillun: me, and Mary, and Frances, and Mack," she counted on the fingers of one hand. "Marse Alec let Marse Jim Johnson have Mack for his bodyguard. Frances, she wuked in de field, and Mary was de baby—she was too little to wuk. Me, I was 14 years old when de war was over. I swept yards, toted water to de field, and played 'round de house and yard wid de rest of de chillun.

"De long, log houses what us lived in was called

"shotgun" houses 'cause dey had three rooms, one behind de other in a row lak de barrel of a shotgun. All de chillun slept in one end room and de grown folkses slept in de other end room. De kitchen whar us cooked and et was de middle room. Beds was made out of pine poles put together wid cords. Dem wheat-straw mattresses was for grown folkses mostly 'cause nigh all de chillun slept on pallets. How-some-ever, dere was some few slave chillun what had beds to sleep on. Pillows! Dem days us never knowed what pillows was. Gals slept on one side of de room and boys on de other in de chilluns room. Uncle Jim, he was de bed-maker, and he made up a heap of little beds lak what dey calls cots now.

"Becky and Stafford Stephens was my Grandma and Grandpa. Marse Alec bought 'em in Old Virginny. I don't know what my Grandma done 'cause she died 'fore I was borned, but I 'members Grandpa Stafford well enough. I can see him now. He was a old man what slept on a trundle bed in the kitchen, and all he done was to set by de fire all day wid a switch in his hand and tend de chillun whilst dere mammies was at wuk. Chillun minded better dem days dan dey does now. Grandpa Stafford never had to holler at 'em but one time. Dey knowed dey would git de switch next if dey didn't behave.

"Now dere you is axin' 'bout dat somepin' t'eat us had dem days! Ida, ain't dere a piece of watermelon in de ice box?" Georgia lifted the lid of a small ice box, got out a piece of melon, and began to smack her thick lips as she devoured it with an air of ineffable satisfaction. When she had tilted the rind to swallow the last drop of pink juice, she indicated that she was fortified and ready to exercise her now well lubricated throat, by resuming her story:

"Oh, yessum! Marse Alec, had plenty for his slaves to eat. Dere was meat, bread, collard greens, snap beans, 'taters, peas, all sorts of dried fruit, and just lots of milk and butter. Marse Alec had 12 cows and dat's whar I learned to love milk so good. De same Uncle Jim what made our beds made our wooden bowls what dey kept filled wid bread and milk for de chillun all day. You might want to call dat place whar Marse Alec had our veg'tables raised a gyarden, but it looked more lak a big field to me, it was so big. You jus' ought to have seed dat dere fireplace whar dey cooked all us had to eat. It was one sho 'nough big somepin, all full of pots, skillets, and ovens. Dey warn't never 'lowed to git full of smut neither. Dey had to be cleant and shined up atter evvy meal, and dey sho was pretty hangin' dar in dat big old fireplace.

"George and Mack was de hunters. When dey went huntin' dey brought back jus' evvything: possums, rabbits, coons, squirrels, birds, and wild turkeys. Yessum, wild turkeys is some sort of birds I reckon, but when us talked about birds to eat us meant part'idges. Some folkses calls 'em quails. De fishes us had in summertime was a sight to see. Us sho et good dem days. Now us jus' eats what-some-ever us can git.

"Summertime us jus' wore what us wanted to. Dresses was made wid full skirts gathered on to tight fittin' waisties. Winter clothes was good and warm; dresses made of yarn cloth made up jus' lak dem summertime clothes, and petticoats and draw's made out of osnaburg. Chillun what was big enough done de spinnin' and Aunt Betsey and Aunt Tinny, dey wove most evvy night 'til dey rung de bell at 10:00 o'clock for us to go to bed. Us made bolts and bolts of cloth evvy year.

"Us went bar'foots in summer, but bless your sweet life us had good shoes in winter and wore good stockin's too. It tuk three shoemakers for our plantation. Dey was Uncle Isom, Uncle Jim, and Uncle Stafford. Dey made up hole-stock shoes for de 'omans and gals and brass-toed brogans for de mens and boys.

"Us had pretty white dresses for Sunday. Marse Alec wanted evvybody on his place dressed up dat day. He sont his houseboy, Uncle Harris, down to de cabins evvy Sunday mornin' to tell evvy slave to clean hisself up. Dey warn't never give no chance to forgit. Dere was a big old room sot aside for a wash-room. Folkses laughs at me now 'cause I ain't never stopped takin' a bath evvy Sunday mornin'.

"Marse Lordnorth Stephens was de boss on Marse Alec's plantation. Course Marse Alec owned us and he was our sho 'nough Marster. Neither one of 'em ever married. Marse Lordnorth was a good man, but he didn't have no use for 'omans—he was a sissy. Dere warn't no Marster no whar no better dan our Marse Alec Stephens, but he never stayed home enough to tend to things hisself much 'cause he was all de time too busy on de outside. He was de President or somepin of our side durin' de war.

"Uncle Pierce went wid Marse Alec evvy whar he went. His dog, Rio, had more sense dan most folkses. Marse Alec, he was all de time havin' big mens visit him up at de big house. One time, out in de yard, him and one of dem 'portant mens got in a argyment 'bout somepin. Us chillun snuck up close to hear what dey was makin' such a rukus 'bout. I heared Marse Alec say: 'I got more sense in my big toe dan you is got in your whole body.' And he was right—he did have more sense dan most folkses. Ain't I been a-tellin' you he was de President or somepin lak dat, dem days?

"Ma, she was Marse Alec's cook and looked atter de house. Atter she died Marse Lordnorth got Mrs. Mary Berry from Habersham County to keep house at de big house, but Aunt 'Liza, she done de cookin' atter Miss Mary got dar. Us little Niggers sho' did love Miss Mary. Us called her "Mammy Mary" sometimes. Miss Mary had three sons and one of 'em was named Jeff Davis. I 'members when dey come and got him and tuk him off to war. Marse Lordnorth built a four-room house on de plantation for Miss Mary and her boys. Evvybody loved our Miss Mary, 'cause she was so good and sweet, and dere warn't nothin' us wouldn't have done for her.

"No Lord! Marse Lordnorth never needed no overseer or no carriage driver neither. Uncle Jim was de head man wat got de Niggers up evvy mornin' and started 'em off to wuk right. De big house sho was a pretty place, a-settin' up on a high hill. De squirrels was so tame dar dey jus' played all 'round de yard. Marse Alec's dog is buried in dat yard.

"No Mam, I never knowed how many acres dere was in de plantation us lived on, and Marse Alec had other places too. He had land scattered evvywhar. Lord, dere was a heap of Niggers on dat place, and all of us was kin to one another. Grandma Becky and Grandpa Stafford was de fust slaves Marse Alec ever had, and dey sho had a passel of chillun. One thing sho Marse Lordnorth wouldn't keep no bright colored Nigger on dat plantation if he could help it. Aunt Mary was a bright colored Nigger and dey said dat Marse John, Marse Lordnorth's brother, was her Pa, but anyhow Marse Lordnorth never had no use for her 'cause she was a bright colored Nigger.

"Marse Lordnorth never had no certain early time for his slaves to git up nor no special late time for 'em to quit wuk. De hours dey wuked was 'cordin' to how much wuk was ahead to be done. Folks in Crawfordville called us 'Stephens' Free Niggers.'

"Us minded Marse Lordnorth—us had to do dat—but he let us do pretty much as us pleased. Us never had no sorry piece of a Marster. He was a good man and he made a sho 'nough good Marster. I never seed no Nigger git a beatin', and what's more I never heared of nothin' lak dat on our place. Dere was a jail in Crawfordville, but none of us Niggers on Marse Alec's place warn't never put in it.

"No Lord! None of us Niggers never knowed nothin' 'bout readin' and writin'. Dere warn't no school for Niggers den, and I ain't never been to school a day in my life. Niggers was more skeered of newspapers dan dey is of snakes now, and us never knowed what a Bible was dem days.

"Niggers never had no churches of deir own den. Dey went to de white folkses' churches and sot in de gallery. One Sunday when me and my sister Frances went to church I found 50¢ in Confederate money and showed it to her. She tuk it away from me. Dat's de onliest money I seed durin' slavery time. Course you knows dey throwed Confederate money away for trash atter de war was over. Den us young chaps used to play wid it.

"I never went to no baptizin's nor no funerals neither den. Funerals warn't de style. When a Nigger died dem days, dey jus' put his body in a box and buried it. I 'members very well when Aunt Sallie and Aunt Catherine died, but I was little den, and I didn't take it in what dey done bout buryin' 'em.

"None of Marse Alec's slaves never run away to de North, 'cause he was so good to 'em dey never wanted to leave him. De onliest Nigger what left Marse Alec's place was Uncle Dave, and he wouldn't have left 'cept he got in trouble wid a white 'oman. You needn't ax me her name 'cause I ain't gwine to tell it, but I knows it well as I does my own name. Anyhow Marse Alec give Uncle Dave some money and told him to leave, and nobody never seed him no more atter dat.

"Oh yessum! Us heared 'bout 'em, but none of us never seed no patterollers on Marse Alec's plantation. He never 'lowed 'em on his land, and he let 'em know dat he kept his slaves supplied wid passes whenever dey wanted to go places so as dey could come and go when dey got good and ready. Thursday and Sadday nights was de main nights dey went off. Uncle Stafford's wife was Miss Mary Stephen's cook, Uncle Jim's wife lived on de Finley place, and Uncle Isom's belonged to de Hollises, so dey had regular passes all de time and no patterollers never bothered 'em none.

"Whenever Marse Alec or Marse Lordnorth wanted to send a message dey jus' put George or Mack on a horse and sont 'em on but one thing sho, dere warn't no slave knowed what was in dem letters.

"Marse Alec sho had plenty of mules. Some of 'em

was named: Pete, Clay, Rollin, Jack, and Sal. Sal was Allen's slow mule, and he set a heap of store by her. Dere was a heap more mules on dat place, but I can't call back dere names right now.

"Most times when slaves went to deir quarters at night, mens rested, but sometimes dey holped de 'omans cyard de cotton and wool. Young folkses frolicked, sung songs, and visited from cabin to cabin. When dey got behind wid de field wuk, sometimes slaves wuked atter dinner Saddays, but dat warn't often. But, Oh, dem Sadday nights! Dat was when slaves got together and danced. George, he blowed de quills, and he sho could blow grand dance music on 'em. Dem Niggers would jus' dance down. Dere warn't no foolishment 'lowed atter 10:00 o'clock no night. Sundays dey went to church and visited 'round, but folks didn't spend as much time gaddin' 'bout lak dey does now days.

"Christmas Day! Oh, what a time us Niggers did have dat day! Marse Lordnorth and Marse Alec give us evvything you could name to eat: cake of all kinds, fresh meat, lightbread, turkeys, chickens, ducks, geese, and all kinds of wild game. Dere was allus plenty of pecans, apples, and dried peaches too at Christmas. Marse Alec had some trees what had fruit dat looked lak bananas on 'em, but I done forgot what was de name of dem trees. Marse Alec would call de grown folkses to de big house early in de mornin' and pass 'round a big pewter pitcher full of whiskey, den he would put a little whiskey in dat same pitcher and fill it wid sweetened water and give dat to us chillun. Us called dat 'toddy' or 'dram'. Marse Alex allus had plenty of good whiskey, 'cause Uncle Willis made it up for him and it was made jus' right. De night atter

Christmas Day us pulled syrup candy, drunk more liquor, and danced. Us had a big time for a whole week and den on New Year's Day us done a little wuk jus' to start de year right and us feasted dat day on fresh meat, plenty of cake, and whiskey. Dere was allus a big pile of ash-roasted 'taters on hand to go wid dat good old baked meat. Us allus tried to raise enough 'taters to last all through de winter 'cause Niggers sho does love dem sweet 'taters. No Mam, us never knowed nothin' 'bout Santa Claus 'til atter de war.

"No Mam, dere warn't no special cornshuckin's and cotton pickin's on Marse Alec's place, but of course dey did quilt in de winter 'cause dere had to be lots of quiltin' done for all dem slaves to have plenty of warm kivver, and you knows, Lady, 'omens can quilt better if dey gits a passel of 'em together to do it. Marse Alec and Marse Lordnorth never 'lowed dere slaves to mix up wid other folkses business much.

"Oh Lord! Us never played no games in slavery times, 'cept jus' to run around in a ring and pat our hands. I never sung no songs 'cause I warn't no singer, and don't talk 'bout no Raw Head and Bloody Bones or nothin' lak dat. Dey used to skeer us chillun so bad 'bout dem sort of things dat us used to lay in bed at night a-shakin' lak us was havin' chills. I've seed plenty of ha'nts right here in Athens. Not long atter I had left Crawfordville and moved to Athens, I had been in bed jus' a little while one night, and was jus' dozin' off to sleep when I woke up and sot right spang up in bed. I seed a white man, dressed in white, standin' before me. I sho didn't say nothin' to him for I was too skeered. De very last time I went to a dance, somepin got atter me and skeered me so my hair riz up 'til I couldn't git my hat on my haid, and dat cyored me of gwine to dances. I ain't never been to no more sich doin's.

"Old Marster was powerful good to his Niggers when dey got sick. He had 'em seed atter soon as it was 'ported to him dat dey was ailin'. Yessum, dere warn't nothin' short 'bout our good Marsters, 'deed dere warn't! Grandpa Stafford had a sore laig and Marse Lordnorth looked atter him and had Uncle Jim dress dat pore old sore laig evvy day. Slaves didn't git sick as often as Niggers does now days. Mammy Mary had all sorts of teas made up for us, 'cordin' to whatever ailment us had. Boneset tea was for colds. De fust thing dey allus done for sore throat was give us tea made of red oak bark wid alum. Scurvy grass tea cleant us out in the springtime, and dey made us wear little sacks of assfiddy (asafetida) 'round our necks to keep off lots of sorts of miseries. Some folkses hung de left hind foot of a mole on a string 'round deir babies necks to make 'em teethe easier. I never done nothin' lak dat to my babies 'cause I never believed in no such foolishment. Some babies is jus' natchelly gwine to teethe easier dan others anyhow.

"I 'members jus' as good as if it was yesterday what Mammy Mary said when she told us de fust news of freedom. 'You all is free now,' she said. 'You don't none of you belong to Mister Lordnorth nor Mister Alec no more, but I does hope you will all stay on wid 'em, 'cause dey will allus be jus' as good to you as dey has done been in de past.' Me, I warn't even studyin' nothin' 'bout leavin' Marse Alec, but Sarah Ann and Aunt Mary, dey threwed down deir hoes and jus' whooped and hollered 'cause dey was so glad. When dem Yankees come to our place Mammy Mary axed 'em if dey warn't tired of war. 'What does you know 'bout no war?' Dey axed her right back. 'No, us won't never git tired of doin' good.'

"I stayed on wid my two good Marsters 'til most 3 years atter de war, and den went to wuk for Marse Tye Elder in Crawfordville. Atter dat I wuked for Miss Puss King, and when she left Crawfordville I come on here to Athens and wuked for Miss Tildy Upson on Prince Avenue. Den I went to Atlanta to wuk for Miss Ruth Evage (probably Elliott). Miss Ruth was a niece of Abraham Lincoln's. Her father was President Lincoln's brother and he was a Methodist preacher what lived in Mailpack, New York. I went evvywhar wid Miss Ruth. When me and Miss Ruth was in Philadelphia, I got sick and she sont me home to Athens and I done been here wid my daughter ever since.

"Lawdy, Miss! I ain't never been married, but I did live wid Major Baker 18 years and us had five chillun. Dey is all daid but two. Niggers didn't pay so much 'tention to gittin' married dem days as dey does now. I stays here wid my gal, Ida Baker. My son lives in Cleveland, Ohio. My fust child was borned when I warn't but 14 years old. De war ended in April and she was borned in November of dat year. Now, Miss! I ain't never told but one white 'oman who her Pa was, so you needn't start axin' me nothin' 'bout dat. She had done been walkin' evvywhar 'fore she died when she was jus' 10 months old and I'm a-tellin' you de truth when I say she had more sense dan a heap of white chillun has when dey is lots older dan she was. Whilst I was off in New York wid Miss Ruth, Major, he up and got married. I reckon he's daid by now. I don't keer nohow, atter de way he done me. I made a good livin' for Major 'til he married again. I seed de 'oman he married once.

"Yes Mam," there was strong emphasis in this reply. "I sho would ruther have slavery days back if I could have my same good Marsters 'cause I never had no hard times den lak I went through atter dey give us freedom. I ain't never got over not bein' able to see Marse Alec no more. I was livin' at Marse Tye Elder's when de gate fell on Marse Alec, and he was crippled and lamed up from dat time on 'til he died. He got to be Governor of Georgia whilst he was crippled. When he got hurt by dat gate, smallpox was evvywhar and dey wouldn't let me go to see 'bout him. Dat most killed me 'cause I did want to go see if dere was somepin' I could do for him.

"Lordy Mussy, Miss! I had a time jinin' up wid de church. I was in Mailpack, New York, wid Miss Ruth when I had de urge to jine up. I told Miss Ruth 'bout it and she said: 'Dere ain't no Baptist church in 10 miles of here.' 'Lord, have mussy!' I said. 'Miss Ruth, what I gwine do? Dese is all Methodist churches up here and I jus' can't jine up wid no Methodists.' 'Yes you can,' she snapped at me, 'cause my own Pa's a-holdin a 'vival in dis very town and de Methodist church is de best anyhow.' Well, I went on and jined de Reverend Lincoln's Methodist church, but I never felt right 'bout it. Den us went to Philadelphia and soon as I could find a Baptist church dar, I jined up wid it. Northern churches ain't lak our southern churches 'cause de black and white folkses all belong to de same church dar and goes to church together. On dat account I still didn't feel lak I had jined de church. Bless your sweet life, Honey, when I come back to de South, I was quick as I could be to jine up wid a good old southern Baptist church. I sho didn't mean to live outdoors, 'specially atter I dies." Georgia's eyes sparkled and her flow of speech was smooth as she told of her religious experiences. When that subject was exhausted her eyes dimmed again and her speech became less articulate.

Georgia's reeking pipe had been laid aside for the watermelon and not long after that was consumed the restless black fingers sought occupation sewing gay pieces for a quilt. "Miss, I warn't born to be lazy, I warn't raised dat way, and I sho ain't skeered to die.

"Good-bye, Honey," said Georgia, as the interviewer arose and made her way toward the street. "Hurry back and don't forget to fetch me dat purty pink dress you is a-wearin'. I don't lak white dresses and I ain't never gwine to wear a black one nohow."

## [TR: Return Visit]

Georgia was on the back porch washing her face and hands and quarrelling with Ida for not having her breakfast ready at nine-thirty when the interviewer arrived for a re-visit.

"Come in," Georgia invited, "and have a cheer. But, Miss I done told you all I knows 'bout Marse Alec and dem deys when I lived on his plantation. You know chillun den warn't 'lowed to hang 'round de grown folks whar dey could hear things what was talked about."

About this time Ida came down from a second-floor kitchen with her mother's breakfast. She was grumbling a little louder on each step of the rickety stairway. "Lord, have mussy! Ma is still a-talkin' 'bout dat old slavery stuff, and it ain't nothin' nohow." After Ida's eyes had rested on the yellow crepe frock just presented Georgia in appreciation of the three hours she had given for the first interview, she became reconciled for the story to be resumed, and even offered her assistance in rousing the recollections of her parent.

"Did I tell you" Georgia began, "dat de man what looked atter Marse Alec's business was his fust cousin? He was de Marse Lordnorth I'se all time talkin' 'bout, and Marse John was Marse Lordnorth's brother. Dere warn't no cook or house gal up at de big house but Ma 'til atter she died, and den when Miss Mary Berry tuk charge of de house dey made Uncle Harry and his wife, Aunt 'Liza, house boy and cook.

"Marse Alec growed all his corn on his Googer Crick plantation. He planned for evvything us needed and dere warn't but mighty little dat he didn't have raised to take keer of our needs. Lordy, didn't I tell you what sort of shoes, holestock shoes is? Dem was de shoes de 'omans wore and dey had extra pieces on de sides so us wouldn't knock holes in 'em too quick.

"De fust time I ever seed Marse Alec to know who he was, I warn't more'n 6 years old. Uncle Stafford had went fishin' and cotched de nicest mess of fish you ever seed. He cleant 'em and put 'em in a pan of water, and told me to take 'em up to de big house to Marse Alec. I was skeered when I went in de big house yard and axed, what looked lak a little boy, whar Marse Alec was, and I was wuss skeered when he said: 'Dis is Marse Alec you is talkin' to. What you want?' I tole him Uncle Stafford sont him de fishes and he told me: 'Take 'em to de kitchen and tell 'Liza to cook 'em for me.' I sho ain't never gwine to forgit dat.

"One day dey sont me wid a bucket of water to de field, and I had to go through de peach orchard. I et so many peaches, I was 'most daid when I got back to de house. Dey had to drench me down wid sweet milk, and from dat day to dis I ain't never laked peaches. From den on Marse Alec called me de 'peach gal.'

"Marse Alec warn't home much of de time, but when he was dar he used to walk down to de cabins and laugh and talk to his Niggers. He used to sing a song for de slave chillun dat run somepin lak dis:

> 'Walk light ladies
> De cake's all dough,
> You needn't mind de weather,
> If de wind don't blow.'"

Georgia giggled when she came to the end of the stanza. "Us didn't know when he was a-singin' dat tune to us chillun dat when us growed up us would be cake walkin' to de same song.

"On Sundays, whenever Marse Alec was home, he done lots of readin' out of a great big old book. I didn't know what it was, but he was pow'ful busy wid it. He never had no parties or dancin' dat I knows 'bout, but he was all time havin' dem big 'portant mens at his house talkin' 'bout de business what tuk him off from home so much. I used to see Lawyer Coombs dere heaps of times. He was a big, fine lookin' man. Another big lawyer was all time comin' dar too, but I done lost his name. Marse Alec had so awful much sense in his haid dat folkses said it stunted his growin'. Anyhow, long as he lived he warn't no bigger dan a boy.

"When Uncle Harry's and Aunt 'Liza's daughter what was named 'Liza, got married he was in Washin'ton or some place lak dat. He writ word to Marse Linton, his half-brother, to pervide a weddin' for her. I knows 'bout dat 'cause I et some of dat barbecue. Dat's all I 'members 'bout her weddin'. I done forgot de name of de bridegroom. He lived on some other plantation. Aunt 'Liza had two gals and one boy. He was named Allen.

"Whilst Marse Alec was President or somepin, he got sick and had to come back home, and it wern't long atter dat 'fore de surrender. Allen was 'pinted to watch for de blue coats. When dey come to take Marse Alec off, dey was all over the place wid deir guns. Us Niggers hollered and cried and tuk on pow'ful 'cause us sho thought dey was gwine to kill him on account of his bein' such a high up man on de side what dey was fightin'. All de Niggers followed 'em to de depot when dey tuk Marse Alec and Uncle Pierce away. Dey kept Marse Alec in prison off somewhar a long time but dey sont Pierce back home 'fore long.

"I seed Jeff Davis when dey brung him through Crawfordville on de train. Dey had him all fastened up wid chains. Dey told me dat a Nigger 'oman put pizen in Jeff Davis' somepin t'eat and dat was what kilt him. One thing sho, our Marse Alec warn't pizened by nobody. He was comin' from de field one day when a big old heavy gate fell down on him, and even if he did live a long time atterwards dat was what was de cause of his death.

"I seed Uncle Pierce 'fore he died and us sot and talked and cried 'bout Marse Alec. Yessum, us sho did have de best Marster in de world. If ever a man went to Heaven, Marse Alec did. I sho does wish our good old Marster was livin' now. Now, Miss, I done told you all I can ricollec' 'bout dem days. I thanks you a lot for dat purty yaller dress, and I hopes you comes back to see me again sometime."

ALICE BATTLE, EX-SLAVE
Hawkinsville, Georgia

(Interviewed By Elizabeth Watson—1936)
[JUL 20, 1937]

# ALICE BATTLE

During the 1840's, Emanuel Caldwell—born in North Carolina, and Neal Anne Caldwell—born in South Carolina, were brought to Macon by "speculators" and sold to Mr. Ed Marshal of Bibb County. Some time thereafter, this couple married on Mr. Marshal's plantation, and their second child, born about 1850, was Alice Battle. From her birth until freedom, Alice was a chattel of this Mr. Marshal, whom she refers to as a humane man, though inclined to use the whip when occasion demanded.

Followed to its conclusion, Alice's life history is void of thrills and simply an average ex-slave's story. As a slave, she was well fed, well clothed, and well treated, as were her brother and sister slaves. Her mother was a weaver, her father—a field hand, and she did both housework and plantation labor.

Alice saw the Yankee pass her ex-master's home with their famous prisoner, Jeff Davis, after his capture, in '65. The Yankee band, says she, was playing "We'll hang Jeff Davis on a Sour Apple Tree". Some of the soldiers "took time out" to rob the Marshal smokehouse. The Whites and Negroes were all badly frightened, but the "damyankees didn't harm nobody".

After freedom, Alice remained with the Marshals until Christmas, when she moved away. Later, she and her family moved back to the Marshal plantation for a few years. A few years still later, Alice married a Battle "Nigger".

Since the early '70's, Alice has "drifted around" quite a bit. She and her husband are now too old and feeble to work. They live with one of their sons, and are objects of charity.

## PLANTATION LIFE

JASPER BATTLE, Age 80
112 Berry St.,
Athens, Ga.

Written by:
Grace McCune [HW: (White)]
Athens

Edited by:
Sarah H. Hall
Athens

Leila Harris
Augusta

and
John N. Booth
District Supervisor
Federal Writers' Project
Residencies 6 & 7

# JASPER BATTLE

The shade of the large water oaks in Jasper's yard was a welcome sight when the interviewer completed the long walk to the old Negro's place in the sweltering heat of a sunny July afternoon. The old house appeared to be in good condition and the yard was clean and tidy. Jasper's wife, Lula, came around the side of the house in answer to the call for Jasper. A large checked apron almost covered her blue dress and a clean white headcloth concealed her hair. Despite her advanced age, she seemed to be quite spry.

"Jus' come back here whar I'se a-doin' de white folks' washin'," she said. "Jasper's done been powerful sick and I can't leave him by hisself none. I brung him out here in de shade so I could watch him and 'tend to him whilst I wuks. Jasper stepped on a old plank what had two rusty nails in it, and both of 'em went up in his foot a fur ways. I done driv dem nails plumb up to dey haids in de north side of a tree and put jimpson weed poultices on Jasper's foot, but it's still powerful bad off."

By this time we had arrived within sight and earshot of the old rocking chair where Jasper sat with his foot propped high in another chair. His chair had long ago been deprived of its rockers. The injured member appeared to be swollen and was covered with several layers of the jimpson weed leaves. The old man's thin form was clothed in a faded blue shirt and old gray cotton trousers. His clothes were clean and his white hair was in marked contrast to his shining but wrinkled black face. He smiled when Lula explained the nature of the proposed interview. "'Scuse me, Missy," he apologized, "for not gittin' up, 'cause I jus' can't use dis old foot much, but you jus' have a seat here in de shade and rest yourself." Lula now excused herself, saying: "I jus' got to hurry and git de white folks' clothes washed and dried 'fore it rains," and she resumed her work in the shade of another huge tree where a fire was burning brightly under her washpot and a row of sud-filled tubs occupied a long bench.

"Lula, she has to wuk all de time," Jasper explained, "and she don't never have time to listen to me talk. I'se powerful glad somebody is willin' to stop long enough to pay some heed whilst I talks 'bout somepin. Dem days 'fore de war was good old days, 'specially for de colored folks. I know, 'cause my Mammy done told me so. You see I was mighty little and young when de war was over, but I heared de old folks do lots of talkin' 'bout dem times whilst I was a-growin' up, and den too, I stayed right dar on dat same place 'til I was 'bout grown. It was Marse Henry Jones' plantation 'way off down in Taliaferro County, nigh Crawfordville, Georgy. Mammy b'longed to Marse Henry. She was Harriet Jones. Daddy was Simon Battle and his owner was Marse Billie Battle. De Battle's plantation was off down dar nigh de Jones' place. When my Mammy and Daddy got married Marse Henry wouldn't sell Mammy, and Marse Billie wouldn't sell Daddy, so dey didn't git to see one another but twice a week—dat was on Wednesday and Sadday nights—'til atter de war was done over. I kin still 'member Daddy comin' over to Marse Henry's plantation to see us.

"Marse Henry kept a lot of slaves to wuk his big old plantation whar he growed jus' evvything us needed to eat and wear 'cept sugar and coffee and de brass toes for our home-made, brogan shoes. Dere allus was a-plenty t'eat and wear on dat place.

"Slave quarters was log cabins built in long rows. Some had chimblies in de middle, twixt two rooms, but de most of 'em was jus' one-room cabins wid a stick and mud chimbly at de end. Dem chimblies was awful bad 'bout ketchin' on fire. Didn't nobody have no glass windows. Dey jus' had plain plank shutters for blinds and de doors was made de same way, out of rough planks. All de beds was home-made and de best of 'em was corded. Dey made holes in de sides and foots and haidpieces, and run heavy home-made cords in dem holes. Dey wove 'em crossways in and out of dem holes from one side to another 'til dey had 'em ready to lay de mattress mat on. I'se helped to pull dem cords tight many a time. Our mattress ticks was made of homespun cloth and was stuffed wid wheat straw. 'Fore de mattress tick was put on de bed a stiff mat wove out of white oak splits was laid on top of de cords to pertect de mattress and make it lay smooth. Us was 'lowed to pick up all de old dirty cotton 'round de place to make our pillows out of.

"Jus' a few of de slave famblies was 'lowed to do deir own cookin' 'cause Marster kept cooks up at de big house what never had nothin' else to do but cook for de white folks and slaves. De big old fireplace in dat kitchen at de big house was more dan eight feet wide and you could pile whole sticks of cord-wood on it. It had racks acrost to hang de pots on and big ovens and little ovens and big, thick, iron fryin' pans wid long handles and hefty iron lids. Dey could cook for a hunderd people at one time in dat big old kitchen easy. At one time dere was tables acrost one end of de kitchen for de slaves t'eat at, and de slave chillun et dar too.

"Marster was mighty good to slave chillun. He never sont us out to wuk in de fields 'til us was 'most growed-up, say 12 or 14 years old. A Nigger 12 or 14 years old dem days was big as a white child 17 or 18 years old. Why Miss, Niggers growed so fast, dat most of de Nigger nurses warn't no older dan de white chillun dey tuk keer of. Marster said he warn't gwine to send no babies to de fields. When slave chillun got to be 'bout 9 or 10 years old dey started 'em to fetchin' in wood and water, cleanin' de yards, and drivin' up de cows at night. De bigges' boys was 'lowed to measure out and fix de stock feed, but de most of us chillun jus' played in de cricks and woods all de time. Sometimes us played Injuns and made so much fuss dat old Aunt Nancy would come out to de woods to see what was wrong, and den when she found us was jus' a-havin' fun, she stropped us good for skeerin' her.

"Mammy's job was to make all de cloth. Dat was what she done all de time; jus' wove cloth. Some of de others cyarded de bats and spun thread, but Mammy, she jus' wove on so reg'lar dat she made enough cloth for clothes for all dem slaves on de plantation and, it's a fact, us did have plenty of clothes. All de nigger babies wore dresses made jus' alak for boys and gals. I was sho'ly mighty glad when dey 'lowed me to git rid of dem dresses and wear shirts. I was 'bout 5 years old den, but dat boys' shirt made me feel powerful mannish. Slave gals wore homespun cotton dresses, and dey had plenty of dem dresses, so as dey could keep nice and clean all de time. Dey knitted all de socks and stockin's for winter. Dem gals wore shawls, and dere poke bonnets had ruffles 'round 'em. All de shoes was home-made too. Marster kept one man on de plantation what didn't do nothin' but make shoes. Lordy, Missy! What would gals say now if dey had to wear dem kind of clothes? Dey would raise de roof plumb offen de house. But jus' let me tell you, a purty young gal dressed in dem sort of clothes would look mighty sweet to me right now.

"Us never could eat all de meat in Marster's big old smokehouse. Sometimes he tuk hams to de store and traded 'em for sugar and coffee. Plenty of 'bacco was raised on dat plantation for all de white folks and de growed-up Niggers. Slave chillun warn't sposen to have none, so us had to swipe what 'bacco us got. If our Mammies found out 'bout us gittin' 'bacco, dey stropped us 'til de skin was most off our backs, but sometimes us got away wid a little. If us seed any of de old folks was watchin' us, us slipped de 'bacco from one to another of us whilst dey s'arched us, and it went mighty bad on us if dey found it.

"Slaves went to de white folks' church and listened to de white preachers. Dere warn't no colored preacher 'lowed to preach in dem churches den. Dey preached to de white folks fust and den dey let de colored folks come inside and hear some preachin' atter dey was through wid de white folks. But on de big 'vival meetin' days dey 'lowed de Niggers to come in and set in de gallery and listen at de same time dey preached to de white folks. When de sermon was over dey had a big dinner spread out on de grounds and dey had jus' evvything good t'eat lak chickens, barbecued hogs and lambs, pies, and lots of watermelons. Us kept de watermelons in de crick 'til dey was ready to cut 'em. A white gentleman, what dey called Mr. Kilpatrick, done most of de preachin'. He was from de White Plains neighborhood. He sho' did try mighty hard to git evvybody to 'bey de Good Lord and keep his commandments.

"Mr. Kilpatrick preached all de funerals too. It 'pears lak a heap more folks is a-dyin' out dese days dan died den, and folks was a heap better den to folks in trouble. Dey would go miles and miles den when dey didn't have no auto'biles, to help folks what was in trouble. Now, dey won't go next door when dere's death in de house. Den, when anybody died de fust thing dey done was to shroud 'em and lay 'em out on de coolin' board 'til Old Marster's cyarpenter could git de coffin made up. Dere warn't no embalmers dem days and us had to bury folks de next day atter dey died. De coffins was jus' de same for white folks and deir slaves. On evvy plantation dere was a piece of ground fenced in for a graveyard whar dey buried white folks and slaves too. My old Daddy is buried down yonder on Marse Henry's plantation right now.

"When a slave wanted to git married up wid a gal, he didn't ax de gal, but he went and told Marster 'bout it. Marster would talk to de gal and if she was willin', den Marster would tell all de other Niggers us was a-goin' to have a weddin'. Dey would all come up to de big house and Marster would tell de couple to jine hands and jump backwards over a broomstick, and den he pernounced 'em man and wife. Dey didn't have to have no licenses or nothin' lak dey does now. If a man married up wid somebody on another place, he had to git a pass from his Marster, so as he could go see his wife evvy Wednesday and Sadday nights. When de patterollers cotched slaves out widout no passes, dey evermore did beat 'em up. Leastways dat's what Mammy told me.

"Durin' de big war all de white folkses was off a-fightin' 'cept dem what was too old to fight or what was too bad crippled and 'flicted. Dey stayed home and looked atter de 'omans and chillun. Somebody sont Mist'ess word dat dem yankees was on de way to our plantation and she hid evvything she could, den had de hogs and hosses driv off to de swamps and hid. Mammy was crazy 'bout a pet pig what Marster had done give her, so Mist'ess told her to go on down to dat swamp quick, and hide dat little pig. Jus' as she was a-runnin' back in de yard, dem yankees rid in and she seed 'em a-laughin' fit to kill. She looked 'round to see what dey was tickled 'bout and dere followin' her lak a baby was dat pig. Dem yankees was perlite lak, and dey never bothered nothin' on our place, but dey jus' plumb ruint evvything on some of de plantations right close to our'n. Dey tuk nigh evvything some of our neighbors had t'eat, most all deir good hosses, and anything else dey wanted. Us never did know why dey never bothered our white folkses' things.

"When dey give us our freedom us went right on over to Marse Billie Battle's place and stayed dar wid Daddy 'bout a year; den Daddy come wid us back to Marse Henry's, and dar us stayed 'til Old Marster died. Long as he lived atter de war, he wukked most of his help on sheers, and seed dat us was tuk keer of jus' lak he had done when us all b'longed to him. Us never went to school much 'cause Mammy said white folks didn't lak for Niggers to have no larnin', but atter de war was done over our Old Mist'ess let colored chillun have some lessons in a little cabin what was built in de back yard for de white chillun to go to school in.

"Atter dey buried our Old Marster, us moved down to Hancock County and farmed dar, 'cause dat was all us knowed how to do. Us got together and raised money to buy ground enough for a churchyard and a graveyard for colored folks. Dat graveyard filled up so fast dat dey had to buy more land several times. Us holped 'em build de fust colored church in Hancock County.

"School for colored chillun was held den in our church house. Our teacher was a white man, Mr. Tom Andrews, and he was a mighty good teacher, but Lordy, how strick he was! Dese here chillun don't know nothin' 'bout school. Us went early in de mornin', tuk our dinner in a bucket, and never left 'til four o'clock, and sometimes dat was 'most nigh sundown. All day us studied dat blue back speller, and dat white teacher of ours sho' tuk de skin offen our backs if us didn't mind him. Dere warn't no fussin' and fightin' and foolin' 'round on de way home, 'cause dat white teacher 'lowed he had control of us 'til us got to our Mammies' doors and if us didn't git for home in a hurry, it was jus' too bad for us when he tuk it out on us next day wid dat long hick'ry switch.

"Things is sho' diffunt now. Folks ain't good now as dey was den, but dere is gwine to be a change. I may not be here to see it, but it's a-comin' 'cause de Good Lord is done 'sied (prophesied) it, and it's got to be. God's sayin' is comin' to pass jus' as sho' as us is livin' and settin' in de shade of dis here tree.

"Lordy, Miss! How come you axes 'bout colored folks'es weddin's? I was a-courtin' a little 14-year old gal named Lovie Williams, but her Mammy runned me off and said she warn't gwine to let Lovie git married up wid nobody 'til she got big enough. I jus' bought dem licenses and watched for my chanct and den I stole dat gal right from under her Mammy's eyes. My Mammy knowed all 'bout it and helped us git away. Us didn't have no time for no weddin'. De best us could do was jus' to git ourselfs married up. Lovie's Mammy raised de Old Ned, but us didn't keer den, 'cause it was too late for her to do nothin' to part us. Lovie was one of the bestest gals what ever lived. Us raised 12 chillun and I never had one speck of trouble wid her. Lovie's done been daid 15 years now."

His voice trembled as he talked about his first wife, and Lula almost stopped her work to listen. This kind of talk did not please her and her expression grew stern. "You done talked a-plenty," she told him. "You ain't strong 'nough to do no more talkin'," but Jasper was not willing to be silenced. "I reckon I knows when I'se tired. I ain't gwine to hush 'til I gits good and ready," was his protest. "Yes Missy," he continued. "All our chillun is done daid now 'cept four and dey is 'way off up North. Ain't nobody left here 'cept me and Lula. Lula is pow'ful good to me. I done got too old to wuk, and can't do nothin' nohow wid dis old foot so bad off. I'se ready and even anxious to go when de Good Lord calls for old Jasper to come to de Heav'nly Home.

"I ain't heared nothin' from my only brother in over 7 years. I 'spose he still lives in Crawfordville. Missy, I wishes I could go back down to Crawfordville one more time. I kin jus' see our old homeplace on de plantation down dar now. Lula a-washin' here, makes me study 'bout de old washplace on Marse Henry's plantation. Dere was a long bench full of old wood tubs, and a great big iron pot for bilin' de clothes, and de batten block and stick. Chillun beat de clothes wid de batten stick and kept up de fire 'round de pot whilst de 'omans leaned over de tubs washin' and a-singin' dem old songs. You could hear 'em 'most a mile away. Now and den one of de 'omans would stop singin' long enough to yell at de chillun to 'git more wood on dat fire 'fore I lash de skin offen your back.'

"Oh Missy, dem was good old days. Us would be lucky to have 'em back again, 'specially when harvest time comes 'round. You could hear Niggers a-singin' in de fields 'cause dey didn't have no worries lak dey got now. When us got de corn up from de fields, Niggers come from far and nigh to Marster's cornshuckin'. Dat cornshuckin' wuk was easy wid evvybody singin' and havin' a good time together whilst dey made dem shucks fly. De cornshuckin' captain led all de singin' and he set right up on top of de highes' pile of corn. De chillun was kept busy a-passin' de liquor jug 'round. Atter it started gittin' dark, Marster had big bonfires built up and plenty of torches set 'round so as dere would be plenty of light. Atter dey et all dey wanted of dem good things what had done been cooked up for de big supper, den de wrastlin' matches started, and Marster allus give prizes to de best wrastlers. Dere warn't no fussin' and fightin' 'lowed on our place, and dem wrastlin' matches was all in good humor and was kept orderly. Marster wanted evvybody to be friends on our plantation and to stay dat way, for says he: 'De Blessed Saviour done said for us to love our neighbor as ourselfs, and to give and what us gives is gwine to come back to us.' Missy, de Good Lord's word is always right."

The interviewer was preparing to leave when one of Jasper's old friends approached the sheltering tree in the yard, where the interview was drawing to a close. "Brudder Paul," said Jasper, "I wisht you had come sooner 'cause Missy, here, and me is done had de bestes' time a-goin' back over dem old times when folks loved one another better dan dey does now. Good-bye Missy, you done been mighty kind and patient wid old Jasper. Come back again some time."

[HW: Dist. --
Ex-Slv. #10]

ARRIE BINNS OF WASHINGTON-WILKES

by
Minnie Branham Stonestreet
Washington-Wilkes
Georgia
[MAY 8 1937]

# ARRIE BINNS

Arrie Binns lives in Baltimore, a negro suburb of Washington-Wilkes, in a little old tumbled down kind of a cottage that used to be one of the neatest and best houses of the settlement and where she has lived for the past sixty-odd years. In the yard of her home is one of the most beautiful holly trees to be found anywhere. She set it there herself over fifty years ago. She recalled how her friends predicted bad luck would befall her because she "sot out er holly", but not being in the least bit superstitious she paid them "no mind" and has enjoyed her beautiful tree all these years. Many lovely oaks are around her house; she set them there long ago when she was young and with her husband moved into their new home and wanted to make it as attractive as possible. She is all alone now. Her husband died some years ago and three of her four children have passed on. Her "preacher son" who was her delight, died not very long ago. All this sorrow has left Aunt Arrie old and sad; her face is no longer lighted by the smile it used to know.

She is a tiny little scrap of a woman with the softest voice and is as neat as can be. She wears an oldfashioned apron all the time and in cool weather there is always a little black cape around her frail shoulders and held together with a plain old gold "breastpin".

She was born in Lincoln County (Georgia), her mother was Emeline Sybert and her father Jordan Sybert. They belonged to Mr. Jones Sybert and his wife "Miss Peggy". After freedom they changed their surname to Gullatt as they liked that better. Arrie was among the oldest of nine children. The night she was born the stork brought a little baby girl to the home of a white family just across the creek from the Syberts. The little white girl was named Arine so "Miss Peggy" named the little new black baby girl Arrie, and that is how it happened she was given such an odd name.

Arrie said she was "15 or 16 years old when the war broke (1865), I wuz big enough to be lookin' at boys an' dey lookin' at me." She remembers the days of war, how when the battle of Atlanta was raging they heard the distant rumble of cannon, and how "upsot" they all were. Her master died of "the consumption" during the war. She recalls how hard it was after his death. The Syberts had no children and there was no one to turn to after his death. Arrie tells of her Master's illness, how she was the housemaid and was called upon to fan him and how she would get so tired and sleepy she would nod a little, the fan dropping from hands into his face. He would take it up and "crack my haid with the handle to wake me up. I wuz allus so sorry when I done that, but I jest had ter nod."

She told about how bad the overseers were and the

trouble they gave until finally "old Miss turned off ther one she had an' put my Pa in his place to manage things and look after the work." Arrie was never punished, (not any more than having her head cracked by her Master when she nodded while fanning him.) "No mam, not none of our niggers wuz whipped. Why I recollect once, my brother wuz out without a pass an' de patter rollers kotch him and brung him to old Miss and said he'd have ter be whipped, old Miss got so mad she didn't know what ter do, she said nobody wuz a goin' ter whip her niggers, but the patter roller men 'sisted so she said after er while, 'Well, but I'm goin' ter stan' right here an' when I say stop, yer got ter stop', an' they 'greed to dat, an' the third time dey hit him she raised her han' an' said 'STOP' an' dey had ter let my brother go. My Miss wuz a big 'oman, she'd weigh nigh on ter three hundred pound, I 'spect."

After her master's death Arrie had to go into the field to work. She recalled with a little chuckle, the old cream horse, "Toby" she use to plow. She loved Toby, she said, and they did good work. When not plowing she said she "picked er round in the fields" doing whatever she could. She and the other slaves were not required to do very hard work. Her mother was a field hand, but in the evenings she spun and wove down in their cabin. Aunt Arrie added "an' I did love to hear that old spinnin' wheel. It made a low kind of a whirring sound that made me sleepy." She said her mother, with all the other negro women on the place, had "a task of spinnin' a spool at night", and they spun and wove on rainy days too. "Ma made our clothes an' we had pretty dresses too. She dyed some blue and brown striped. We growed the indigo she used fer the blue, right dar on the plantation, and she used bark and leaves to make the tan and brown colors."

Aunt Arrie said the Doctor was always called in when they were sick, "but we never sont fer him lesse'n somebody wuz real sick. De old folks doctored us jest fer little ailments. Dey give us lye tea fer colds. (This was made by taking a few clean ashes from the fire place, putting them in a little thin bag and pouring boiling water over them and let set for a few minutes. This had to be given very weak or else it would be harmful, Aunt Arrie explained.) Garlic and whiskey, and den, dar ain't nothin' better fer the pneumony dan splinter tea. I've cured bad cases with it." (That is made by pouring boiling water over lightwood splinters.)

Aunt Arrie told of their life on the plantation and it was not unlike that of other slaves who had good masters who looked after them. They had plenty to eat and to wear. Their food was given them and they cooked and ate their meals in the cabins in family groups. Santa Claus always found his way to the Quarters and brought them stick candy and other things to eat. She said for their Christmas dinner there was always a big fat hen and a hog head.

In slavery days the negroes had quiltings, dances, picnics and everybody had a good time, Aunt Arrie said, "an' I kin dance yit when I hears a fiddle." They had their work to do in the week days, but when Sundays came there was no work, everybody rested and on "preachin' days" went to Church. Her father took them all to old Rehoboth, the neighborhood white church, and they worshiped together, white and black, the negroes in the gallery. That was back in the days when there was "no lookin' neither to the right nor to the left" when in church; no matter what happened, no one could even half way smile. This all was much harder than having to listen to the long tiresome sermons of those days, Arrie thinks, specially when she recalled on one occasion "when Mr. Sutton wuz a preachin' a old goat [HW: got] up under the Church an' every time Mr. Sutton would say something out real loud that old goat would go 'Bah-a-a Bah ba-a-a' an' we couldn't laugh a bit. I most busted, I wanted ter laugh so bad."

"Yassum, in dem days" continued Aunt Arrie, "all us colored folks went to the white folks church kase us didn't have no churches of our own and day want no colored preachers den, but some what wuz called "Chairbacks". The Chairback fellows went er round preachin' an' singin' in the cabins down in the Quarters and dey use ter have the bes' meetin's, folks would be converted an' change dey way. De hymns dey sung de most wuz "Amazin' Grace" an' "Am I Born ter Die?" I 'members de meetin's us use ter have down in our cabin an' how everybody would pray an' sing."

"Dey ain't nothin' lak it use ter be," sighed Aunt Arrie, "Now when I first could recollect, when a nigger died they sot up with de corpse all night and de next day had de funeral an' when dey started to the burial ground with the body every body in the whole procession would sing hymns. I've heard 'em 'nough times clear 'cross the fields, singin' and moanin' as they went. Dem days of real feelin' an' keerin' is gone."

When freedom came there were sad times on the Sybert plantation, Arrie said. "Old Miss cried and cried, and all us cried too. Old Miss said 'You'al jest goin' off to perish.' Aunt Jennie, one of the oldest women slaves stayed on with her and took keer of her, but all us stayed on a while. Us didn't know whar to go an' what ter do, an' den come Dr. Peters and Mr. Allen frum Arkansas to git han's to go out dar an' work fer dem. My Pa took his family and we stayed two years. It took us might nigh ar whole week to git dar, we went part way on de train and den rid de steam boat up de Mississippi River ter de landin'. We worked in the cotton field out dar and done all kinds er work on de farm, but us didn't like an' Dr. Peters an' Mr. Allen give my Pa money fer us ter come home on. 'Fore we could git started my oldest brother wanted to come home so bad he jest pitched out and walked all de way frum Arkansas to our old home in Georgy. We come back by Memphis and den come on home on de train. When we wuz out dar I went to school an' got as far as 'Baker'. Dat's de only schoolin' I ever had."

Aunt Arrie told about her courtship and marriage, she remembers all about it and grew rather sentimental and sad while she talked. She said that Franklin Binns was going with her before she went to live in Arkansas and when she came home he picked up the courtship where he had left off when she went away. He would ride 20 miles on horseback to see her. He brought her candy and nice things to eat, but she still wouldn't "give him no satisfaction 'bout whether she keered fer him er not." She said other men wanted to come to see her, but she paid them not one bit of attention. "No mam, I wouldn't 'cept of them, I never did go with in an' everybody, I don't do dat yit." She said one day Franklin was to see her and said "Less us marry, I think 'nough of you to marry." She said she wouldn't tell him nothin' so he went to see her parents and they agreed, so she married him sometime later. They were married by a white minister, Mr. Joe Carter.

Aunt Arrie leads a lonely life now. She grieves for her loved ones more than negroes usually do. She doesn't get about much, but "I does go over to see Sis Lou (a neighbor) every now an' den fer consolation." She says she is living on borrowed time because she has always taken care of herself and worked and been honest. She said that now she is almost at the close of her life waiting day by day for the call to come, she is glad she knew slavery, glad she was reared by good white people who taught her the right way to live, and she added: "Mistess, I'se so glad I allus worked hard an' been honest—hit has sho paid me time an' time agin."

[HW: Dist. 5
ExSlv. #7
Driskell]

HENRY BLAND—EX-SLAVE
[MAY -- --]

# HENRY BLAND

Henry Bland is one of the few living ex-slaves who was born on a plantation near Edenton, Ga., in 1851. His parents were Martha and Sam Coxton. In this family group were three other children, two girls and one boy, who was the oldest. When questioned regarding the birthplace and the movements of his parents, Mr. Bland stated that his father was born in Hancock County, Ga. His mother along with her mother was brought to Georgia by the speculator with a drove of other slaves. The first thing that he remembers of his parents is when he was quite small and was allowed to remain in the Master's kitchen in the "big house" where his mother was cook.

Mr. Coxton, who was the owner of Mr. Bland and his family, was described as being very rich and influential man in the community where he lived. Says Mr. Bland, "His only fault was that of drinking too much of the whisky that he distilled on the plantation." Unlike some of the other slave owners in that section, Mr. Coxton was very kind to his slaves. His plantation was a large one and on it was raised cotton, corn, cane[TR:?], vegetables, and live stock. More cotton was grown than anything else.

From the time he was 1 year and 6 months of age until he was 9 years old he lived in the "big house" with his mother. At night he slept on the floor there. In spite of this, his and his mother's treatment was considerably better than that received by those slaves who worked in the fields. While their food consisted of the same things as did that of the field slaves, sometimes choice morsels came back to the kitchen from the Master's table. He says that his mother's clothes were of better quality than the other slave women (those who were not employed in the house).

As a child his first job was to cut wood for the stove, pick up chips, and to drive the cows to and from the pasture. When 9 years old he was sent to the field as a plow boy. Here he worked with a large number of other slaves (he does not know the exact number) who were divided into two groups, the plow group and the hoe group. His father happened to be the foreman of the hoe gang. His brothers and sisters also worked here in the fields being required to hoe as well as plow. When picking time came, everyone was required to pick. The usual amount of cotton each person was required to pick was 200 lbs. per day. However, when this amount was not picked by some they were not punished by the overseer, as was the case on neighboring plantations, because Mr. Coxton realized that some could do more work than others. Mr. Coxton often told his overseer that he had not been hired to whip the slaves, but to teach them how to work.

Says Mr. Bland: "Our working hours were the same as on any other plantation. We had to get up every morning before sun-up and when it was good and light we were in the field. A bugle was blown to wake us." All the slaves stayed in the field until dark. After leaving the field they were never required to do any work but could spend their time as they saw fit to. No work was required on Saturday or Sunday with the exception that the stock had to be cared for. Besides those days when no work was required, there was the 4th of July and Christmas on which the slaves were permitted to do as they pleased. These two latter dates were usually spent in true holiday spirit as the master usually gave a big feast in the form of a barbecue and allowed them to invite their friends.

When darkness came they sang and danced and this was what they called a "frolic." As a general rule this same thing was permitted after the crops had been gathered. Music for these occasions was furnished by violin, banjo and a clapping of hands. Mr. Bland says that he used to help furnish this music as Mr. Coxton had bought him a violin.

On the Coxton plantation all slaves always had a sufficient amount of clothing. These clothes which were issued when needed and not at any certain time included articles for Sunday wear as well as articles for work. Those servants who worked in the "big house" wore practically the same clothes as the master and his wife with the possible exception that it met the qualification of being second-handed. An issue of work clothing included a heavy pair of work shoes called brogans, homespun shirts and a pair of jeans pants. A pair of knitted socks was also included The women wore homespun dresses for their working clothes. For Sunday wear the men were given white cotton shirts and the women white cotton dresses. All clothing was made on the plantation by those women who were too old for field work.

In the same manner that clothing was sufficient, so was food plentiful. At the end of each week each family was given 4 lbs. of meat, 1 peck of meal, and some syrup. Each person in a family was allowed to raise a garden and so they had vegetables whenever they wished to. In addition to this they were allowed to raise chickens, to hunt and to fish. However, none of the food that was secured in any of the ways mentioned above could be sold. When anyone wished to hunt, Mr. Coxton supplied the gun and the shot.

Although the slaves cooked for themselves, their breakfast and dinner were usually sent to them in the fields after it had been prepared in the cook house. The reason for this was that they had to get up too soon in the morning, and at noon too much time would be lost if they were permitted to go to their cabins for lunch.

The children who were too young to work in the field were cared for by some old slave who likewise was unable to do field work. The children were usually fed pot liquor, corn bread, milk, syrup, and vegetables. Each one had his individual cup to eat from. The food on Sunday was usually no different from that of any other day of the week. However, Mr. Bland says that they never had to break in the smokehouse because of hunger.

When asked to describe the living quarters of the slaves on his plantation he looked around his room and muttered: "Dey wuz a lot better than dis one." Some of the cabins were made of logs and some of weatherboards. The chinks in the walls were sealed with mud. In some instances boards were used on the inside to keep the weather out. There were usually two windows, shutters being used in the place of window panes. The chimney and fireplace were made of mud and stones. All cooking was done at the fireplace as none of them were provided with stoves. Iron cooking utensils were used. To boil food a pot was hung over the fire by means of a hook. The remaining furniture was a bench which served as a chair, and a crude bed. Rope running from side to side served as bed springs. The mattress was made of straw or hay. For lighting purposes, pine knots and candles were used. The slaves on the Coxton plantation were also fortunate in that all cabins had good floors. All cabins and their furnishings were built by the slaves who learned the use of hammer and saw from white artisans whom Mr. Coxton employed from time to time. Mr. Bland remarked that his father was a blacksmith, having learned the trade in this manner.

A doctor was employed regularly by Mr. Coxton to minister to the needs of the slaves in time of illness. "We also had our own medicine," says Mr. Bland. At different times excursions were made to the woods where "yarbs" (herbs) were gathered. Various kinds of teas and medicines were made by boiling these roots in water. The usual causes of illness on this plantation were colds, fevers, and constipation. Castor oil and salts were also used to a great extent. If an individual was too ill to work an older slave had to nurse this person.

No effort was made by Mr. Coxton to teach his slaves anything except manual training. A slave who could use his hands at skilled work was more valuable than the ordinary field hand. If, however, a slave secured a book, Mr. Coxton would help him learn to read it. Above all, religious training was not denied. As a matter of fact, Mr. Coxton required each one of his servants to dress in his

Sunday clothes and to go to church every Sunday. Services for all were held at the white church—the slaves sitting on one side and the masters on the other. All preaching was done by a white pastor.

No promiscuous relationships were allowed. If a man wanted to marry he merely pointed out the woman of his choice to the master. He in turn called her and told her that such and such an individual wished her for a wife. If she agreed they were pronounced man and wife and were permitted to live together.

The slaves on his plantation were great believers in roots and their values in the use of conjuring people.

Mr. Bland doesn't remember ever seeing anyone sold by Mr. Coxton, but he heard that on other nearby plantations slaves were placed on an auction block and sold like cattle.

None of the slaves were ever whipped or beaten by Mr. Coxton or by anyone else. If a rule was broken the offender was called before Mr. Coxton where he was talked to. In some cases a whipping was promised and that ended the matter. The "Paddie Rollers" whipped the slaves from other plantations when they were caught off of their premises without a "pass" but this was never the case when a slave belonging to Mr. Coxton broke this rule. Mr. Bland remembers that once he and some of his fellow slaves were away from home without a pass when they were seen by the "Paddie Rollers" who started after them. When they were recognized as belonging to Mr. Coxton one of them (Paddie Rollers) said: "Don't bother them; that's them d---- 'free niggers'." The Paddie Rollers were not allowed to come on the Coxton plantation to whip his slaves or any other owner's slaves who happened to be visiting at the time. Mr. Coxton required that they all be on the plantation by nightfall.

(The above seems to be rather conclusive proof of Mr. Coxton's influence in the community.) [TR: Parentheses added by hand.]

Whenever a slave committed a crime against the State, his master usually had to pay for the damage done or pay the slave's fine. It was then up to him to see that the offender was punished.

Mr. Coxton once saw him (Mr. Bland) beat another slave (who was a guest at a frolic) when this visitor attempted to draw a pistol on him. Mr. Bland was upheld in his action and told by Mr. Coxton that he had better always fight back when anyone struck him, whether the person was white or black. Further, if he (Mr. Coxton) heard of his not fighting back a whipping would be in store for him.

Mr. Coxton was different from some of the slave owners in that he gave the head of each family spending money at Christmas time—the amount varying with the size of the family.

"When the Civil war was begun the master seemed to be worried all the time" states Mr. Bland. "He was afraid that we would be freed and then he would have to hire us to do his work."

When asked to describe his feelings about the war and the possibility of his being freed, Mr. Bland said that he had no particular feeling of gladness at all. The outcome of the war did not interest him at all because Mr. Coxton was such a good master he didn't care whether he was freed or not. His fellow slaves felt the same way.

When Sherman and the Yankees were marching through they took all of the live stock but bothered nothing else. The buildings on the adjoining plantation were all burned. A small skirmish took place about 2 miles away from Mr. Coxton's plantation when the Yankees and Confederates met. Mr. Coxton's two sons took part in the war.

Mr. Bland was taken by Sherman's army to Savannah and then to Macon. He says that he saw President Jeff Davis give up his sword to General Sherman in surrender.

After the war Mr. Coxton was still well off in spite of the fact that he had lost quite a bit of money as a result of the war. He saved a great deal of his cash by burying it when Sherman came through. The cattle might have been saved if he (Mr. Bland) could have driven them into the woods before he was seen by some of the soldiers.

At the close of the war Mr. Coxton informed all the slaves that they were free to go where they wished, but they all refused to leave. Most of them died on the plantation. Mr. Bland says that when he became of age his former master gave him a wagon, two mules, a horse and buggy and ten pigs.

Mr. Bland thinks that old age is a characteristic in his family. His grandmother lived to be 115 years old and his mother 107 years old. Although in his 80's, Mr. Bland is an almost perfect picture of health. He thinks that he will live to become at least 100 years old because he is going to continue to live as sane a life as he has in the past.

J.R. Jones

RIAS BODY, Ex-Slave.
Place of birth: Harris County, near Waverly Hall, Georgia
Date of birth: April 9, 1846
Present residence: 1419-24th Street, Columbus, Georgia
Interviewed: July 24, 1936
[JUL 8, 1937]

# RIAS BODY

Rias Body was born the slave property of Mr. Ben Body, a Harris County planter. He states that he was about fifteen years old when the Civil War started and, many years ago, his old time white folks told him that April 9, 1846, was the date of his birth.

The "patarolers," according to "Uncle" Rias, were always quite active in ante-bellum days. The regular patrol consisted of six men who rode nightly, different planters and overseers taking turns about to do patrol duty in each militia district in the County.

All slaves were required to procure passes from their owners or their plantation overseers before they could go visiting or leave their home premises. If the "patarolers" caught a "Nigger" without a pass, they whipped him and sent him home. Sometimes, however, if the "Nigger" didn't run and told a straight story, he was let off with a lecture and a warning. Slave children, though early taught to make themselves useful, had lots of time for playing and frolicking with the white children.

Rias was a great hand to go seining with a certain clique of white boys, who always gave him a generous or better than equal share of the fish caught.

At Christmas, every slave on the Body plantation received a present. The Negro children received candy, raisins and "nigger-toes", balls, marbles, etc.

As for food, the slaves had, with the exception of "fancy trimmins", about the same food that the whites ate. No darky in Harris County that he ever heard of ever went hungry or suffered for clothes until after freedom.

Every Saturday was a wash day. The clothes and bed linen of all Whites and Blacks went into wash every Saturday. And "Niggers", whether they liked it or not, had to "scrub" themselves every Saturday night.

The usual laundry and toilet soap was a homemade lye product, some of it a soft-solid, and some as liquid as water. The latter was stored in jugs and demijohns. Either would "fetch the dirt, or take the hide off"; in short, when applied "with rag and water, something had to come".

Many of the Body slaves had wives and husbands living on other plantations and belonging to other planters. As a courtesy to the principals of such matrimonial alliances, their owners furnished the men passes permitting them to visit their wives once or twice a week. Children born to such unions were the property of the wife's owner; the father's owner had no claim to them whatsoever.

"Uncle" Rias used to frequently come to Columbus with his master before the war, where he often saw "Niggers oxioned off" at the old slave mart which was located at what is now 1225 Broadway. Negroes to be offered for sale were driven to Columbus in droves—like cattle—by "Nawthon speckulatahs". And prospective buyers would visit the "block" accompanied by doctors, who would feel of, thump, and examine the "Nigger" to see if sound. A young or middle-aged Negro man, specially or even well trained in some trade or out-of-the-ordinary line of work, often sold for from $2000.00 to $4000.00 in gold. Women and "runty Nigger men" commanded a price of from $600.00 up, each. A good "breedin oman", though, says "Uncle" Rias, would sometimes sell for as high as $1200.00.

Rias Body had twelve brothers, eight of whom were "big buck Niggers," and older than himself. The planters and "patarolers" accorded these "big Niggers" unusual privileges—to the end that he estimates that they "wuz de daddies uv least a hunnert head o' chillun in Harris County before de war broke out." Some of these children were "scattered" over a wide area.

Sin, according to Rias Body, who voices the sentiment of the great majority of aged Negroes, is that, or everything, which one does and says "not in the name of the Master". The holy command, "Whatever ye do, do it in My name," is subjected to some very unorthodox interpretations by many members of the colored race. Indeed, by their peculiar interpretation of this command, it is established that "two clean sheets can't smut", which means that a devout man and woman may indulge in the primal passion without committing sin.

The old man rather boasts of the fact that he received a number of whippings when a slave: says he now knows that he deserved them, "an thout 'em", he would have no doubt "been hung 'fore he wuz thutty years ole."

Among the very old slaves whom he knew as a boy were quite a few whom the Negroes looked up to, respected, and feared as witches, wizzards, and magic-workers. These either brought their "learnin" with them from Africa or absorbed it from their immediate African forebears. Mentally, these people wern't brilliant, but highly sensitized, and Rias gave "all sich" as wide a berth as opportunity permitted him, though he knows "dat dey had secret doins an carrying-ons". In truth, had the Southern Whites not curbed the mumbo-jumboism of his people, he is of the opinion that it would not now be safe to step "out his doe at night".

Incidentally, Rias Body is more fond of rabbit than any other meat "in de wurrul", and says that he could— if he were able to get them—eat three rabbits a day, 365 days in the year, and two for breakfast on Christmas morning. He also states that pork, though killed in the hottest of July weather, will not spoil if it is packed down in shucked corn-on-the-cob. This he learned in slavery days when, as a "run-away", he "knocked a shoat in the head" one summer and tried it—proving it.

EX-SLAVE INTERVIEW

JAMES BOLTON
Athens, Georgia

Written by:
Mrs. Sarah H. Hall
Federal Writers' Project
Residency 4
Athens, Georgia

Edited by:
Miss Maude Barragan
Residency 13
Augusta, Georgia

# JAMES BOLTON

"It never was the same on our plantation atter we done laid Mistess away," said James Bolton, 85 year old mulatto ex-slave. "I ain't never forget when Mistess died—she had been so good to every nigger on our plantation. When we got sick, Mistess allus had us tended to. The niggers on our plantation all walked to church to hear her funeral sermon and then walked to the graveyard to the buryin'."

James, shrivelled and wrinkled, with his bright eyes taking in everything on one of his rare visits to town, seemed glad of the chance to talk about slavery days. He spoke of his owner as "my employer" and hastily corrected himself by saying, "I means, my marster."

"My employer, I means my marster, and my mistess, they was sho' all right white folkses," he continued.

"They lived in the big 'ouse. Hit was all painted brown. I heard tell they was more'n 900 acres in our plantation and lots of folkses lived on it. The biggest portion was woods. My paw, he was name Whitfield Bolton and Liza Bolton was my maw. Charlie, Edmund, Thomas and John Bolton was my brothers and I had one sister, she was Rosa. We belonged to Marse Whitfield Bolton and we lived on his plantation in Oglethorpe County near Lexington, not far from the Wilkes County line.

"We stayed in a one room log cabin with a dirt floor. A frame made outen pine poles was fastened to the wall to hold up the mattresses. Our mattresses was made outen cotton bagging stuffed with wheat straw. Our kivers was quilts made outen old clothes. Slave 'omens too old to work in the fields made the quilts.

"Maw, she went up to the big house onc't a week to git the 'lowance or vittles. They 'lowanced us a week's rations at a time. Hit were generally hog meat, corn meal and sometimes a little flour. Maw, she done our cookin' on the coals in the fireplace at our cabin. We had plenty of 'possums and rabbits and fishes and sometimes we had wild tukkeys and partidges. Slaves warn't spozen to go huntin' at night and everybody know you can't ketch no 'possums 'ceppin' at night! Jus' the same, we had plenty 'possums and nobody ax how we cotch 'em!" James laughed and nodded. "Now, 'bout them rabbits! Slaves warn't 'lowed to have no guns and no dogs of they own. All the dogs on our plantation belonged to my employer—I means, to my marster, and he 'lowed us to use his dogs to run down the rabbits. Nigger mens and boys 'ud go in crowds, sometimes as many as twelve at one time, and a rabbit ain't got no chance 'ginst a lot of niggers and dogs when they light out for to run 'im down!

"What wild critters we wanted to eat and couldn't run down, we was right smart 'bout ketchin' in traps. We cotch lots of wild tukkeys and partidges in traps and nets. Long Crick runned through our plantation and the river warn't no fur piece off. We sho' did ketch the fishes, mostly cats, and perch and heaps and heaps of suckers. We cotch our fishes mos'n generally with hook and line, but the carpenters on our plantation knowed how to make basket traps that sho' nuff did lay in the fishes! God only knows how long it's been since this old nigger pulled a big shad out of the river. Ain't no shads been cotch in the river round here in so long I disremembers when!

"We didn' have no gardens of our own round our cabins. My employer—I means, my marster—had one big gyarden for our whole plantation and all his niggers had to work in it whensomever he wanted 'em to, then he give 'em all plenty good gyarden sass for theyselfs. They was collards and cabbage and turnips and beets and english peas and beans and onions, and they was allus some garlic for ailments. Garlic was mostly to cure wums (worms). They roasted the garlic in the hot ashes and squez the juice outen it and made the chilluns take it. Sometimes they made poultices outen garlic for the pneumony.

"We saved a heap of bark from wild cherry and poplar and black haw and slippery ellum trees and we dried out mullein leaves. They was all mixed and brewed to make bitters. Whensomever a nigger got sick, them bitters was good for—well ma'am, they was good for what ailed 'em! We tuk 'em for rheumatiz, for fever, and for the misery in the stummick and for most all sorts of sickness. Red oak bark tea was good for sore throat.

"I never seed no store bought clothes twel long atter freedom done come! One slave 'oman done all the weavin' in a separate room called the 'loom house.' The cloth was dyed with home-made coloring. They used indigo for blue, red oak bark for brown, green husks offen warnicks (walnuts) for black, and sumacs for red and they'd mix these colors to make other colors. Other slave 'omans larned to sew and they made all the clothes. Endurin' the summertime we jus' wore shirts and pants made outen plain cotton cloth. They wove wool in with the cotton to make the cloth for our winter clothes. The wool was raised right thar on our plantation. We had our own shoemaker man—he was a slave named Buck Bolton and he made all the shoes the niggers on our plantation wore.

"I waren't nothin' but chillun when freedom come. In slavery-time chilluns waren't 'lowed to do no wuk kazen the marsters wanted they niggers to grow up big and strong and didn' want 'em stunted none. Tha's howcome I didn' git no mo' beatin's than I did! My employer—I means, my marster, never did give me but one lickin'. He had done told me to watch the cows and keep 'em in the pastur'. I cotch lots of grasshoppers and started fishin' in the crick runnin' through the pastur' and fust thing I knowed, the overseer was roundin' up all the other niggers to git the cows outen the cornfields! I knowed then my time had done come!"

James was enjoying the spotlight now, and his audience did not have to prompt him. Plantation recollections crowded together in his old mind.

"We had one overseer at a time," he said, "and he allus lived at the big 'ouse. The overseers warn't quality white folkses like our marster and mistess but we never heard nuffin' 'bout no poor white trash in them days, and effen we had heard sumpin' like that we'd have knowed better'n to let Marster hear us make such talk! Marster made us call his overseer 'Mister.' We had one overseer named Mr. Andrew Smith and another time we had a overseer named Mr. Pope Short. Overseers was jus' there on the business of gettin' the work done—they seed atter everybody doin' his wuk 'cordin' to order.

"My employer—I means, my marster, never 'lowed no overseer to whup none of his niggers! Marster done all the whuppin' on our plantation hisself. He never did make no big bruises and he never drawed no blood, but he sho' could burn 'em up with that lash! Niggers on our plantation was whupped for laziness mostly. Next to that, whuppings was for stealin' eggs and chickens. They fed us good and plenty but a nigger is jus' bound to pick up chickens and eggs effen he kin, no matter how much he done eat! He jus' can't help it. Effen a nigger ain't busy he gwine to git into mischief!

"Now and then slaves 'ud run away and go in the woods and dig dens and live in 'em. Sometimes they runned away on 'count of cruel treatment, but most of the time they runned away kazen they jus' didn't want to wuk, and wanted to laze around for a spell. The marsters allus put the dogs atter 'em and git 'em back. They had black and brown dogs called 'nigger hounds' what waren't used for nothin' but to track down niggers.

"They waren't no such place as a jail whar we was. Effen a nigger done sumpin' disorderly they jus' natcherly tuk a lash to 'im. I ain't never seed no nigger in chains twel long atter freedom done come when I seed 'em on the chain gangs.

"The overseer woke us up at sunrise—leas'n they called it sunrise! We would finish our vittles and be in the fields ready for wuk befo' we seed any sun! We laid off wuk at sunset and they didn't drive us hard. Leas'wise, they didn' on our plantation. I done heard they was moughty hard on 'em on other plantations. My marster never did 'low his niggers to wuk atter sundown. My employer, I means my marster, didn't have no bell. He had 'em blow bugles to wake up his hands and to call 'em from the fields. Sometimes the overseer blowed it. Mistess done larned the cook to count the clock, but none of the rest of our niggers could count the clock.

"I never knowed Marster to sell but one slave and he jus' had bought her from the market at New Orleans. She say it lonesome off on the plantation and axed Marster for to sell her to folkses livin' in town. Atter he done sold her, every time he got to town she beg 'im to buy her back! But he didn' pay her no more 'tention. When they had sales of slaves on the plantations they let everybody know what time the sale gwine to be. When the crowd git togedder they put the niggers on the block and sell 'em. Leas'wise, they call it 'puttin' on the block'—they jus' fotch 'em out and show 'em and sell 'em.

"They waren't no church for niggers on our plantation and we went to white folkses church and listened to the white preachers. We set behind a partition. Sometimes on a plantation a nigger claim he done been called to preach and effen he kin git his marster's cawn-sent he kin preach round under trees and in cabins when t'aint wuk time. These nigger preachers in slavery time was called 'chairbackers.' They waren't no chairbackers 'lowed to baptize none of Marster's niggers. White preachers done our baptizin' in Long Crick. When we went to be baptized they allus sang, 'Amazing Grace! How sweet the sound!'"

The old negro's quavery voice rose in the familiar song. For a moment he sat thinking of those long-ago Sundays. His eyes brightened again, and he went on:

"We never done no wuk on Sundays on our plantation. The church was 'bout nine miles from the plantation and we all walked there. Anybody too old and feeble to walk the nine miles jus' stayed home, kazen Marster didn't 'low his mules used none on Sunday. All along the way niggers from other plantations 'ud jine us and sometimes befo' we git to the church house they'd be forty or fifty slaves comin' along the road in a crowd! Preaching generally lasted twel bout three o'clock. In summertime we had dinner on the ground at the church. Howsomever we didn' have no barbecue like they does now. Everybody cooked enough on Sadday and fotched it in baskets.

"I was thirty years old when I jined the church. Nobody ought to jine no church twels't he is truly borned of God, and effen he is truly borned of God he gwine know it. Effen you want a restin' place atter you leaves this old world you ought to git ready for it now!

"When folkses on our plantation died Marster allus let many of us as wanted to go, lay offen wuk twel atter the buryin'. Sometimes it were two or three months atter the buryin' befo' the funeral sermon was preached. Right now I can't rekelleck no song we sung at funerals cep'n 'Hark from the tombs a doleful sound.'"

The reedy old voice carried the funeral hymn for a few minutes and then trailed off. James was thinking back into the past again.

"Spring plowin' and hoein' times we wukked all day Saddays, but mos'en generally we laid off wuk at twelve o'clock Sadday. That was dinnertime. Sadday nights we played and danced. Sometimes in the cabins, sometimes in the yards. Effen we didn' have a big stack of fat kindling wood lit up to dance by, sometimes the mens and 'omans would carry torches of kindling wood whils't they danced and it sho' was a sight to see! We danced the 'Turkey Trot' and 'Buzzard Lope', and how we did love to dance the 'Mary Jane!' We would git in a ring and when the music started we would begin wukkin' our footses while we sang 'You steal my true love and I steal your'n!'

"Atter supper we used to gether round and knock tin buckets and pans, we beat 'em like drums. Some used they fingers and some used sticks for to make the drum sounds and somebody allus blowed on quills. Quills was a row of whistles made outen reeds, or sometimes they made 'em outen bark. Every whistle in the row was a different tone and you could play any kind of tune you wants effen you had a good row of quills. They sho' did sound sweet!

"'Bout the most fun we had was at corn shuckin's whar they put the corn in long piles and called in the folkses from the plantations nigh round to shuck it. Sometimes four or five hunnert head of niggers 'ud be shuckin' corn at one time. When the corn all done been shucked they'd drink the likker the marsters give 'em and then frolic and dance from sundown to sunup. We started shuckin' corn 'bout dinnertime and tried to finish by sundown so we could have the whole night for frolic. Some years we 'ud go to ten or twelve corn shuckin's in one year!

"We would sing and pray Easter Sunday and on Easter Monday we frolicked and danced all day long! Christmas we allus had plenty good sumpin' to eat and we all got togedder and had lots of fun. We runned up to the big 'ouse early Christmas mornin' and holler out: 'Mornin', Christmas Gif'!' Then they'd give us plenty of Sandy Claus and we would go back to our cabins to have fun twel New Year's day. We knowed Christmas was over and gone when New Year's day come, kazen we got back to wuk that day atter frolickin' all Christmas week.

"We didn' know nuttin' 'bout games to play. We played with the white folkses chilluns and watched atter 'em but most of the time we played in the crick what runned through the pastur'. Nigger chilluns was allus skeered to go in the woods atter dark. Folkses done told us Raw-Head-and-Bloody Bones lived in the woods and git little chilluns and eat 'em up effen they got out in the woods atter dark!

"'Rockabye baby in the tree trops' was the onliest song I heard my maw sing to git her babies to sleep. Slave folkses sung most all the time but we didn' think of what we sang much. We jus' got happy and started singin'. Sometimes we 'ud sing effen we felt sad and lowdown, but soon as we could, we 'ud go off whar we could go to sleep and forgit all 'bout trouble!" James nodded his gray head with a wise look in his bright eyes. "When you hear a nigger singin' sad songs hit's jus' kazen he can't stop what he is doin' long enough to go to sleep!"

The laughter that greeted this sally brought an answering grin to the wrinkled old face. Asked about marriage customs, James said:

"Folkses didn' make no big to-do over weddings like they do now. When slaves got married they jus' laid down the broom on the floor and the couple jined hands and jumped back-uds over the broomstick. I done seed 'em married that way many a time. Sometimes my marster would fetch Mistess down to the slave quarters to see a weddin'. Effen the slaves gittin' married was house servants, sometimes they married on the back porch or in the back yard at the big 'ouse but plantation niggers what was field hands married in they own cabins. The bride and groom jus' wore plain clothes kazen they didn' have no more.

"When the young marsters and mistesses at the big houses got married they 'lowed the slaves to gadder on the porch and peep through the windows at the weddin'. Mos'en generally they 'ud give the young couple a slave or two to take with them to they new home. My marster's chilluns was too young to git married befo' the war was over. They was seven of them chilluns; four of 'em was gals.

"What sort of tales did they tell 'mongs't the slaves 'bout the Norf befo' the war? To tell the troof, they didn't talk much like they does now 'bout them sort of things. None of our niggers ever runned away and we didn' know nuthin' 'bout no Norf twel long atter freedom come. We visited round each other's cabins at night. I did hear tell 'bout the patterollers. Folkses said effen they cotched niggers out at night they 'ud give 'em 'what Paddy give the drum'.

"Jus' befo' freedom comed 'bout 50 Yankee sojers come through our plantation and told us that the bull-wh-ups and cow-hides was all dead and buried. Them sojers jus' passed on in a hurry and didn' stop for a meal or vittles or nuffin'. We didn't talk much 'bout Mr. Abbieham Lincum endurin' slavery time kazen we was skeered of him atter the war got started. I don't know nothin' 'bout Mr. Jef'son Davis, I don't remember ever hearin' 'bout him. I is heard about Mr. Booker Washin'ton and they do say he runned a moughty good school for niggers.

"One mornin' Marster blowed the bugle his own self and called us all up to the big 'ouse yard. He told us: 'You all jus' as free as I is. You are free from under the task-marster but you ain't free from labor. You gotter labor and wuk hard effen you aims to live and eet and have clothes to wear. You kin stay here and wuk for me, or you kin go wharsomever you please.' He said he 'ud pay us what was right, and Lady, hit's the troof, they didn't nary a nigger on our plantation leave our marster then! I wukked on with Marster for 40 years atter the war!"

James had no fear of the Ku Klux.

"Right soon atter the war we saw plenty of Ku Kluxers but they never bothered nobody on our plantation. They allus seemed to be havin' heaps of fun. 'Course, they did have to straighten out some of them brash young nigger bucks on some of the other farms round about. Mos' of the niggers the Ku Kluxers got atter was'n on no farm, but was jus' roamin' 'round talkin' too much and makin' trouble. They had to take 'em in hand two or three times befo' some of them fool free niggers could be larned to behave theyselfs! But them Ku Kluxers kept on atter 'em twels't they larned they jus got to be good effen they 'spects to stay round here.

"Hit was about 40 years atter the war befo' many niggers 'gun to own they own lan'. They didn' know nothin' 'bout tendin' to money business when the war done ended and it take 'em a long time to larn how to buy and sell and take care of what they makes." James shook his head sadly. "Ma'am, heaps of niggers ain't never larned nothin' 'bout them things yit!

"A long time atter the war I married Lizy Yerby. I didn' give Liza no chanc't for to dress up. Jus' went and tuk her right outer the white folkses' kitchen and married her at the church in her workin' clothes. We had 13 chilluns but they ain't but two of 'em livin' now. Mos' of our chilluns died babies. Endurin' slavery Mistess tuk care of all the nigger babies borned on our plantations and looked atter they mammies too, but atter freedom come heap of nigger babies died out."

James said he had two wives, both widows.

"I married my second wife 37 years ago. To tell the troof, I don't rightly know how many grandchilluns I got, kazen I ain't seed some of 'em for thirty years. My chilluns is off fum here and I wouldn' know to save my life whar they is or what they does. My sister and brothers they is done dead out what ain't gone off, I don't know for sho' whar none of 'em is now."

A sigh punctuated James' monologue, and his old face was shadowed by a look of fear.

"Now I gwine tell you the troof. Now that it's all over I don't find life so good in my old age, as it was in slavery time when I was chillun down on Marster's plantation. Then I didn' have to worry 'bout whar my clothes and my somepin' to eat was comin' from or whar I was gwine to sleep. Marster tuk keer of all that. Now I ain't able for to wuk and make a livin' and hit's sho' moughty hard on this old nigger."

ALEC BOSTWICK
Ex-Slave—Age 76

*[TR: Preceding page that would usually contain information regarding the interview was marked 'Placeholder'.]*

# ALEC BOSTWICK

All of Uncle Alec Bostwick's people are dead and he lives in his tiny home with a young Negress named Emma Vergal. It was a beautiful April morning when his visitor arrived and while he was cordial enough he seemed very reluctant about talking. However, as one question followed another his interest gradually overcame his hesitancy and he began to unfold his life's story.

"I wuz born in Morgan County, an' I warn't mo' dan four year old when de War ended so I don't ricollect nothin' 'bout slav'ry days. I don't know much 'bout my ma, but her name was Martha an' pa's name was Jordan Bostwick, I don't know whar dey come from. When I knowed nothin' I wuz dar on de plantation. I had three brothers; George, John an' Reeje, an' dey's all dead. I dis'members my sister's name. Dar warn't but one gal an' she died when she wuz little.

"Ain't much to tell 'bout what wuz done in de quarters. Slaves wuz gyarded all de time jus' lak Niggers on de chain gang now. De overseer always sot by wid a gun.

"'Bout de beds, Nigger boys didn't pay no 'tention to sich as dat 'cause all dey keered 'bout wuz a place to sleep but 'peers lak to me dey wuz corded beds, made wid four high posties, put together wid iron pegs, an' holes what you run de cords thoo', bored in de sides. De cords wuz made out of b'ar grass woun' tight together. Dey put straw an' old quilts on 'em, an' called 'em beds.

"Gran'pa Berry wuz too old to wuk in de field so he stayed 'roun' de house an' piddled. He cut up wood, tended to de gyarden an' yard, an' bottomed chairs. Gran'ma Liza done de cookin' an' nussed de white folkses chilluns.

"I wukked in de field 'long side da rest of de Niggers, totin' water an' sich lak, wid de overseer dar all de time wid dat gun.

"What you talkin' 'bout Miss? Us didn't have no money. Sho' us didn't. Dey had to feed us an' plenty of it, 'cause us couldn't wuk if dey didn't feed us good.

"Us et cornbread, sweet 'tatoes, peas, home-made syrup an' sich lak. De meat wuz fried sometimes, but mos' of de time it wuz biled wid de greens. All de somethin' t'eat wuz cooked in de fireplace. Dey didn't know what stoves wuz in dem days. Yes Ma'am, us went 'possum huntin' at night, an' us had plenty 'possums too. Dey put sweet 'tatoes an' fat meat roun' 'em, an' baked 'em in a oven what had eyes on each side of it to put hooks in to take it off de fire wid.

"No Ma'am, us didn't go fishin', or rabbit huntin' nuther. Us had to wuk an' warn't no Nigger 'lowed to do no frolickin' lak dat in daytime. De white folkses done all de fishin' an' daytime huntin'. I don't 'member lakin' no sartin' somethin'. I wuz jus' too glad to git anythin'.

Slaves didn't have no gyardens of dey own. Old Marster had one big gyarden what all de slaves et out of.

"Tell you 'bout our clo'es: us wore home-made clo'es, pants an' shirts made out of cotton in summer an' in de winter dey give us mo' home-made clo'es only dey wuz made of wool. All de clawf wuz made on de loom right dar on de plantation. Us wore de same things on Sunday what us did in de week, no diffunt. Our shoes wuz jus' common brogans what dey made at home. I ain't seed no socks 'til long atter de War. Co'se some folkses mought a had 'em, but us didn't have none.

"Marster Berry Bostwick an' Mist'ess Mary Bostwick, had a passel of chillun, I don't 'member none 'cept young Marse John. De others drifted off an' didn't come back, but young Marse John stayed on wid Old Marster an' Old Mist'ess 'til dey died. Old Marster, he warn't good. Truth is de light, an' he wuz one mean white man. Old Mist'ess wuz heaps better dan him. Dar wuz 'bout 150 mens an' 75 'omans. I couldn't keep up wid de chilluns. Dere wuz too many for me.

"Marster an' Mist'ess lived in a big fine house, but de slave quarters wuz made of logs, 'bout de size of box cyars wid two rooms.

"'Bout dat overseer he wuz a mean man, if one ever lived. He got de slaves up wid a gun at five o'clock an' wukked 'em 'til way atter sundown, standin' right over 'em wid a gun all de time. If a Nigger lagged or tuk his eyes off his wuk, right den an' dar he would make him strip down his clo'es to his waist, an' he whup him wid a cat-o-nine tails. Evvy lick dey struck him meant he wuz hit nine times, an' it fotch da red evvy time it struck.

"Oh! Yes Ma'am, dey had a cyar'iage driver, he didn't do much 'cept look attar de hawses an' drive de white folkses 'roun'.

"I done tole you 'bout dat overseer; all he done wuz sot 'roun' all day wid a gun an' make de Niggers wuk. But I'se gwine tell you de trufe, he sho' wuz poor white trash wid a house full of snotty-nose chilluns. Old Marster tole him he wuz jus' lak a rabbit, he had so many chillun. I means dis; if dem days comes back I hope de good Lord takes me fus'.

"Dey had a house whar dey put de Niggers, what wuz called de gyard house, an' us didn't know nothin' 'bout no jail dat day an' time. I seed 'em drive de Niggers by old Marster's place in droves takin' 'em to Watkinsville. Morgan County, whar us lived, touched Oconee an' dat wuz the nighes' town. One day I went wid old Marster to Watkinsville an' I seed 'em sell Niggers on de block. I warn't sold. When I knowed nothin' I wuz right whar I wuz at.

"No Ma'am, dey warn't no schools for de Niggers in dem days. If a Nigger wuz seed wid a paper, de white folks would pretty nigh knock his head off him.

"Us didn't have no church in de country for Niggers, an' dey went to church wid deir white folkses, if dey went a tall. De white folks sot in front, an' de Niggers sot in de back. All de time dat overseer wuz right dar wid his gun. When dey baptized de Niggers dey tuk 'em down to de river and plunged 'em in, while dem what had done been baptized sang: "Dar's a Love Feast in Heb'en Today."

"Yes Ma'am, de white folkses had deir cemetery, an'

dey had one for de slaves. When dere wuz a funeral 'mong de Niggers us sung:

> 'Dark was de night
> And cold was de groun'
> Whar my Marster was laid
> De drops of sweat
> Lak blood run down
> In agony He prayed.'

"Dem coffins sho' wuz mournful lookin' things, made out of pine boa'ds an' painted wid lampblack; dey wuz black as de night. Dey wuz big at de head an' little at de foot, sort a lak airplanes is. De inside wuz lined wid white clawf, what dey spun on de plantation.

"De patterollers wuz right on dey job. Slaves use' to frame up on 'em if dey knowed whar dey wuz hidin', 'waitin' to cotch a Nigger. Dey would git hot ashes an' dash over 'em, an' dem patterollers dey sho' would run, but de slaves would git worse dan dat, if dey was cotched.

"Miss, in slav'ry time when Niggers come from de fields at night dey warn't no frolickin'. Dey jus' went to sleep. De mens wukked all day Sadday, but de 'omans knocked off at twelve o'clock to wash an' sich lak.

"Christmas times dey give us a week off an' brung us a little candy an' stuff 'roun'. Not much, not much. On New Year's Day us had to git back on de job.

"Chilluns what wuz big enough to wuk didn't have time in week days to play no games on Marse Bostwick's place. On Sunday us played wid marbles made out of clay, but dat's all. I heered my ma sing a little song to de baby what soun' lak dis:

> 'Hush little baby
> Don't you cry
> You'll be an angel
> Bye-an'-bye.'

"Yes Ma'am, dere wuz one thing dey wuz good 'bout. When de Niggers got sick dey sont for de doctor. I heered 'em say dey biled jimson weeds an' made tea for colds, an' rhubarb tea wuz to cure worms in chillun. I wuz too young to be bothered 'bout witches an' charms, Rawhead an' Bloody Bones an' sich. I didn't take it in.

"When de Yankees come thoo' an' 'lowed us wuz free, us thought dey wuz jus' dem patterollers, an' us made for de woods. Dey tole us to come out, dat us wuz free Niggers. Marster Berry said: 'You dam Niggers am free. You don't b'long to me no more.'

"Us married long time atter de War, an' us had a little feast: cake, wine, fried chicken, an' ham, an' danced 'til 'mos' daybreak. I 'members how good she looked wid dat pretty dove colored dress, all trimmed wid lace. Us didn't have no chillun. She wuz lak a tree what's sposen to bear fruit an' don't. She died 'bout thirteen years ago.

"When de Ku Kluxers come thoo', us chillun thought de devil wuz atter us for sho'. I wuz sich a young chap I didn't take in what dey said 'bout Mr. Abyham Lincoln, an' Mr. Jeff Davis. Us would a been slaves 'til yit, if Mr. Lincoln hadn't sot us free. Dey wuz bofe of 'em, good mens. I sho' had ruther be free. Who wants a gun over 'em lak a prisoner? A pusson is better off dead.

"I jined de church 'cause dis is a bad place at de bes' an' dere's so many mean folkses, what's out to seem good an' ain't. An' if you serve God in de right way, I'se sho' when you die he'll give you a place to rest for evermore. An' 'cordin' to my notion dat's de way evvybody oughta live."

In conclusion, Alec said: "I don't want to talk no more. I'se disappointed, I thought sho' you wuz one of dem pension ladies what come for to fetch me some money. I sho' wish dey would come. Good-bye Miss." Then he hobbled into the house.

United States. Work Projects Administration

Barragan-Harris
[TR: Miss Maude Barragan (interviewer), Mrs. Leila Harris (editor)]

NANCY BOUDRY, THOMSON, GEORGIA

# NANCY BOUDRY

"If I ain't a hunnard," said Nancy, nodding her white-turbaned head, "I sho' is close to it, 'cause I got a grandson 50 years old."

Nancy's silky white hair showed long and wavy under her headband. Her gingham dress was clean, and her wrinkled skin was a reddish-yellow color, showing a large proportion of Indian and white blood. Har eyes ware a faded blue.

"I speck I is mos' white," acknowledged Nancy, "but I ain't never knowed who my father was. My mother was a dark color."

The cottage faced the pine grove behind an old church. Pink ramblers grew everywhere, and the sandy yard was neatly kept. Nancy's paralyzed granddaughter-in-law hovered in the doorway, her long smooth braids hanging over Indian-brown shoulders, a loose wrapper of dark blue denim flowing around her tall unsteady figure. She was eager to taka part in the conversation but hampered by a thick tongue induced, as Nancy put it, "by a bad sore throat she ain't got over."

Nancy's recollections of plantation days were colored

to a somber hue by overwork, childbearing, poor food and long working hours.

"Master was a hard taskmaster," said Nancy. "My husband didn't live on de same plantation where I was, de Jerrell places in Columbia County. He never did have nuthin' to give me 'cause he never got nuthin'. He had to come and ask my white folks for me. Dey had to carry passes everywhere dey went, if dey didn't, dey'd git in trouble.

"I had to work hard, plow and go and split wood jus' like a man. Sometimes dey whup me. Dey whup me bad, pull de cloes off down to de wais'—my master did it, our folks didn'have overseer.

"We had to ask 'em to let us go to ohurch. Went to white folks church, 'tell de black folks get one of dere own. No'm I dunno how to read. Never had no schools at all, didn' 'low us to pick up a piece paper and look at it."

"Nancy, wasn't your mistress kind to you?"

"Mistis was sorta kin' to me, sometimes. But dey only give me meat and bread, didn' give me nothin' good—I ain' gwine tell no story. I had a heap to undergo wid. I had to scour at night at de Big House—two planks one night, two more de nex'. De women peoples spun at night and reeled, so many cuts a night. Us had to git up befo' daybreak be ready to go to de fiel's.

"My master didn' have but three cullud people, dis yuh was what I stayed wid, my young master, had not been long married and dus' de han's dey give him when he marry was all he had.

"Didn' have no such house as dis," Nancy looked into the open door of the comfortable octtage, "sometimes dey have a house built, it would be daubed. Dus' one family, didn' no two families double up."

"But the children had a good time, didn't they? They played games?"

"Maybe dey did play ring games, I never had no time to see what games my chillus play, I work so hard. Heap o' little chillun slep' on de flo'. Never had no frolics neither, no ma'm, and didn' go to none. We would have prayer meetings on Saturday nights, and one might in de week us had a chairback preacher, and sometimes a regular preacher would come in."

Nancy did not remember ever having seen the Patterollers.

"I hearn talk of 'em you know, heap o' times dey come out and make out like dey gwine shoot you at night, dey mus' been Patterollers, dey was gettin' hold of a heap of 'em."

"What did you do about funerals, Nancy?"

"Dey let us knock off for funerals, I tell de truth. Us stay up all night, singin' and prayin'. Dey make de coffin outter pine boards."

"Did you suffer during the war?"

"We done de bes' we could, we et what we could get, sometimes didn' have nothin' to eat but piece of cornbread, but de white folks allus had chicken."

"But you had clothes to wear?"

"Us had clothes 'cause we spun de thread and weaved 'em. Dey bought dem dere great big ole brogans where you couldn' hardly walk in 'em. Not like dese shoes I got on." Nancy thrust out her foot, easy in "Old Ladies' Comforts."

"When they told you were free, Nancy, did the master appear to be angry?"

"No'm, white folks didn' 'pear to be mad. My master dus' tole us we was free. Us moved right off, but not so far I couldn' go backwards and forwards to see 'um." (So it was evident that even if Nancy's life had been hard, there was a bond between her and her former owners.) "I didn' do no mo' work for 'um, I work for somebody else. Us rented land and made what we could, so we could have little somethin' to eat. I scoured and waited on white people in town, got little piece of money, and was dus' as proud!"

Nancy savored the recollection of her first earned money a moment, thinking back to the old days.

"I had a preacher for my second marriage," she continued, "Fo' chillun died on me—one girl, de yuthers was babies. White doctor tended me."

Asked about midwifery, Nancy smiled.

"I was a midwife myself, to black and white, after freedom. De Thomson doctors all liked me and tole people to 'git Nancy.' I used 'tansy tea'—heap o' little root— made black pepper tea, fotch de pains on 'em. When I would git to de place where I had a hard case, I would send for de doctor, and he would help me out, yes, doctor help me out of all of 'em."

Asked about signs and superstitions, Nancy nodded.

"I have seed things. Day look dus' like a person, walkin' in de woods. I would look off and look back to see it again and it be gone." Nancy lowered her voice mysteriously, and looked back into the little room where Vanna's unsteady figure moved from bed to chair. "I seed a coffin floatin' in de air in dat room—" she shivered, "and I heard a heap o' knockings. I dunno what it bees— but de sounds come in de house. I runs ev'y squeech owl away what comes close, too." Nancy clasped her hands, right thumb over left thumb, "does dat—and it goes on away—dey quits hollerin', you chokin' 'em when you does dat."

"Do you plant by the moon, Nancy?"

"Plant when de moon change, my garden, corn, beans. I planted some beans once on de wrong time of de moon and dey didn' bear nothing—I hated it so bad, I didn' know what to do, so I been mindful ever since when I plant. Women peoples come down on de moon, too. I ain't know no signs to raise chillun. I whup mine when dey didn' do right, I sho' did. I didn' 'low my chillun to take nothin'—no aigs and nothin' 'tall and bring 'em to my house. I say 'put dem right whar you git 'em.''

"Did you sing spirituals, Nancy?"

"I sang regular meetin' songs," she said, "like 'lay dis body down' and 'let yo' joys be known'—but I can't sing now, not any mo'."

Nancy was proud of her quilt-making ability.

"Git 'um, Vanna, let de ladies see 'um," she said;

and when Vanna brought the gay pieces made up in a "double-burst" (sunburst) pattern, Nancy fingered the squares with loving fingers. "Hit's pooty, ain't it?" she asked wistfully, "I made one for a white lady two years ago, but dey hurts my fingers now—makes 'em stiff."

**FOLKLORE INTERVIEW**

ALICE BRADLEY
Hull Street near Corner of Hoyt Street
Athens, Georgia

KIZZIE COLQUITT
243 Macon Avenue
Athens, Georgia

Written by:
Miss Grace McCune
Athens, Georgia

Edited by:
Mrs. Leila Harris
Editor
Federal Writers' Project
Augusta, Georgia
[APR 20 1938]

*[TR: These two interviews were filed together, though not recorded at the same place or time.]*

# ALICE BRADLEY

Alice Bradley, or "Aunt Alice" as she is known to everybody, "runs cards" and claims to be a seeress. Apologetic and embarrassed because she had overslept and was straightening her room, she explained that she hadn't slept well because a dog had howled all night and she was uneasy because of this certain forerunner of disaster.

"Here t'is Sunday mornin' and what wid my back, de dog, and de rheumatics in my feets, its [TR: 'done' crossed out] too late to go to church, so come in honey

I'se glad to hab somebody to talk to. Dere is sho' goin' to be a corpse close 'round here. One night a long time ago two dogs howled all night long and on de nex' Sunday dere wuz two corpses in de church at de same time. Dat's one sign dat neber fails, when a dog howls dat certain way somebody is sho' goin' to be daid."

When asked what her full name was, she said: "My whole name is Alice Bradley now. I used to be a Hill, but when I married dat th'owed me out of bein' a Hill, so I'se jus' a Bradley now. I wuz born on January 14th but I don't 'member what year. My ma had three chillun durin' de war and one jus' atter de war. I think dat las' one wuz me, but I ain't sho'. My pa's name wuz Jim Hill, and ma's name wuz Ca'line Hill. Both of 'em is daid now. Pa died October 12, 1896 and wuz 88 years old. Ma died November 20, 1900; she wuz 80 years old. I knows dem years is right 'cause I got 'em from dat old fambly Bible so I kin git 'em jus' right. One of my sisters, older dan I is, stays in Atlanta wid her son. Since she los' one of her sons, her mind's done gone. My other sister ain't as old as I is but her mind is all right and she is well."

"I wuz raised in Washin'ton, Wilkes County, and de fust I 'members was stayin' wid Miss Alice Rayle. She had three chillun and I nussed 'em. One of de boys is a doctor now, and has a fambly of his own, and de las' I heared of 'im, he wuz stayin' in Atlanta.

"I'se been married' two times. I runned away wid Will Grisham, when I wuz 'bout 14 years old. Mr. Carter, a Justice of de Peace, met us under a 'simmon tree and tied de knot right dar. My folks ketched us, but us wuz already married and so it didn't make no diffunce.

"I lived on a farm wid my fust husband, and us had three chillun, but dey is all gone now. I 'members when my oldes' gal wuz 'bout 2 years old, dey wuz playin' out on de porch wid dey little dog, when a mad dog come by and bit my chillun's dog. Folks kilt our dog, and jus' 'bout one week atterwards my little gal wuz daid too. She did love dat little dog, and he sho' did mind 'er. She jus' grieved herself to death 'bout dat dog.

"Atter my fust husband died, I married Rich Bradley. Rich wuz a railroad man, and he went off to Washin'ton, D.C., to wuk. He sont me money all de time den, but when he went from dar to Shecargo to wuk I didn't hear from 'im long, and I don't know what's happened to 'im 'til now, for it's been a long time since I heared from 'im.

"I loves to run de cyards for my friends. I always tells 'em when I sees dere's trouble in de cyards for 'em, and shows 'em how to git 'round it, if I kin. None of de res' of my folks ever run de cyards, but I'se been at it ever since I wuz jus' a little gal, pickin' up old wore out cyards, dat had bean th'owed away, 'cause I could see things in 'em. I 'members one time when I wuz small and didn't know so good what de cyards wuz tellin' me, dat a rich man, one of de riches' in Wilkes County, wuz at our place, I tol 'im de cyards when I run 'em. I saw sompin' wuz goin' to happen on his place, dat two colored mens would be tangled up wid, but I didn't know jus' what wuz goin' to happen. And sho' 'nuff, two colored mens sot fire to his barns and burned up all his horses and mules, de onlies' thing dey saved wuz one ridin' horse. Dey ketched de mens, and dey served time for what dey done. One of 'em died way out yonder where dey sont 'em.

"I 'members one white lady way out in Alabama sont

a note axin' me to run de cyards for her. I runned 'em and got one of my friends to writer her what I seed. Dey had run bright and dat wuz good luck. One time I runned de cyards for two sisters dat had done married two brothers, and de cyards run so close kin date I wuz able to tell 'em how dey wuz married and dey tol me dat I wuz right.

"And jus' a few days ago a old man come to see me thinkin' dat he wuz pizened. When I runned de cyards, I seed his trouble. He had been drinkin' and wuz sick, so I jus' give him a big dose of soda and cream of tartar and he got better. Den I tole him to go on home; dat nobody hadn't done nothin' to 'im and all he needed wuz a little medicine.

"I told Mr. Dick Armell of how he wuz goin' to git kilt if he went up in his airyplane dat day and begged him not to try it but to wait. He wouldn't listen and went on and got kilt jus' lak I tole 'im he would. I runned de cyards for Mrs. Armell lots of times for I liked 'im, and he wuz a fine man. I runned de cyards for 'im one time 'fore he went to de World's Fair, and de cyards run bright, and his trip wuz a good one jus' lak I tole 'im it would be.

"All de old white folks dat I wuz raised up wid, de Hills from Washin'ton, Wilkes, is gone now, 'cept I think one of de gals is wukin' at de capitol in Atlanta, but she done married now and I don't 'member her name."

Alice excused herself to answer a knock at the door. Upon her return she said: "Dat wuz one of my white chillun. I wukked for 'em so long and one of 'em comes by every now an' den to see if I needs sompin'. Her ma done had a new picture of herself took and wanted me to see it. Dey sho' is good to me."

Alice doesn't charge for "running the cards." She says she doesn't have a license, and is very thankful for anything that visitors may care to give her. She will not run the cards on Sunday. "Dat's bad luck," she said. "Come back some day when tain't Sunday, and I'll see whats in de cyards for you!"

United States. Work Projects Administration

# KIZZIE COLQUITT

Old Aunt Kizzie Colquitt, about 75 years old, was busily washing in her neat kitchen. She opened the door and window frequently to let out the smoke, saying: "Dis old wore out stove don't draw so good." Her hands and feet were badly swollen and she seemed to be suffering.

"I'll be glad to tell all I kin 'member 'bout dem old times," she said. "I wuz borned durin' de war, but I don't 'member what year. My pa wuz Mitchell Long. He b'longed to Marster Sam Long of Elbert County. Us lived on Broad River. My ma wuz Sallie Long, and she b'longed to Marster Billie Lattimore. Dey stayed on de other side of Broad River and my pa and ma had to cross de river to see one another. Atter de war wuz over, and dey wuz free, my pa went to Jefferson, Georgia, and dar he died.

"My ma married some nigger from way out in Indiana. He promised her he would send money back for her chillun, but us never heered nothin' from 'im no mo'. I wuz wid' my w'ite folks, de Lattimores, when my ma died, way out in Indiana.

"Atter Marse Bob died, I stayed wid my old Missus, and slep' by her bed at night. She wuz good to me, and de hardes' wuk I done wuz pickin' up acorns to fatten de hogs. I stayed dar wid her 'til she died. Us had plenty t'eat, a smokehouse filled wid hams, and all de other things us needed. Dey had a great big fireplace and a big old time oven whar dey baked bread, and it sho' wuz good bread.

"My old Missus died when I wuz 'bout 6 years old, and I wus sont to Lexin'ton, Georgia, to live wid my sister. Dere wuz jus' da two of us chilluns. Den us wukked every day, and went to bed by dark; not lak de young folks now, gallivantin' 'bout all night long.

"When I wuz 'bout 14 I married and come to live on Dr. Willingham's place. It wuz a big plantation, and dey really lived. When de crops wuz all in and all de wuk done, dey had big times 'round dar.

"Dere wuz de corn shuckin' wid one house for de corn and another house for de shucks. Atter all de shuckin' wuz done, dere wuz eatin' and dancin'. And it wuz eatin' too! Dey kilt hogs, barbecued 'em, and roasted some wid apples in dey mouf's to give 'em a good flavor, and course a little corn likker went wid it. Dey had big doin's at syrup makin' time too, but dat wuz hard wuk den. Makin' syrup sho' wuz a heap of trouble.

"Later us lived wid de Johnson fambly, and atter my old man died, I come to dis town wid de Johnsons. Dere wuz three chilluns, Percy, Lewis, and a gal. I stayed wid 'em 'til de chilluns wuz all growed up and eddicated. All my other w'ite folks is gone; my sister done gone too, and my son; all de chillun dat I had, deys done daid too.

"Now I has to wash so I kin live. I used to have plenty, but times is changed and now sometimes I don't have nothin' but bread, and jus' bread is hard to git, heap of de time.

"I put in for one of dem old age pensions, but dey ain't give me nothin' yet, so I jus' wuk when I kin, and hope dat it won't be long 'fore I has plenty again."

OLD SLAVE STORY

DELLA BRISCOE
Macon, Georgia

By Adella S. Dixon [HW: (Colored)]
[JUL 28 1937]

# DELLA BRISCOE

Della Briscoe, now living in Macon, is a former slave of Mr. David Ross, who owned a large plantation in Putnam County. Della, when a very tiny child, was carried there with her father and mother, Sam and Mary Ross. Soon after their arrival the mother was sent to work at the "big house" in Eatonton. This arrangement left Della, her brother and sister to the care of their grandmother, who really posed as their mother. The children grew up under the impression that their mother was an older sister and did not know the truth until just after the close of the Civil War, when the mother became seriously ill and called the children to her bedside to tell them goodbye.

Mr. David Ross had a large family and was considered the richest planter in the county. Nearly every type of soil was found on his vast estate, composed of hilly sections as well as acres of lowlands. The highway entering Eatonton divided the plantation and, down this road every Friday, Della's father drove the wagon to town with a supply of fresh butter, for Mrs. Ross' thirty head of cows supplied enough milk to furnish the city dwellers with butter.

Refrigeration was practically unknown, so a well was used to keep the butter fresh. This cool well was eighty feet deep and passed through a layer of solid rock. A rope ladder was suspended from the mouth of the well to the place where the butter was lowered for preservation. For safety, and to shield it from the sun, reeds were planted all around the well. And as they grew very tall, a stranger would not suspect a well being there.

In addition to marketing, Della's father trapped beavers which were plentiful in the swampy part of the plantation bordering the Oconee, selling their pelts to traders in the nearby towns of Augusta and Savannah, where Mr. Ross also marketed his cotton and large quantities of corn. Oxen, instead of mules, were used to make the trips to market and return, each trip consuming six or seven days.

The young children were assigned small tasks, such as piling brush in "new grounds", carrying water to field hands, and driving the calves to pasture.

Punishment was administered, though not as often as on some plantations. The little girl, Della, was whipped only once—for breaking up a turkey's nest she had found. Several were accused of this, and because the master could not find the guilty party, he whipped each of the children.

Crime was practically unknown and Mr. Ross' slaves never heard of a jail until they were freed.

Men were sometimes placed in "bucks", which meant

they were laid across blocks with their hands and feet securely tied. An iron bar was run between the blocks to prevent any movement; then, after being stripped, they were whipped. Della said that she knew of but one case of this type of punishment being administered a Ross slave. Sickness was negligible—childbirth being practically the only form of a Negro woman's "coming down".

As a precaution against disease, a tonic was given each slave every spring. Three were also, every spring, taken from the field each day until every one had been given a dose of calomel and salts. Mr. Ross once bought two slaves who became ill with smallpox soon after their arrival. They were isolated in a small house located in the center of a field, while one other slave was sent there to nurse them. All three were burned to death when their hut was destroyed by fire.

In case of death, even on a neighboring place, all work was suspended until the dead was buried.

Sunday, the only day of rest, was often spent in attending religious services, and because these were irregularly held, brush arbor meetings were common. This arbor was constructed of a brush roof supported by posts and crude joists. The seats were usually made of small saplings nailed to short stumps.

Religion was greatly stressed and every child was christened shortly after its birth. An adult who desired to join the church went first to the master to obtain his permission. He was then sent to the home of a minister who lived a short distance away at a place called Flat Rock. Here, his confession was made and, at the next regular service, he was formally received into the church.

Courtships were brief.

The "old man", who was past the age for work and only had to watch what went on at the quarters, was usually the first to notice a budding friendship, which he reported to the master. The couple was then questioned and, if they consented, were married without the benefit of clergy.

Food was distributed on Monday night, and for each adult slave the following staple products were allowed—

| Weekly ration: | On Sunday: |
|---|---|
| 3-1/2 lbs. meat | One qt. syrup |
| 1 pk. of meal | One gal. flour |
| 1 gal. shorts | One cup lard |

Vegetables, milk, etc., could be obtained at the "big house", but fresh meat and chickens were never given. The desire for these delicacies often overcame the slaves' better natures, and some frequently went night foraging for small shoats and chickens.

The "old man" kept account of the increase or decrease in live stock and poultry and reported anything missing each day. When suspicion fell on a visitor of the previous night, this information was given to his master, who then searched the accused's dinner pail and cabin. If meat was found in either the culprit was turned over to his accuser for punishment. After being whipped, he was forbidden for three months to visit the plantation where he had committed the theft.

One of Della's grandmother's favorite recipes was made of dried beef and wheat. The wheat was brought from the field and husked by hand. This, added to the rapidly boiling beef, was cooked until a mush resulted, which was then eaten from wooden bowls with spoons of the same material. White plates were never used by the slaves.

Cloth for clothing was woven on the place. Della's grandmother did most of the spinning, and she taught her child to spin when she was so small that she had to stand on a raised plank to reach the wheel. After the cloth was spun it was dyed with dye made from "shoemake" (sumac) leaves, green walnuts, reeds, and copperas. One person cut and others sewed. The dresses for women were straight, like slips, and the garments of the small boys resembled night shirts. If desired, a bias fold of contrasting colour was placed at the waist line or at the bottom of dresses. The crudely made garments were starched with a solution of flour or meal and water which was strained and then boiled.

As a small child Della remembers hearing a peculiar knock on the door during the night, and a voice which replied to queries, "No one to hurt you, but keep that red flannel in your mouth. Have you plenty to eat? Don't worry; you'll be free." No one would ever tell, if they knew, to whom this voice belonged.

Just before the beginning of the Civil War a comet appeared which was so bright that the elder people amused themselves by sitting on the rail fence and throwing pins upon the ground where the reflection was cast. The children scrambled madly to see who could find the most pins.

During the early part of the war Mr. Ross fought

with the Confederates, leaving his young son, Robert, in charge of his affairs. The young master was very fond of horses and his favorite horse—"Bill"—was trained to do tricks. One of these was to lie down when tickled on his flanks. The Yankees visited the plantation and tried to take this horse. Robert, who loved him dearly, refused to dismount, and as they were about to shoot the horse beneath him, the slaves began to plead. They explained that the boy was kind to every one and devoted to animals, after which explanation, he was allowed to keep his horse.

The breastworks at Savannah required many laborers to complete their construction, and as the commanders desired to save the strength of their soldiers, slave labor was solicited. Two slaves from each nearby plantation were sent to work for a limited number of days. The round trip from the Ross plantation required seven days.

Nearly every man had a family and when they returned from these long trips they drove to the quarters and fell on their knees to receive the welcome caresses of their small children.

Recreational facilities were not provided and slave children had little knowledge of how to play. Their two main amusements were building frog houses and sliding down a steep bank on a long board. One day, as they played up and down the highway, building frog houses at irregular intervals, little Della looked up and saw a group of Yankee calvarymen approaching. She screamed and began running and so attracted the attention of Mr. Ross who was at home on a furlough.

He saw the men in time to find a hiding place. Meanwhile, the soldiers arrived and the leader, springing from his horse, snatched Della up and spanked her soundly for giving the alarm, as they had hoped to take her master by surprise. Della said this was the first "white slap" she ever received.

Some of the Yankees entered the house, tore up the interior, and threw the furniture out doors. Another group robbed the smokehouse and smashed so many barrels of syrup that it ran in a stream through the yard. They carried much of the meat off with them and gave the remainder to the slaves. Chickens were caught, dressed, and fried on the spot as each soldier carried his own frying pan, and a piece of flint rock and a sponge with which to make a fire. The men were skilled in dressing fowls and cleaned them in a few strokes.

When they had eaten as much as they desired, a search for the corral was made, but the mules were so well hidden that they were not able to find them. Della's father's hands were tied behind him and he was then forced to show them the hiding place. These fine beasts, used for plowing, were named by the slaves who worked them. Characteristic names were: "Jule", "Pigeon", "Little Deal", "Vic", (the carriage horse), "Streaked leg," "Kicking Kid", "Sore-back Janie". Every one was carried off.

This raid took place on Christmas Eve and the slaves were frantic as they had been told that Yankees were mean people, especially was Sherman so pictured.

When Sherman had gone, Mr. Ross came from his hiding place in the "cool well" and spoke to his slaves. To the elder ones he said, "I saw you give away my meat and mules."

"Master, we were afraid. We didn't want to do it, but we were afraid not to."

"Yes, I understand that you could not help yourselves." He then turned to the children, saying, "Bless all of you, but to little Della, I owe my life. From now on she shall never be whipped, and she shall have a home of her own for life."

She shook with laughter as she said, "Master thought I screamed to warn him and I was only frightened."

True to his word, after freedom he gave her a three-acre plot of land upon which he built a house and added a mule, buggy, cow, hogs, etc. Della lived there until after her marriage, when she had to leave with her husband. She later lost her home. Having been married twice, she now bears the name of Briscoe, her last husband's name.

When the family had again settled down to the ordinary routine, a new plague, body lice, said to have been left by the invaders, made life almost unbearable for both races.

Della now lives with her granddaughter, for she has been unable to work for twenty-eight years. Macon's Department of Public Welfare assists in contributing to her livelihood, as the granddaughter can only pay the room rent.

She does not know her age but believes that she is above ninety. Her keen old eyes seemed to look back into those bygone days as she said, "I got along better den dan I eber hab since. We didn't know nuthin 'bout jail houses, paying for our burial grounds, and de rent. We had plenty o' food."

[HW: Dist. 6
Ex. Slv. #11]

GEORGE BROOKS, EX-SLAVE
Date of birth: Year unknown (See below)
Place of birth: In Muscogee County, near Columbus, Georgia
Present Residence: 502 East 8th Street, Columbus, Georgia
Interviewed: August 4, 1936
[MAY 8 1937]

# GEORGE BROOKS

This old darky, probably the oldest ex-slave in West Georgia, claims to be 112 years of age. His colored friends are also of the opinion that he is fully that old or older—but, since none of his former (two) owners' people can be located, and no records concerning his birth can be found, his definite age cannot be positively established.

"Uncle" George claims to have worked in the fields, "some", the year the "stars fell"—1833.

His original owner was Mr. Henry Williams—to whom he was greatly attached. As a young man, he was—for a number of years—Mr. Williams' personal body-servant. After Mr. Williams' death—during the 1850's, "Uncle" George was sold to a white man—whose name he doesn't remember—of Dadeville, Alabama, with whom he subsequently spent five months in the Confederate service.

One of "Uncle" George's stories is to the effect that he once left a chore he was doing for his second "Marster's" wife, "stepped" to a nearby well to get a drink of water and, impelled by some strange, irresistible "power", "jes kep on walkin 'til he run slap-dab inter de Yankees", who corraled him and kept him for three months.

Still another story he tells is that of his being sold after freedom! According to his version of this incident, he was sold along with two bales of cotton in the fall of 1865—either the cotton being sold and he "thrown in" with it, or vice versa—he doesn't know which, but he does know that he and the cotton were "sold" together! And very soon after this transaction occurred, the seller was clapped in jail! Then, "somebody" (he doesn't remember who) gave him some money, put him on a stage-coach at night and "shipped" him to Columbus, where he learned that he was a free man and has since remained.

"Uncle" George has been married once and is the father of several children. His wife, however, died fifty-odd years ago and he knows nothing of the whereabouts of his children—doesn't even know whether or not any of them are living, having lost "all track o'all kin fokes too long ago to tawk about."

Unfortunately, "Uncle" George's mind is clouded and his memory badly impaired, otherwise his life story would perhaps be quite interesting. For more than twenty years, he has been supported and cared for by kind hearted members of his race, who say that they intend to continue "to look after the old man 'til he passes on."

EX-SLAVE INTERVIEW

EASTER BROWN
1020 S. Lumpkin Street
Athens, Georgia

Written By:
Mrs. Sadie B. Hornsby

Edited By:
John N. Booth
Federal Writers' Project
WPA Residency No. 7

# EASTER BROWN

"Aunt" Easter Brown, 78 years old, was sweeping chips into a basket out in front of her cabin. "Go right in honey, I'se comin' soon as I git some chips for my fire. Does I lak to talk 'bout when I wuz a chile? I sho does. I warn't but 4 years old when de war wuz over, but I knows all 'bout it."

"I wuz born in Floyd County sometime in October. My pa wuz Erwin and my ma wuz Liza Lorie. I don't know whar dey come from, but I knows dey wuz from way down de country somewhars. Dere wuz six of us chilluns. All of us wuz sold. Yessum, I wuz sold too. My oldest brother wuz named Jim. I don't riccolec' de others, dey wuz all sold off to diffunt parts of de country, and us never heared from 'em no more. My brother, my pa and me wuz sold on de block in Rome, Georgia. Marster Frank Glenn buyed me. I wuz so little dat when dey bid me off, dey had to hold me up so folkses could see me. I don't 'member my real ma and pa, and I called Marster 'pa' an' Mist'ess 'ma', 'til I wuz 'bout 'leven years old.

"I don't know much 'bout slave quarters, or what dey had in 'em, 'cause I wuz raised in de house wid de white folkses. I does know beds in de quarters wuz lak shelves. Holes wuz bored in de side of de house, two in de wall and de floor, and poles runnin' from de wall and de floor, fastened together wid pegs; on 'em dey put planks, and cross de foot of de bed dey put a plank to hold de straw and keep de little 'uns from fallin' out.

"What did us have to eat? Lordy mussy! Mist'ess! us had everything. Summertime dere wuz beans, cabbage, squashes, irish 'tatoes, roas'en ears, 'matoes, cucumbers, cornbread, and fat meat, but de Nigger boys, dey wuz plum fools 'bout hog head. In winter dey et sweet 'tatoes, collards, turnips and sich, but I et lak de white folkses. I sho does lak 'possums and rabbits. Yessum, some of de slaves had gyardens, some of 'em sholy did.

"No'm, us Niggers never wore no clothes in summer, I means us little 'uns. In de winter us wore cotton clothes, but us went barefoots. My uncle Sam and some of de other Niggers went 'bout wid dey foots popped open from de cold. Marster had 110 slaves on his plantation.

"Mist'ess wuz good to me. Pa begged her to buy me, 'cause she wuz his young Mist'ess and he knowed she would be good to me, but Marster wuz real cruel. He'd beat his hoss down on his knees and he kilt one of 'em. He whupped de Niggers when dey didn't do right. Niggers is lak dis; dey wuz brought to dis here land wild as bucks, and dey is lak chicken roosters in a pen. You just have to make 'em 'have deyselves. Its lak dat now; if dey'd 'have deyselves, white folkses would let 'em be.

"Dere warn't no jails in dem days. Dey had a gyuard house what dey whupped 'em in, and Mondays and Tuesdays wuz set aside for de whuppin's, when de Niggers what had done wrong got so many lashes, 'cordin' to what devilment dey had been doin'. De overseer didn't do de whuppin', Marster done dat. Dem patterrollers wuz sompin else. Mankind! If dey ketched a Nigger out atter dark widout no pass dey'd most nigh tear de hide offen his back.

"I'll tell you what dat overseer done one night. Some enemy of Marster's sot fire to de big frame house whar him and Mist'ess and de chillun lived. De overseer seed it burnin', and run and clam up de tree what wuz close to de house, went in de window and got Marster's two little gals out dat burnin' house 'fore you could say scat. Dat sho fixed de overseer wid old Marster. Atter dat Marster give him a nice house to live in but Marster's fine old house sho wuz burnt to de ground.

"De cyarriage driver wuz uncle Sam. He drove de chillun to school, tuk Marster and Mist'ess to church, and done de wuk 'round de house; such as, totin' in wood, keepin' de yards and waitin' on de cook. No'm us slaves didn't go to church; de Niggers wuz so wore out on Sundays, dey wuz glad to stay home and rest up, 'cause de overseer had 'em up way 'fore day and wuked 'em 'til long atter dark. On Saddays dey had to wash deir clothes and git ready for de next week. Some slaves might a had special things give to 'em on Christmas and New Years Day, but not on Marster's plantation; dey rested up a day and dat wuz all. I heared tell dey had Christmas fixin's and doin's on other plantations, but not on Marse Frank's place. All corn shuckin's, cotton pickin's, log rollin's, and de lak was when de boss made 'em do it, an' den dere sho warn't no extra sompin t'eat.

"De onliest game I ever played wuz to take my doll made out of a stick wid a rag on it and play under a tree. When I wuz big 'nough to wuk, all I done wuz to help de cook in de kitchen and play wid old Mist'ess' baby.

"Some of de Niggers runned away. Webster, Hagar, Atney, an' Jane runned away a little while 'fore freedom. Old Marster didn't try to git 'em back, 'cause 'bout dat time de war wuz over. Marster and Mist'ess sho looked atter de Niggers when dey got sick for dey knowed dat if a Nigger died dat much property wuz lost. Yessum, dey had a doctor sometime, but de most dey done wuz give 'em hoarhound, yellow root and tansy. When a baby wuz cuttin' teeth, dey biled ground ivy and give 'em.

"Louisa, de cook wuz married in de front yard. All I 'members 'bout it wuz dat all de Niggers gathered in de yard, Louisa had on a white dress; de white folkses sho fixed Louisa up, 'cause she wuz deir cook.

"Jus' lemme tell you 'bout my weddin' I buyed myself a dress and had it laid out on de bed, den some triflin', no 'count Nigger wench tuk and stole it 'fore I had a chance to git married in it. I had done buyed dat dress for two pupposes; fust to git married in it, and second to be buried in. I stayed on wid Old Miss 'til I got 'bout grown and den I drifted to Athens. When I married my fust husband, Charlie Montgomery, I wuz wukkin' for Mrs. W.R. Booth, and us married in her dinin' room. Charlie died out and I married James Hoshier. Us had one baby. Hit wuz a boy. James an' our boy is both daid now and I'se all by myself.

"What de slaves done when dey wuz told dat dey wuz free? I wuz too little to know what dey meant by freedom, but Old Marster called de overseer and told him to ring de bell for de Niggers to come to de big house. He told 'em dey wuz free devils and dey could go whar dey pleased and do what dey pleased—dey could stay wid him if dey wanted to. Some stayed wid Old Marster and some went away. I never seed no yankee sojers. I heared tell of 'em comin' but I never seed none of 'em.

"No'm I don't know nothin' 'bout Abraham Lincoln, Booker T. Washington or Jefferson Davis. I didn't try to ketch on to any of 'em. As for slavery days; some of de Niggers ought to be free and some oughtn't to be. I don't know nuttin much 'bout it. I had a good time den, and I gits on pretty good now.

"How come I jined de church? Well I felt lak it wuz time for me to live better and git ready for a home in de next world. Chile you sho has axed me a pile of questions, and I has sho 'joyed tellin' you what I knowed."

United States. Work Projects Administration

JULIA BROWN (Aunt Sally)
710 Griffin Place, N.W.
Atlanta, Ga.
July 25, 1936[TR:?]

by
Geneva Tonsill

[TR: One page of this interview was repeated in typescript; where there was a discrepancy, the clearer version was used.]

# JULIA BROWN

## Ah Always Had A Hard Time

Aunt Sally rocked back and forth incessantly. She mopped her wrinkled face with a dirty rag as she talked. "Ah wuz born fo' miles frum Commerce, Georgia, and wuz thirteen year ole at surrender. Ah belonged to the Nash fambly—three ole maid sisters. My mama belonged to the Nashes and my papa belonged to General Burns; he wuz a officer in the war. There wuz six of us chilluns, Lucy, Malvina, Johnnie, Callie, Joe and me. We didn't stay together long, as we wuz give out to different people. The Nashes didn't believe in selling slaves but we wuz known as their niggers. They sold one once 'cause the other slaves said they would kill him 'cause he had a baby by his own daughter. So to keep him frum bein' kilt, they sold him.

"My mama died the year of surrender. Ah didn't fare well after her death, Ah had sicha hard time. Ah wuz give to the Mitchell fambly and they done every cruel thing they could to me. Ah slept on the flo' nine years, winter and summer, sick or well. Ah never wore anything but a cotton dress, a shimmy and draw's. That 'oman didn't care what happened to the niggers. Sometimes she would take us to church. We'd walk to the church house. Ah never went nowhere else. That 'oman took delight in sellin' slaves. She'd lash us with a cowhide whip. Ah had to shift fur mahself.

"They didn't mind the slaves matin', but they wanted their niggers to marry only amongst them on their place. They didn't 'low 'em to mate with other slaves frum other places. When the wimmen had babies they wuz treated kind and they let 'em stay in. We called it 'lay-in', just about lak they do now. We didn't go to no horspitals as they do now, we jest had our babies and had a granny to catch 'em. We didn't have all the pain-easin' medicines then. The granny would put a rusty piece of tin or a ax under the mattress and this would ease the pains. The granny put a ax under my mattress once. This wuz to cut off the after-pains and it sho did too, honey. We'd set up the fifth day and after the 'layin-in' time wuz up we wuz 'lowed to walk out doors and they tole us to walk around the house jest once and come in the house. This wuz to keep us frum takin' a 'lapse.

"We wuzn't 'lowed to go around and have pleasure as the folks does today. We had to have passes to go wherever we wanted. When we'd git out there wuz a bunch of white men called the 'patty rollers'. They'd come in and see if all us had passes and if they found any who didn't have a pass he wuz whipped; give fifty or more lashes—and they'd count them lashes. If they said a hundred you got a hundred. They wuz somethin' lak the Klu Klux. We wuz 'fraid to tell our masters about the patty rollers because we wuz skeered they'd whip us again, fur we wuz tole not to tell. They'd sing a little ditty. Ah wish Ah could remember the words, but it went somethin' lak this:

> 'Run, Niggah, run, de Patty Rollers'll git you,
> Run Niggah, ran, you'd bettah git away.'

"We wuz 'fraid to go any place.

"Slaves ware treated in most cases lak cattle. A man went about the country buyin' up slaves lak buyin' up cattle and the like, and he wuz called a 'speculator', then he'd sell 'em to the highest bidder. Oh! it wuz pitiful to see chil'en taken frum their mothers' breast, mothers sold, husbands sold frum wives. One 'oman he wuz to buy had a baby, and of course the baby come befo' he bought her and he wouldn't buy the baby; said he hadn't bargained to buy the baby too, and he jest wouldn't. My uncle wuz married but he wuz owned by one master and his wife wuz owned by another. He wuz 'lowed to visit his wife on Wednesday and Saturday, that's the onliest time he could git off. He went on Wednesday and when he went back on Saturday his wife had been bought by the speculator and he never did know where she wuz.

"Ah worked hard always. Honey, you can't 'magine what a hard time Ah had. Ah split rails lak a man. How did Ah do it? Ah used a huge glut, and a iron wedge drove into the wood with a maul, and this would split the wood.

"Ah help spin the cotton into thread fur our clothes. The thread wuz made into big broaches—four broaches made four cuts, or one hank. After the thread wuz made we used a loom to weave the cloth. We had no sewin' machine—had to sew by hand. My mistress had a big silver bird and she would always catch the cloth in the bird's bill and this would hold it fur her to sew.

"Ah didn't git to handle money when I wuz young. Ah worked frum sunup to sundown. We never had overseers lak some of the slaves. We wuz give so much work to do in a day and if the white folks went off on a vacation they would give us so much work to do while they wuz gone and we better have all of that done too when they'd come home. Some of the white folks wuz very kind to their slaves. Some did not believe in slavery and some freed them befo' the war and even give 'em land and homes. Some would give the niggers meal, lard and lak that. They made me hoe when Ah wuz a chile and Ah'd keep rat up with the others, 'cause they'd tell me that if Ah got behind a run-a-way nigger would git me and split open my head and git the milk out'n it. Of course Ah didn't know then that wuzn't true—Ah believed everything they tole me and that made me work the harder.

"There wuz a white man, Mister Jim, that wuz very mean to the slaves. He'd go 'round and beat 'em. He'd even go to the little homes, tear down the chimneys and do all sorts of cruel things. The chimneys wuz made of mud 'n straw 'n sticks; they wuz powerful strong too. Mister Jim wuz jest a mean man, and when he died we all said God got tired of Mister Jim being so mean and kilt him. When they laid him out on the coolin' board, everybody wuz settin' 'round, moanin' over his death, and all of a sudden Mister Jim rolled off'n the coolin' board, and sich a runnin' and gittin' out'n that room you never saw. We said Mister Jim wuz tryin' to run the niggers and we wuz 'fraid to go about at night. Ah believed it then; now that they's 'mbalmin' Ah know that must have been gas and he wuz purgin', fur they didn't know nothin' 'bout 'mbalmin' then. They didn't keep dead folks out'n the ground long in them days.

"Doctors wuzn't so plentiful then. They'd go 'round in buggies and on hosses. Them that rode on a hoss had saddle pockets jest filled with little bottles and lots of them. He'd try one medicine and if it didn't do not [TR: no?] good he'd try another until it did do good and when the doctor went to see a sick pusson he'd stay rat there until he wuz better. He didn't jest come in and write a 'scription fur somebody to take to a drug store. We used herbs a lots in them days. When a body had dropsy we'd set him in a tepid bath made of mullein leaves. There wuz a jimson weed we'd use fur rheumatism, and fur asthma we'd use tea made of chestnut leaves. We'd git the chestnut leaves, dry them in the sun jest lak tea leaves, and we wouldn't let them leaves git wet fur nothin' in the world while they wuz dryin'. We'd take poke salad roots, boil them and then take sugar and make a syrup. This wuz the best thing fur asthma. It was known to cure it too. Fur colds and sich we used ho'hound; made candy out'n it with brown sugar. We used a lots of rock candy and whiskey fur colds too. They had a remedy that they used fur consumption—take dry cow manure, make a tea of this and flavor it with mint and give it to the sick pusson. We didn't need many doctors then fur we didn't have so much sickness in them days, and nachelly they didn't die so fast; folks lived a long time then. They used a lot of peachtree leaves too for fever, and when the stomach got upsot we'd crush the leaves, pour water over them and wouldn't let them drink any other kind of water 'till they wuz better. Ah still believes in them ole ho'made medicines too and ah don't believe in so many doctors.

"We didn't have stoves plentiful then: just ovens we set in the fireplace. Ah's toted a many a armful of bark—good ole hickory bark to cook with. We'd cook light bread—both flour and corn. The yeast fur this bread wuz made frum hops. Coals of fire wuz put on top of the oven and under the bottom, too. Everything wuz cooked on coals frum a wood fire—coffee and all. Wait, let me show you my coffee tribet. Have you ever seen one? Well, Ah'll show you mine." Aunt Sally got up and hobbled to the kitchen to get the trivet. After a few moments search she came back into the room.

"No, it's not there. Ah guess it's been put in the basement. Ah'll show it to you when you come back. It's a rack made of iron that the pot is set on befo' puttin' it on the fire coals. The victuals wuz good in them days; we got our vegetables out'n the garden in season and didn't have all the hot-house vegetables. Ah don't eat many vegetables now unless they come out'n the garden and I know it. Well, as I said, there wuz racks fitted in the fireplace to put pots on. Once there wuz a big pot settin' on the fire, jest bilin' away with a big roast in it. As the water biled, the meat turned over and over, comin' up to the top and goin' down again, Ole Sandy, the dog, come in the kitchen. He sot there a while and watched that meat roll over and over in the pot, and all of a sudden-like he grabbed at that meat and pulls it out'n the pot. 'Course he couldn't eat it 'cause it wuz hot and they got the meat befo' he et it. The kitchen wuz away frum the big house, so the victuals wuz cooked and carried up to the house. Ah'd carry it up mahse'f. We couldn't eat all the different kinds of victuals the white folks et and one mornin' when I was carryin' the breakfast to the big house we had waffles that wuz a pretty golden brown and pipin' hot. They wuz a picture to look at and ah jest couldn't keep frum takin' one, and that wuz the hardest waffle fur me to eat befo' I got to the big house I ever saw. Ah jest couldn't git rid of that waffle 'cause my conscience whipped me so.

"They taught me to do everything. Ah'd use battlin' blocks and battlin' sticks to wash the clothes; we all did. The clothes wuz taken out of the water an put on the block and beat with a battlin' stick, which was made like a paddle. On wash days you could hear them battlin' sticks poundin' every which-away. We made our own soap, used ole meat and grease, and poured water over wood ashes which wuz kept in a rack-like thing and the water would drip through the ashes. This made strong lye. We used a lot 'o sich lye, too, to bile with.

"Sometimes the slaves would run away. Their masters wuz mean to them that caused them to run away. Sometimes they would live in caves. How did they get along? Well, chile, they got along all right—what with other people slippin' things in to 'em. And, too, they'd steal hogs, chickens, and anything else they could git their hands on. Some white people would help, too, fur there wuz some white people who didn't believe in slavery. Yes, they'd try to find them slaves that run away and if they wuz found they'd be beat or sold to somebody else. My grandmother run away frum her master. She stayed in the woods and she washed her clothes in the branches. She used sand fur soap. Yes, chile, I reckon they got 'long all right in the caves. They had babies in thar and raised 'em too.

"Ah stayed with the Mitchells 'til Miss Hannah died. Ah even helped to lay her out. Ah didn't go to the graveyard though. Ah didn't have a home after she died and Ah wandered from place to place, stayin' with a white fambly this time and then a nigger fambly the next time. Ah moved to Jackson County and stayed with a Mister Frank Dowdy. Ah didn't stay there long though. Then Ah moved to Winder, Georgia. They called it 'Jug Tavern' in them days, 'cause jugs wuz made there. Ah married Green Hinton in Winder. Got along well after marryin' him. He farmed fur a livin' and made a good livin' fur me and the eight chilluns, all born in Winder. The chilluns wuz grown nearly when he died and wuz able to help me with the smalles ones. Ah got along all right after his death and didn't have sich a hard time raisin' the chilluns. Then Ah married Jim Brown and moved to Atlanta. Jim farmed at first fur a livin' and then he worked on the railroad—the Seaboard. He helped to grade the first railroad track for that line. He wuz a sand-dryer."

Aunt Sally broke off her story here. "Lord, honey, Ah got sich a pain in mah stomach Ah don't believe Ah can go on. It's a gnawin' kind of pain. Jest keeps me weak all over." Naturally I suggested that we complete the story at another time. So I left, promisin' to return in a few days. A block from the house I stopped in a store to order some groceries for Aunt Sally. The proprietress, a Jewish woman, spoke up when I gave the delivery address. She explained in broken English that she knew Aunt Sally.

"I tink you vas very kind to do dis for Aunt Sally. She neets it. I often gif her son food. He's very old and feeble. He passed here yesterday and he look so wasted and hungry. His stomick look like it vas drawn in, you know. I gif him some fresh hocks. I know dey could not eat all of them in a day and I'm afrait it von't be goof [TR: goot? or good?] for dem today. I vas trained to help people in neet. It's pert of my religion. See, if ve sit on de stritcar and an olt person comes in and finds no seat, ve get up and gif him one. If ve see a person loaded vid bundles and he iss old and barely able to go, ve gif a hand. See, ve Jews—you colored—but ve know no difference. Anyvon neeting help, ve gif."

A couple of days later I was back at Aunt Sally's. I had brought some groceries for the old woman. I knocked a long time on the front door, and, getting no answer, I picked my way through the rank growth of weeds and grass surrounding the house and went around to the back door. It opened into the kitchen, where Aunt Sally and her son were having breakfast. The room was small and dark and I could hardly see the couple, but Aunt Sally welcomed me. "Lawd, honey, you come right on in. I tole John I heard somebody knockin' at the do'."

"You been hearin' things all mornin'," John spoke up. He turned to me. "You must've been thinkin' about mamma just when we started eatin' breakfast because she asked me did I hear somebody call her. I tole her the Lawd Jesus is always a-callin' poor niggers, but she said it sounded like the lady's voice who was here the other day. Well I didn't hear anything and I tole her she mus' be hearin' things."

I'd put the bag of groceries on the table unobtrusively, but Aunt Sally wasn't one to let such gifts pass unnoticed. Eagerly she tore the bag open and began pulling out the packages. "Lawd bless you, chile, and He sho will bless you! I feels rich seein' what you brought me. Jest look at this—Lawdy mercy!—rolls, butter, milk, balogny...! Oh, this balogny, jest looky there! You must a knowed what I wanted!" She was stuffing it in her mouth as she talked. "And these aigs...! Honey, you knows God is goin' to bless you and let you live long. Ah'se goin' to cook one at a time. And Ah sho been wantin' some milk. Ah'se gonna cook me a hoecake rat now."

She went about putting the things in little cans and placing them on shelves or in the dilapidated little cupboard that stood in a corner. I sat down near the door and listened while she rambled on.

"Ah used to say young people didn't care bout ole folks but Ah is takin' that back now. Ah jest tole my son the other day that its turned round, the young folks thinks of the ole and tries to help 'em and the ole folks don't try to think of each other; some of them, they is too mean. Ah can't understand it; Ah jest know I heard you call me when Ah started to eat, and tole my son so. Had you been to the do' befo'?" She talked on not waiting for a reply. "Ah sho did enjoy the victuals you sent day befo' yistidy. They send me surplus food frum the gove'nment but Ah don't like what they send. The skim milk gripes me and Ah don't like that yellow meal. A friend brought me some white meal t'other day. And that wheat cereal they send! Ah eats it with water when Ah don't have milk and Ah don't like it but when you don't have nothin' else you got to eat what you have. They send me 75¢ ever two weeks but that don't go very fur. Ah ain't complainin' fur Ah'm thankful fur what Ah git.

"They send a girl to help me around the house, too. She's frum the housekeepin' department. She's very nice to me. Yes, she sho'ly is a sweet girl, and her foreman is sweet too. She comes in now 'n then to see me and see how the girl is gittin' along. She washes, too. Ah's been on relief a long time. Now when Ah first got on it wuz when they first started givin' me. They give me plenty of anything Ah asked fur and my visitor wuz Mrs. Tompkins. She wuz so good to me. Well they stopped that and then the DPW (Department of Public Welfare) took care of me. When they first started Ah got more than I do now and they've cut me down 'till Ah gits only a mighty little.

"Yes, Ah wuz talkin' about my husband when you wuz here t'other day. He wuz killed on the railroad. After he moved here he bought this home. Ah'se lived here twenty years. Jim wuz comin' in the railroad yard one day and stepped off the little engine they used for the workers rat in the path of the L. & M. train. He wuz cut up and crushed to pieces. He didn't have a sign of a head. They used a rake to git up the pieces they did git. A man brought a few pieces out here in a bundle and Ah wouldn't even look at them. Ah got a little money frum the railroad but the lawyer got most of it. He brought me a few dollars out and tole me not to discuss it with anyone nor tell how much Ah got. Ah tried to git some of the men that worked with him to tell me just how it all happened, but they wouldn't talk, and it wuz scand'lous how them niggers held their peace and wouldn't tell me anything. The boss man came out later but he didn't seem intrusted in it at all, so Ah got little or nothing fur his death. The lawyer got it fur hisse'f.

"All my chilluns died 'cept my son and he is ole and sick and can't do nothin' fur me or hisse'f. He gets relief too, 75¢ every two weeks. He goes 'round and people gives him a little t'eat. He has a hard time tryin' to git 'long.

"Ah had a double bed in t'other room and let a woman have it so she could git some of the delegates to the Baptist World Alliance and she wuz goin' to pay me fur lettin' her use the bed, but she didn't git anybody 'cept two. They come there on Friday and left the next day. She wuz tole that they didn't act right 'bout the delegates and lots of people went to the expense to prepare fur them and didn't git a one. Ah wuz sorry, for Ah intended to use what she paid me fur my water bill. Ah owes $3.80 and had to give my deeds to my house to a lady to pay the water bill fur me and it worries me 'cause Ah ain't got no money to pay it, fur this is all Ah got and Ah hates to loose my house. Ah wisht it wuz some way to pay it. Ah ain't been able to do fur mahse'f in many years now, and has to depend on what others gives me.

"Tell you mo' about the ole times? Lawd, honey, times has changed so frum when Ah was young. You don't hear of haints as you did when I growed up. The Lawd had to show His work in miracles 'cause we didn't have learnin' in them days as they has now. And you may not believe it but them things happened. Ah knows a old man what died, and after his death he would come to our house where he always cut wood, and at night we could hear a chain bein' drug along in the yard, jest as if a big log-chain wuz bein' pulled by somebody. It would drag on up to the woodpile and stop, then we could hear the thump-thump of the ax on the wood. The woodpile was near the chimney and it would chop-chop on, then stop and we could hear the chain bein' drug back the way it come. This went on fur several nights until my father got tired and one night after he heard it so long, the chop-chop, papa got mad and hollered at the haint, 'G---- D---- you, go to hell!!!' and that spirit went off and never did come back!

"We'd always know somebody wuz goin' to die when we heard a owl come to a house and start screechin'. We always said, 'somebody is gwine to die!' Honey, you don't hear it now and it's good you don't fur it would skeer you to death nearly. It sounded so mo'nful like and we'd put the poker or the shovel in the fire and that always run him away; it burned his tongue out and he couldn't holler no more. If they'd let us go out lak we always wanted to, Ah don't 'spects we'd a-done it, 'cause we wuz too skeered. Lawdy, chile, them wuz tryin' days. Ah sho is glad God let me live to see these 'uns.

"Ah tried to git the ole-age pension fur Ah sho'ly needed it and wuz 'titled to it too. Sho wuz. But that visitor jest wouldn't let me go through. She acted lak that money belonged to her. Ah 'plied when it first come out and shoulda been one of the first to get one. Ah worried powerful much at first fur Ah felt how much better off Ah'd be. Ah wouldn't be so dependent lak Ah'm is now. Ah 'spects you know that 'oman. She is a big black 'oman—wuz named Smith at first befo' she married. She is a Johns now. She sho is a mean 'oman. She jest wouldn't do no way. Ah even tole her if she let me go through and Ah got my pension Ah would give her some of the money Ah got, but she jest didn't do no way. She tole me if Ah wuz put on Ah'd get no more than Ah wuz gittin'. Ah sho believes them thats on gits more'n 75¢ every two weeks. Ah sho had a hard time and a roughety road to travel with her my visitor until they sent in the housekeeper. Fur that head 'oman jest went rat out and got me some clothes. Everything Ah needed. When Ah tole her how my visitor wuz doin' me she jest went out and come rat back with all the things Ah needed. Ah don't know why my visitor done me lak that. Ah said at first it wuz because Ah had this house but honey what could Ah do with a house when Ah wuz hongry and not able to work. Ah always worked hard. 'Course Ah didn't git much fur it but Ah lak to work fur what Ah gits."

Aunt Sally was beginning to repeat herself and I began to suspect she was talking just to please me. So I arose to go.

"Lawsy mercy, chile, you sho is sweet to set here and talk to a ole 'oman lak me. Ah sho is glad you come. Ah tole my son you wuz a bundle of sunshine and Ah felt so much better the day you left—and heah you is again! Chile, my nose wuzn't itchin' fur nothin'! You come back to see me real soon. Ah'se always glad to have you. And the Lawd's gonna sho go with you fur bein' so good to me."

My awareness of the obvious fulsomeness in the old woman's praise in no way detracted from my feeling of having done a good deed. Aunt Sally was a clever psychologist and as I carefully picked my way up the weedy path toward the street, I felt indeed that the "Lawd" was "sho goin'" with me.

EX-SLAVE INTERVIEW

JULIA BUNCH, Age 85
Beech Island
South Carolina

Written by:
Leila Harris
Augusta

Edited by:
John N. Booth
District Supervisor
Federal Writers' Project
Res. 6 & 7
[MAY 10 1938]

# JULIA BUNCH

Seated in a comfortable chair in the living room of her home, Julia Bunch, Negress of 85 years, presented a picture of the old South that will soon pass away forever. The little 3-room house, approachable only on foot, was situated on top of a hill. Around the clean-swept yard, petunias, verbena, and other flowers were supplemented by a large patch of old-fashioned ribbon grass. A little black and white kitten was frisking about and a big red hen lazily scratched under a big shade tree in search of food for her brood. Julia's daughter, who was washing "white people's clothes" around the side of the house, invited us into the living room where her mother was seated.

The floors of the front porch and the living room were

scrubbed spotlessly clean. There was a rug on the floor, while a piano across one corner, a chifforobe with mirrored doors, a bureau, and several comfortable chairs completed the room's furnishings. A motley assortment of pictures adorning the walls included: The Virgin Mother, The Sacred Bleeding Heart, several large family photographs, two pictures of the Dionne Quintuplets, and one of President Roosevelt.

Julia was not very talkative, but had a shy, irresistible chuckle, and it was this, together with her personal appearance and the tidiness of her home that left an indelible impression on the minds of her visitors. Her skin was very dark, and her head closely wrapped in a dark bandana, from which this gray hair peeped at intervals forming a frame for her face. She was clad in a black and white flowered print dress and a dark gray sweater, from which a white ruffle was apparent at the neck. Only two buttons of the sweater were fastened and it fell away at the waist displaying her green striped apron. From beneath the long dress, her feet were visible encased in men's black shoes laced with white strings. Her ornaments consisted of a ring on her third finger, earrings, and tortoise-rimmed glasses which plainly displayed their dime-store origin.

"I b'longed to Marse Jackie Dorn of Edgefield County, I was gived to him and his wife when dey was married for a weddin' gift. I nussed deir three chilluns for 'em and slep' on a couch in dier bedroom 'til I was 12 years old, den 'Mancipation come. I loved 'em so and stayed wid 'em for four years atter freedom and when I left 'em I cried and dem chilluns cried.

"Yassir, dey was sho' good white people and very

rich. Dere warn't nothin' lackin' on dat plantation. De big house was part wood and part brick, and de Niggers lived in one or two room box houses built in rows. Marse Jackie runned a big grist mill and done de grindin' for all de neighbors 'round 'bout. Three or four Niggers wukked in de mill all de time. Us runned a big farm and dairy too.

"Dere was allus plenty t'eat 'cause Marster had a 2-acre gyarden and a big fruit orchard. Two cooks was in de kitchen all de time. Dey cooked in a big fireplace, but us had big ovens to cook de meat, biscuits and lightbread in. Us made 'lasses and syrup and put up fruits just lak dey does now.

"My Ma was head weaver. It tuk two or three days to set up de loom 'cause dere was so many little bitty threads to be threaded up. Us had dyes of evvy color. Yassir, us could make wool cloth too. De sheeps was sheered once a year and de wool was manufactured up and us had a loom wid wheels to spin it into thread.

"Old Marster never whupped nobody and dere was only one man dat I kin 'member dat de overseer whupped much and he 'served it 'cause he would run away in spite of evvything. Dey would tie him to a tree way down in de orchard and whup him."

Julia kept repeating and seemed anxious to impress upon the minds of her visitors that her white folks were good and very rich. "Yassir, my white folks had lots of company and visited a lot. Dey rode saddle horses and had deir own carriages wid a high seat for de driver. Nos-ir, she didn't ride wid hoopskirts—you couldn't ride wid dem on.

"Us bought some shoes from de market but dere was a travelin' shoemaker dat wukked by days for all de folks. He was a slave and didn't git no money; it was paid to his Marster. Us had our own blacksmith dat wukked all de time.

"De slaves from all de plantations 'round come to our corn shuckin's. Us had 'em down in de orchard. Lots of white folks comed too. Dey kilt hogs and us had a big supper and den us danced. Nosir, dere warn't no toddy, Marse didn't b'lieve in dat, but dey would beat up apples and us drinked de juice. It sho' was sweet too.

"Folks done dey travelin' in stages and hacks in dem days. Each of de stages had four hosses to 'em. When de cotton and all de other things was ready to go to market, dey would pack 'em and bring 'em to Augusta wid mules and wagons. It would take a week and sometimes longer for de trip, and dey would come back loaded down wid 'visions and clothes, and dere was allus a plenty for all de Niggers too.

"De white folks allus helped deir Niggers wid de weddin's and buyed deir clothes for 'em. I 'members once a man friend of mine come to ax could he marry one of our gals. Marster axed him a right smart of questions and den he told him he could have her, but he mustn't knock or cuff her 'bout when he didn't want her no more, but to turn her loose.

"Us had a big cemetery on our place and de white folks allus let deir Niggers come to de fun'rals. De white folks had deir own sep'rate buryin' ground, but all de coffins was home-made. Even de ones for de settlement peoples was made right in our shop. Yassum, dey sung at de fun'rals and you wants me to sing. I can't sing, but I'll try a little bit." Then with a beautiful and peculiar rhythm only attained by the southern Negro, she chanted:

'Come-ye-dat-love-de-Lord

And-let-your-joys-be-known.'

"A rooster crowin' outside your door means company's comin' and a squinch owl means sho' death. Dose are all de signs I kin 'member and I don't 'member nothin' 'bout slavery remedies.

"Yassir, dey useter give us a nickel or 10 cents sometimes so us could buy candy from de store." Asked if she remembered patterollers she gave her sly chuckle and said: "I sho' does. One time dey come to our house to hunt for some strange Niggers. Dey didn't find 'em but I was so skeered I hid de whole time dey was dar. Yassir, de Ku Kluxers raised cain 'round dar too.

"I 'members de day well when Marster told us us was free. I was glad and didn't know what I was glad 'bout. Den 'bout 200 Yankee soldiers come and dey played music right dar by de roadside. Dat was de fust drum and fife music I ever heared. Lots of de Niggers followed 'em on off wid just what dey had on. None of our Niggers went and lots of 'em stayed right on atter freedom.

"Four years atter dat, I left Edgefield and come here wid my old man. Us had six chilluns. My old man died six years ago right dar 'cross de road and I'se livin' here wid my daughter. I can't wuk no more. I tried to hoe a little out dar in de field last year and I fell down and I hasn't tried no more since.

"I went once not so long ago to see my white folkses. Dey gived me a dollar to spend for myself and I went 'cross de street and buyed me some snuff—de fust I had had for a long time. Dey wanted to know if I had ever got de old age pension and said dat if I had been close to dem I would have had it 'fore now."

[HW: Ex. Slv. #6]

[HW: MARSHAL BUTLER]
Subject: Slavery Days And After
District: No. 1 W.P.A.
Editor and Research: Joseph E. Jaffee
Supervisor: Joseph E. Jaffee

[HW: (This copy has photog. attached.)]

# MARSHAL BUTLER

## Slavery Days And After

I'se Marshal Butler, [HW: 88] years old and was born on December 25. I knows it was Christmas Day for I was a gift to my folks. Anyhow, I'se the only niggah that knows exactly how old he be. I disremembers the year but you white folks can figure et out.

My mammy was Harriet Butler and my pappy was John Butler and we all was raised in Washington-Wilkes.

Mammy was a Frank Collar niggah and her man was of the tribe of Ben Butler, some miles down de road. Et was one of dem trial marriages—they'se tried so hard to see each other but old Ben Butler says two passes a week war enuff to see my mammy on de Collar plantation. When de war was completed pappy came home to us. We wuz a family of ten—four females called Sally, Liza, Ellen and Lottie and six strong bucks called Charlie, Elisha,

Marshal, Jack, Heywood and little Johnnie, [TR: 'cuz he war' marked out] de baby.

De Collar plantation wuz big and I don't know de size of it. Et must have been big for dere war [HW: 250] niggahs aching to go to work—I guess they mus' have been aching after de work wuz done. Marse Frank bossed the place hisself—dere war no overseers. We raised cotton, corn, wheat and everything we un's et. Dere war no market to bring de goods to. Marse Frank wuz like a foodal lord of back history as my good for nothing grandson would say—he is the one with book-larning from Atlanta. Waste of time filling up a nigger's head with dat trash—what that boy needs is muscle-ology—jes' look at my head and hands.

My mammy was maid in de Collar's home and she had many fine dresses—some of them were give to her by her missus. Pappy war a field nigger for ole Ben Butler and I worked in the field when I wuz knee high to a grasshopper. We uns et our breakfast while et war dark and we trooped to the fields at sun-up, carrying our lunch wid us. Nothing fancy but jes' good rib-sticking victuals. We come in from the fields at sun-down and dere were a good meal awaiting us in de slave quarters. My good Master give out rations every second Monday and all day Monday wuz taken to separate the wheat from the chaff—that is—I mean the victuals had to be organized to be marched off to de proper depository.

Before we uns et we took care of our mules. I had a mule named George—I know my mule—he was a good mule.

"Yes, I hollow at the mule, and the

mule would not gee, this mornin'.
Yes, I hollow at the mule, and the
mule would not gee.
An' I hit him across the head with
the single-tree, so soon."

Yes, Boss-man I remembers my mule.

Marse Frank gave mammy four acres of ground to till for herself and us childrens. We raised cotton—yes-sah! one bale of it and lots of garden truck. Our boss-man give us Saturday as a holiday to work our four acres.

All the niggers worked hard—de cotton pickers had to pick 200 pounds of cotton a day and if a nigger didn't, Marse Frank would take de nigger to the barn and beat him with a switch. He would tell de nigger to hollow loud as he could and de nigger would do so. Then the old Mistress would come in and say! "What are you doing Frank?" "Beating a nigger" would be his answer. "You let him alone, he is my nigger" and both Marse Frank and de whipped nigger would come out of the barn. We all loved Marse and the Mistress. No, we wuz never whipped for stealing—we never stole anything in dose days—much.

We sure froliked Saturday nights. Dat wuz our day to howl and we howled. Our gals sure could dance and when we wuz thirsty we had lemonade and whiskey. No sah! we never mixed [HW: no] whiskey with [HW: no] water.—Dem dat wanted lemonade got it—de gals all liked it. Niggers never got drunk those days—we wuz scared of the "Paddle-Rollers." Um-m-h and swell music. A fiddle and a tin can and one nigger would beat his hand on the can and another nigger would beat the strings on the

[HW: fiddle] [TR: 'can' marked out.] with broom straws. It wuz almos' like a banjo. I remembers we sung "Little Liza Jane" and "Green Grows the Willow Tree". De frolik broke up in de morning—about two o'clock—and we all scattered to which ever way we wuz going.

We put on clean clothes on Sunday and go to church. We went to de white church. Us niggars sat on one side and de white folks sat on the other. We wuz baptized in de church—de "pool-room" wuz right in de church.

If we went visiting we had to have a pass. If nigger went out without a pass de "Paddle-Rollers" would get him. De white folks were the "Paddle-Rollers" and had masks on their faces. They looked like niggers wid de devil in dere eyes. They used no paddles—nothing but straps—wid de belt buckle fastened on.

Yes sah! I got paddled. Et happened dis way. I'se left home one Thursday to see a gal on the Palmer plantation—five miles away. Some gal! No, I didn't get a pass—de boss was so busy! Everything was fine until my return trip. I wuz two miles out an' three miles to go. There come de "Paddle-Rollers" I wuz not scared—only I couldn't move. They give me thirty licks—I ran the rest of the way home. There was belt buckles all over me. I ate my victuals off de porch railing. Some gal! Um-m-h. Was worth that paddlin' to see that gal—would do it over again to see Mary de next night.

> "O Jane! love me lak you useter,
> O Jane! chew me lak you useter,
> Ev'y time I figger, my heart gits bigger,
> Sorry, sorry, can't be yo' piper any mo".

Um-m-mh—Some gal!

We Niggers were a healthy lot. If we wuz really sick Marse Frank would send for Doctor Fielding Ficklin of Washington. If jus' a small cold de nigger would go to de woods and git catnip and roots and sich things. If tummy ache—dere was de Castor oil—de white folks say children cry for it—I done my cryin' afterwards. For sore throat dere was alum. Everybody made their own soap—if hand was burned would use soap as a poultice and place it on hand. Soap was made out of grease, potash and water and boiled in a big iron pot. If yo' cut your finger use kerozene wid a rag around it. Turpentine was for sprains and bad cuts. For constipation use tea made from sheep droppings and if away from home de speed of de feet do not match de speed of this remedy.

No, boss, I'se not superstitious and I'se believe in no signs. I jes' carry a rabbits' foot for luck. But I do believe the screeching of an owl is a sign of death. I found et to be true. I had an Uncle named Haywood. He stayed at my house and was sick for a month but wasn't so bad off. One night uncle had a relapse and dat same night a screech owl come along and sat on de top of de house and he—I mean the owl,—"whooed" three times and next morning uncle got "worser" and at eleven o'clock he died.

I does believe in signs. When de rooster crows in the house it is sign of a stranger coming. If foot itches you is going to walk on strange land. If cow lows at house at night death will be 'round de house in short time. If sweeping out ashes at night dat is bad luck for you is sweeping out your best friend. Remember, your closest friend is your worst enemy.

If you want to go a courtin'—et would take a week or so to get your gal. Sometimes some fool nigger would bring a gal a present—like "pulled-candy" and sich like. I had no time for sich foolishness. You would pop the question to boss man to see if he was willing for you to marry de gal. There was no minister or boss man to marry you—no limitations at all. Boss man would jes say: "Don't forget to bring me a little one or two for next year" De Boss man would fix a cottage for two and dere you was established for life.

> "If you want to go a courtin', I sho' you where to go,
> Right down yonder in de house below,
> Clothes all dirty an' ain't got no broom,
> Ole dirty clothes all hangin' in de room.
> Ask'd me to table, thought I'd take a seat,
> First thing I saw was big chunk o'meat.
> Big as my head, hard as a maul,
> ash-cake, corn bread, bran an' all."

Marse Frank had plenty of visitors to see him and his three gals was excuse for anyone for miles around to come trompin' in. He enterained mostly on Tuesday and Thursday nights. I remembers them nights for what was left over from de feasts the niggers would eat.

Dr. Fielding Ficklen [TR: earlier, 'Ficklin'], Bill Pope, Judge Reese,—General Robert Toombs and Alexander Stephens from Crawfordville—all would come to Marse Franks' big house.

General Robert Toombs lived in Washington and had a big plantation 'bout a mile from de city. He was a farmer and very rich. De General wuz a big man—'bout six feet tall—heavy and had a full face. Always had unlighted cigar in his mouth. He was the first man I saw who smoked ten cent cigars. Niggers used to run to get "the stumps" and the lucky nigger who got the "stump" could even sell it for a dime to the other niggers for after all—wasn't it General Toombs' cigar? The General never wore expensive clothes and always carried a crooked-handled walking stick. I'se never heard him say "niggah", never heard him cuss. He always helped us niggars—gave gave us nickles and dimes at times.

Alexander Stephens wuz crippled. He was a little fellow—slim, dark hair and blue eyes. Always used a rolling chair. Marse Frank would see him at least once a month.

I'se saw a red cloud in de west in 1860. I knew war was brewing. Marse Frank went to war. My uncle was his man and went to war with him—Uncle brought him back after the battle at Gettsburg—wounded. He died later. We all loved him. My mistress and her boys ran de plantation.

The blue-coats came to our place in '62 and 63. They took everythin' that was not red-hot or nailed down. The war made no changes—we did the same work and had plenty to eat. The war was now over. We didn't know we wuz free until a year later. I'se stayed on with Marse Frank's boys for twenty years. I'se did the same work fo $35 to $40 a year with rations thrown in.

I lived so long because I tells no lies, I never spent more than fifty cents for a doctor in my life. I believe in whiskey and that kept me going. And let me tell you—I'se always going to be a nigger till I die.

[HW: Dist. 5
Ex. Slave #13]

AN INTERVIEW ON SLAVERY OBTAINED FROM
MRS. SARAH BYRD—EX-SLAVE

# MRS. SARAH BYRD

Mrs. Sarah Byrd claims to be 95 years of age but the first impression one receives when looking at her is that of an old lady who is very active and possessing a sweet clear voice. When she speaks you can easily understand every word and besides this, each thought is well expressed. Often during the interview she would suddenly break out in a merry laugh as if her own thoughts amused her.

Mrs. Sarah Byrd was born in Orange County Virginia the youngest of three children. During the early part of her childhood her family lived in Virginia her mother Judy Newman and father Sam Goodan each belonging to a different master. Later on the family became separated the father was sold to a family in East Tennessee and the mother and children were bought by Doctor Byrd in Augusta, Georgia. Here Mrs. Byrd remarked "Chile in them days so many families were broke up and some went one way and der others went t'other way; and you nebber seed them no more. Virginia wuz a reg'lar slave market."

Dr. Byrd owned a large plantation and raised such products as peas potatoes, cotton corn (etc). There were a large number of slaves. Mrs. Byrd was unable to give the exact number but remarked. "Oh Lordy Chile I nebber could tell just how many slaves that man had t'wuz too many uv em."

The size of the plantation required that the slaves be classified according to the kind of work each was supposed to do. There were the "cotton pickers", the "plow hands," the "hoe hands," the "rail splitters," etc. "My very fust job," remarked Mrs. Byrd, "wuz that uv cotton picking." Mrs Byrd's mother was a full [TR: field?] hand.

Houses on the Byrd Plantation were made of logs and the cracks were daubed with mud. The chimneys were made of mud and supported by sticks.

Each fireplace varied in length from 3 to 4 feet because they serve the purpose of stoves; and the family meals were prepared in those large fireplaces often two and three pots were suspended from a rod running across the fireplace. Most of the log houses consisted of one room; however if the family was very large two rooms were built. The furnishings consisted only of a home-made table, benches, and a home-made bed, the mattress of which was formed by running ropes from side to side forming a framework. Mattresses were made by filling a tick with wheatstraw. The straw was changed each season. Laughing Mrs. Byrd remarked, "Yessirree, them houses wuz warmer than some are ter day."

Doctor Byrd was rather kind and tried to help his slaves as much as possible, but according to Mrs. Byrd his wife was very mean and often punished her slaves without any cause. She never gave them anything but the coarsest foods. Although there of plenty of milk and butter, she only gave it to the families after it had soured.

"Many a day I have seed butter just sittin around in pans day after day till it got good and spoiled then she would call some uv us and give it ter us. Oh she wuz a mean un," remarked Mrs. Byrd. Continuing Mrs. Byrd remarked "she would give us bread that had been cooked a week." Mr. Byrd gave his slave families good clothes. Twice a year clothing was distributed among his families. Every June summer clothes were given and every October winter clothes were given. Here Mrs. Byrd remarked "I nebber knowed what it wuz not ter have a good pair uv shoes." Cloth for the dresses and shirts was spun on the plantation by the slaves.

The treatment of the slaves is told in Mrs. Byrd's own words:

"We wuz always treated nice by Master Byrd and he always tried ter save us punishment at the hands uv his wife but that 'oman wuz somethin' nother. I nebber will ferget once she sent me after some brush broom and told me ter hurry back. Well plums wuz jest gitting ripe so I just took my time and et all the plums I wanted after that I come on back ter the house. When I got there she called me upstairs, 'Sarah come here.' Up the steps I went and thar she stood with that old cow hide. She struck me three licks and I lost my balance and tumbled backward down the stairs. I don't know how come I didn't hurt myself but the Lord wuz wid me and I got up and flew. I could hear her just hollering 'Come back here! come back here!' but I ant stop fer nothing. That night at supper while I wuz fanning the flies from the table she sed ter the doctor. 'Doctor what you think? I had ter whip that little devil ter day. I sent her after brush broom and she went off and eat plums instead of hurrying back.' The doctor just looked at her and rolled his eyes but never sed a word. There wuz very little whipping on Byrd's plantation, but I have gone ter bed many a night and heard 'em gittin whipped on the plantation next ter us. If dey runned away they would put the hounds on 'em." Concluding her story on treatmeant Mrs. Byrd remarked "Yessirree I could tell that 'oman wuz mean the first time I seed her after we came from Virginia cause she had red eyes." "Pader rollers" stayed busy all the time trying to find slaves off their plantations without passes. Marriages were performed by having the couple jump the broom. If the [TR: 'couple' deleted, handwritten words above illegible] belonged to different masters oftentimes one master would purchase the other; but should neither wish to sell the man would then have to get passes to visit his wife on her plantation. "Dey would leave the plantation on Saturday afternoons and on Sunday afternoon you could see 'em coming in just lak they wuz coming from church," remarked Mrs. Byrd.

There were frolics on the Byrd plantation any time that the slaves chose to have them. "Yes sir we could frolic all we want ter. I use ter be so glad when Saturday night came cause I knowed us wuz go have a frolic and I wouldn't have a bit 'uv appetite I would tell my ma we gwine dance ter night I dont want nothin teet. Yes sir us would frolic all night long sometimes when the sun rise on Sunday morning us would all be layin round or settin on the floor. They made music on the banjo, by knocking bones, and blowing quills."

The Byrds did not provide a church on their plantation for their slaves neither were they allowed to attend the white church; instead they had prayer meetings in their own cabins where they could sing pray and shout as much as they wished. "I nebber will fergit the last prayer meeting us had," remarked Mrs. Byrd. "Two woman named Ant Patsy and Ant Prudence came over from the next plantation. I believed they slipped over there wid out gittin a pass. Anyway, they old master came there and whipped 'em and made 'em go home. I reckin he thought us wuz praying ter git free." Continuing—

I nebber will fergit the fust time I set eyes on them thar Yankees. I done already heard 'bout how they wuz going round ter the different plantations taking the horses and carrying away the money and other valuable things, but they had nebber come ter our place. So this day I saw 'em coming cross the railroad track and they look jest lack thunder there wuz so meny 'uv em. When they got ter our house every body wuz sleep and they knocked and knocked. We had a bad dog that didn't take no foolishness off nobody, so when he kept barking them Yankees cursed him and do you know he heshed up? I sid, 'Dear Lord what sort of man is that all he got ter do is curse that dog and he don't even growl.' Well, when they finally got in all they wanted wuz ter know if Mr. Byrd could help feed the soldiers until Monday. Mr. Byrd told 'em he would. Soon after that the war ended and we wuz called ter gether and told us wuz free. Some uv'em stayed there and some uv'em left. Us left and moved ter another plantation."

Mrs. Byrd who had previously given the writer an interview on folk-lore asked the writer to return at a later date and she would try to think up more information concerning superstitions, conjure, etc. The writer thanked her for the interview and promised to make another visit soon.

Ex-Slave #18

INTERVIEW WITH (MRS.) MARIAH CALLAWAY EX-SLAVE

*[TR: A significant portion of this interview was repeated in typescript; where there was a discrepancy, the clearer version was used. Where a completely different word was substituted, 'the original' refers to the typewritten page.]*

# MRS. MARIAH CALLAWAY

Mrs. Mariah Callaway sat in a chair opposite the writer and told her freely of the incidents of slavery as she remembered them. To a casual observer it will come as a surprise to know the woman was blind. She is quite old, but her thoughts were clearly and intelligently related to the writer.

Mrs. Callaway was born in Washington, Wilkes County, Georgia probably during the year 1852, as she estimated her age to be around 12 or 13 years when freedom was declared. She does not remember her mother and father, as her mother died the second day after she was born, so the job of rearing her and a small brother fell on her grandmother, Mariah Willis, for whom she was named. Mrs. Callaway stated that the old master, Jim Willis, kept every Negro's age in a Bible: but after he died the Bible was placed upstairs in the gallery and most of the pages were destroyed. The following is a story of the purchase of Mrs. Callaway's grandfather as related by her.

"My grandfather come directly from Africa and I never shall forget the story he told us of how he and other natives were fooled on board a ship by the white slave traders using red handkerchiefs as enticement. When they reached America, droves of them were put on the block and sold to people all over the United States.

The master and mistress of their plantation were Mr. Jim Willis and Mrs. Nancy Willis who owned hundreds of acres of land and a large number of slaves. Mrs. Callaway was unable to give an exact number but stated the Willises were considered wealthy people. On their plantation were raised sheep, goats, mules, horses, cows, etc. Cotton, corn and vegetables were also raised. The Willis family was a large one consisting of six children. 4 boys and 2 girls. Their home was a large two-story frame house which was set apart from the slave quarters.

Slave homes on the Willis plantation differed in no respect from the usual type found elsewhere. All homes were simple log cabins grouped together, forming what is known as slave quarters.

The Willis family as kind and religious and saw to it that their slaves were given plenty of food to eat. Every Monday night each family was given its share of food for the week. Each grown person was given a peck of corn [TR: meal on original page] and three pounds of meat; besides the vegetables, etc. On Tuesday morning each family was given an ample amount of real flour for biscuits.

Many of the slave families, especially Mrs. Callaway's family, were given the privilege of earning money by selling different products. "My grandfather owned a cotton patch," remarked Mrs. Callaway, "and the master would loan him a mule so he could plow it at night. Two boys would each hold a light for him to work by. He preferred working at night to working on his holidays. My master had a friend in Augusta, Ga., by the name of Steve Heard and just before my grandfather got ready to sell his cotton, the master would write Mr. Heard and tell him that he was sending cotton by Sam and wanted his sold and a receipt returned to him. He also advised him to give all the money received to Sam. When grandfather returned he would be loaded down with sugar, cheese, tea, mackerel, etc. for his family."

When the women came home from the fields they had to spin 7 cuts, so many before supper and so many after supper. A group of women were then selected to weave the cuts of thread into cloth. Dyes were made from red shoe berries and later used to dye this cloth different colors. All slaves received clothing twice a year, spring and winter. Mr. Jim Willis was known for his kindness to his slaves and saw to it that they were kept supplied with Sunday clothes and shoes as well as work clothing. A colored shoemaker was required to keep the plantation supplied with shoes; and everyone was given a pair of Sunday shoes which they kept shined with a mixture of egg white and soot.

The size of the Willis Plantation and the various crops and cattle raised required many different types of work. There were the plow hands, the hoe hands, etc. Each worker had a required amount of work to complete each day and an overseer was hired by slave owners to keep check on this phase of the work. "We often waited until the overseer got behind a hill, and then we would lay down our hoe and call on God to free us, my grandfather told me," remarked Mrs. Callaway. "However, I was a pet in the Willis household and did not have any work to do except play with the small children. I was required to keep their hands and faces clean. Sometimes I brought in chips to make the fires. We often kept so much noise playing in the upstairs bedroom that the master would call to us and ask that we keep quiet." Older women on the plantation acted as nurses for all the small children and babies while their parents worked in the fields. The mistress would keep a sharp eye on the children also to see that they were well cared for. A slave's life was very valuable to their owners.

Punishment was seldom necessary on the Willis plantation as the master and mistress did everything possible to make their slaves happy; and to a certain extent indulged them. They were given whisky liberally from their master's still; and other choice food on special occasions. "I remember once," remarked Mrs. Callaway, "my aunt Rachel burned the biscuits and the young master said to her, "Rachel, you nursed me and I promised not to ever whip you, so don't worry about burning the bread." My mistress was very fond of me, too, and gave me some of everything that she gave her own children, tea cakes, apples, etc. She often told me that she was my mother and was supposed to look after me. In spite of the kindness of the Willis family there were some slaves who were unruly; so the master built a house off to itself and called it the Willis jail. Here he would keep those whom he had to punish. I have known some slaves to run away on other plantations and the hounds would bite plugs out of their legs."

The Willis family did not object to girls and boys courting. There were large trees, and often in the evenings the boys from other plantations would come over to see the girls on the Willis plantation. They would stand in groups around the trees, laughing and talking. If the courtship reached the point of marriage a real marriage ceremony was performed from the Bible and the man was given a pass to visit his wife weekly. Following a marriage a frolic took place and the mistress saw to it that everyone was served nice foods for the occasion.

Frolics were common occurrences on the Willis plantation, also quilting parties. Good foods consisting of pies, cakes, chicken, brandied peaches, etc. "Dancing was always to be expected by anyone attending them," remarked Mrs. Callaway. "Our master always kept two to three hundred gallons of whisky and didn't mind his slaves drinking. I can remember my master taking his sweetened dram every morning, and often he gave me some in a tumbler. On Christmas Day big dinners were given for all of the slaves and a few ate from the family's table after they had finished their dinner."

Medical care was promptly given a slave when he became ill. Special care was always given them for the Willis family had a personal interest in their slaves. "On one occasion," remarked Mrs. Calloway, "the scarlet fever broke out among the slaves and to protect the well ones it became necessary to build houses in a field for those who were sick. This little settlement later became know as "Shant Field." Food was carried to a hill and left so that the sick persons could get it without coming in contact with the others. To kill the fever, sticks of fat pine were dipped in tar and set on fire and then placed all over the field."

Religion played as important part in the lives of the

slaves, and such [TR: much?] importance was attached to their prayer meetings. There were no churches, provided and occasionally they attended the white churches; but more often they held their prayer meetings in their own cabins. Prayers and singing was in a moaning fashion, and you often heard this and nothing more. On Sunday afternoons everyone found a seat around the mulberry tree and the young mistress would conduct Sunday School.

Concerning the Civil War, Mrs. Callaway related the following story:

"When the war broke out my mistress' home became a sewing center and deifferent women in the neighborhood would come there every day to make clothes for the soldiers. On each bed was placed the vests, coats, shirts, pants, and caps. One group did all the cutting, one the stitching, and one the fitting. Many women cried while they served [TR: sewed?] heart-broken because their husbands and sons had to go to the war. One day the Yanks came to our plantation and took all of the best horses. In one of their wagons were bales of money which they had taken. Money then was blue in color; of course, there was silver and gold. After taking the horses they drank as much whisky as they could hold and then filled their canteens. The rest of the whisky they filled with spit. The master didn't interfere for fear of the long guns which they carried."

After the war some of the slaves left the plantation to seek their fortune; others remained, renting land from the Willis family or working with them on a share crop basis.

As a conclusion Mrs. Callaway remarked: "My folks were good and I know [HW: they're] in heaven." Mrs. Callaway is deeply religious and all during the interview would constantly drift to the subject of religion. She is well cared for by her nine children, six girls and three boys.

United States. Work Projects Administration

PLANTATION LIFE AS VIEWED BY EX-SLAVE

SUSAN CASTLE, Age 78
1257 W. Hancock Ave.
Athens, Georgia

Written by:
Sadie B. Hornsby
Athens

Edited by:
Sarah H. Hall
Athens

and
John N. Booth
District Supervisor
Federal Writers' Project
Augusta, Georgia

# SUSAN CASTLE

On a beautiful morning in April, the interviewer found Susan sitting in the door of her cabin. When asked if she would like to talk about the old plantation days, she replied; "Yes Ma'am, I don't mind tellin' what I know, but for dat I done forgot I sho' ain't gwine make nothin' up. For one thing, I ain't never lived on no plantation. I was a house servant in town." She added: "Do you mind me axin' you one favor?" Consent was given and she continued: "Dat is, please don't call me Aunt Susan; it makes me feel lak I was a hundred years old.

"I was borned in Clarke County, March 7, 1860; I believes dat's what dey say. Mudder was named Fannie and

Pappy's name was Willis. Us chillun called 'im Pappy lak he was de onliest one in de world. He fust belonged to Marse Maxwell of Savannah, Georgia. I was so little I disremembers how Pappy come by de name of Castle. In all de seben of us chillun, I didn't have but one brudder, and his name was Johnny. My five sisters was Mary, Louvenia, Rosa, Fannie, and Sarah. All I 'members 'bout us as chilluns was dat us played lak chilluns will do.

"In de quarters us had old timey beds and cheers, but I'll tell you whar I slept most times. Hit was on a cot right at de foot of Mist'ess' bed. I stayed at de big house most of de time at night, and 'fore bedtime I sot close by Mist'ess on a foot stool she had special for me.

"All I ricollects 'bout my gran'ma was she belonged to General Thomas R.R. Cobb, and us called 'im Marse Thomas. Gran'ma Susan wouldn't do right so Marse Thomas sold her on de block.

"Us had evvything good to eat. Marse Thomas was a rich man and fed 'is Niggers well. Dey cooked in a big open fireplace and biled greens and some of de udder vittals in a great big pot what swung on a rack. Meat, fish and chickens was fried in a griddle iron what was sot on a flat topped trivet wid slits to let de fire thoo. Dey called it a trivet 'cause it sot on three legs and hot coals was raked up under it. Hoe cakes made out of cornmeal and wheat flour sho' was good cooked on dat griddle. 'Tatoes was roasted in de ashes, and dey cooked bread what dey called ash cake in de ashes. Pound cake, fruit cake, light bread and biscuits was baked in a great big round pot, only dey warn't as deep as de pots dey biled in; dese was called ovens. Makes me hongry to think 'bout all dem good vittals now.

"Oh! Yes Ma'am, us had plenty 'possums. Pappy used to cotch so many sometimes he jest put 'em in a box and let us eat 'em when us got ready. 'Possums tasted better atter dey was put up in a box and fattened a while. Us didn't have many rabbits; dey warn't as much in style den as dey is now, and de style of eatin' 'possums lak dey done in slav'ry times, dat is 'bout over. Dey eats 'em some yet, but it ain't stylish no mo'. Us chillun used to go fishin' in Moore's Branch; one would stand on one side of de branch wid a stick, and one on de udder side would roust de fishes out. When dey come to de top and jump up, us would hit 'em on de head, and de grown folks would cook 'em. Dere warn't but one gyarden, but dat had plenty in it for evvybody.

"In summer time us wore checkedy dresses made wid low waistes and gethered skirts, but in winter de dresses was made out of linsey-woolsey cloth and underclothes was made out of coarse unbleached cloth. Petticoats had bodice tops and de draw's was made wid waistes too. Us chillun didn't know when Sunday come. Our clothes warn't no diffu'nt den from no udder day. Us wore coarse, heavy shoes in winter, but in summer us went splatter bar feets.

"Marse Thomas was jest as good as he could be, what us knowed of 'im. Miss Marion, my Mist'ess, she won't as good to us as Marse Thomas, but she was all right too. Dey had a heap of chillun. Deir twin boys died, and de gals was Miss Callie, Miss Sallie, Miss Marion (dey called her Miss Birdie), and Miss Lucy, dat Lucy Cobb Institute was named for. My mudder was Miss Lucy's nuss. Marse Thomas had a big fine melonial (colonial) house on Prince Avenue wid slave quarters in de back yard of his

10-acre lot. He owned 'most nigh dat whole block 'long dar.

"Oh! dey had 'bout a hundred slaves I'm sho', for dere was a heap of 'em. De overseer got 'em up 'bout five o'clock in de mornin' and dat breakfust sho' had better be ready by seben or else somebody gwine to have to pay for it. Dey went to deir cabins 'bout ten at night. Marse was good, but he would whup us if we didn't do right. Miss Marion was allus findin' fault wid some of us.

"Jesse was de car'iage driver. Car'iages was called phaetons den. Dey had high seats up in front whar de driver sot, and de white folks sot in de car'iage below. Jesse went to de War wid Marse Thomas, and was wid him when he was kilt at Fred'ricksburg, Virginia. I heard 'em sey one of his men shot 'im by mistake, but I don't know if dat's de trufe or not. I do know dey sho' had a big grand fun'al 'cause he was a big man and a general in de War.

"Some of de slaves on Marse Thomas' place knowed how to read. Aunt Vic was one of de readers what read de Bible. But most of de Niggers didn't have sense enough to learn so dey didn't bother wid 'em. Dey had a church way downtown for de slaves. It was called Landon's Chapel for Rev. Landon, a white man what preached dar. Us went to Sunday School too. Aunt Vic read de Bible sometimes den. When us jined de chu'ch dey sung: 'Amazing Grace How Sweet de Sound.'

"Marse Thomas had lots of slaves to die, and dey was buried in de colored folks cemetery what was on de river back of de Lucas place. I used to know what dey sung at fun'als way back yonder, but I can't bring it to mind now.

"No Ma'am, none of Marse Thomas' Niggers ever run away to de Nawth. He was good to his Niggers. Seems lak to me I 'members dem patterollers run some of Marse Thomas' Niggers down and whupped 'em and put 'em in jail. Old Marse had to git 'em out when dey didn't show up at roll call next mornin'.

"Marse Thomas allus put a man or de overseer on a hoss or a mule when he wanted to send news anywhar. He was a big man and had too many slaves to do anything hisse'f.

"I 'spect dey done den lak dey does now, slipped 'round and got in devilment atter de day's wuk was done. Marse Thomas was allus havin' swell elegant doin's at de big house. De slaves what was house servants didn't have no time off only atter dinner on Sundays.

"Christmas was somepin' else. Us sho' had a good time den. Dey give de chilluns china dolls and dey sont great sacks of apples, oranges, candy, cake, and evvything good out to de quarters. At night endurin' Christmas us had parties, and dere was allus some Nigger ready to pick de banjo. Marse Thomas allus give de slaves a little toddy too, but when dey was havin' deir fun if dey got too loud he sho' would call 'em down. I was allus glad to see Christmas come. On New Year's Day, de General had big dinners and invited all de high-falutin' rich folks.

"My mudder went to de corn shuckin's off on de plantations, but I was too little to go. Yes Ma'am, us sho' did dance and sing funny songs way back in dem days. Us chillun used to play 'Miss Mary Jane,' and us would pat our hands and walk on broom grass. I don't know nothin' 'bout charms. Dey used to tell de chillun dat when old folks died dey turned to witches. I ain't never seed no ghostes, but I sho' has felt 'em. Dey made de rabbits jump over my grave and had me feelin' right cold and clammy. Mudder used to sing to Miss Lucy to git her to sleep, but I don't 'member de songs.

"Marster was mighty good to his slaves when dey got sick. He allus sont for Dr. Crawford Long. He was de doctor for de white folks and Marster had him for de slaves.

"My mudder said she prayed to de Lord not to let Niggers be slaves all deir lifes and sho' 'nough de yankees comed and freed us. Some of de slaves shouted and hollered for joy when Miss Marion called us togedder and said us was free and warn't slaves no more. Most of 'em went right out and left 'er and hired out to make money for deyselfs.

"I stayed on wid my mudder and she stayed on wid Miss Marion. Miss Marion give her a home on Hull Street 'cause mudder was allus faithful and didn't never leave her. Atter Miss Marion died, mudder wukked for Miss Marion's daughter, Miss Callie Hull, in Atlanta. Den Miss Callie died and mudder come on back to Athens. 'Bout ten years ago she died.

"I wukked for Mrs. Burns on Jackson Street a long time, but she warn't no rich lady lak de Cobbs. De last fambly I wukked for was Dr. Hill. I nussed 'til atter de chillun got too big for dat, and den I done de washin' 'til dis misery got in my limbs."

When asked about marriage customs, she laughed and replied: "I was engaged, but I didn't marry though, 'cause my mudder 'posed me marryin'. I had done got my clothes bought and ready. Mrs. Hull helped me fix my things. My dress was a gray silk what had pearl beads on it and was trimmed in purple.

"What does I think 'bout freedom? I think it's best to be free, 'cause you can do pretty well as you please. But in slav'ry time if de Niggers had a-behaved and minded deir Marster and Mist'ess dey wouldn't have had sich a hard time. Mr. Jeff Davis 'posed freedom, but Mr. Abraham Lincoln freed us, and he was all right. Booker Wash-in'ton was a great man, and done all he knowed how to make somepin' out of his race.

"De reason I jined de church was dat de Lord converted me. He is our guide. I think people ought to be 'ligious and do good and let deir lights shine 'cause dat's de safest way to go to Heben."

At the conclusion of the interview Susan asked: "Is dat all you gwine to ax me? Well, I sho' enjoyed talkin' to you. I hopes I didn't talk loud 'nough for dem other Niggers to hear me, 'cause if you open your mouth dey sho' gwine tell it. Yes Ma'am, I'se too old to wuk now and I'se thankful for de old age pension. If it warn't for dat, since dis misery tuk up wid me, I would be done burnt up, I sho' would. Good-bye Mist'ess."

United States. Work Projects Administration

[HW: Dist. 2
Ex-Slave #17]

ELLEN CLAIBOURN
808 Campbell Street
(Richmond County)
Augusta, Georgia

By:
(Mrs.) Margaret Johnson—Editor
Federal Writers' Project
Dist. 2
Augusta, Ga.

# ELLEN CLAIBOURN

Ellen was born August 19, 1852, on the plantation of Mr. Hezie Boyd in Columbia County, her father being owned by Mr. Hamilton on an adjoining plantation. She remembers being given, at the age of seven, to her young mistress, Elizabeth, who afterward was married to Mr. Gabe Hendricks. At her new home she served as maid, and later as nurse. The dignity of her position as house servant has clung to her through the years, forming her speech in a precision unusual in her race.

"I 'member all our young marsters was drillin' way back in 1860, an' the Confed'rate War did not break out till in April 1861. My mistis' young husband went to the war, an' all the other young marsters 'round us. Young marster's bes' friend came to tell us all goodby, an' he was killed in the first battle he fought in.

"Befo' the war, when we was little, we mostly played

dolls, and had doll houses, but sometime young marster would come out on the back porch and play the fiddle for us. When he played 'Ole Dan Tucker' all the peoples uster skip and dance 'bout and have a good time. My young mistis played on the piano.

"My granpa was so trusty and hon'able his old marster give him and granma they freedom when he died. He give him a little piece of land and a mule, and some money, and tole him he didn't b'long to nobody, and couldn't work for nobody 'cept for pay. He couldn't free granpa's chilrun, 'cause they already b'longed to their young marsters and mistises. He worked for Mr. Hezie Boyd one year as overseer, but he say he didn't wanter lose his religion trying to make slaves work, so he took to preaching. He rode 'bout on his mule and preach at all the plantations. I never 'member seein' granma, but granpa came to see us of'en. He wore a long tail coat and a big beaver hat. In that hat granma had always pack a pile of ginger cakes for us chilrun. They was big an' thick, an' longish, an' we all stood 'round to watch him take off his hat. Every time he came to see us, granma sent us clothes and granpa carried 'em in his saddle bags. You ever see any saddle bags, ma'am? Well they could sho' hold a heap of stuff!

"My pa uster come two or three times a week to our plantashun, an' just so he was back by sun-up for work, nobody didn't say nothin' to him. He just lived 'bout three or four miles way from us.

"Yes ma'am we went to church, and the white preachers preached for us. We sat in the back of the church just like we sits in the back of the street cars now-days. Some of the house servants would go one time and some another. All the hands could go but ev'rybody had to has a pass, to sho' who they b'long to.

"Yes ma'am, the slaves was whipped if they didn't do they taskwork, or if they steal off without a pass, but if our marster found a overseer whipped the slaves overmuch he would git rid of him. We was always treated good and kind and well cared for, and we was happy.

"No ma'am, no overseer ever went to marster's table, or in the house 'cept to speak to marster. Marster had his overseers' house and give 'em slaves to cook for 'em and wait on 'em, but they never go anywhere with the fam'ly.

"The house servants' houses was better than the fiel'-hands'—and Marster uster buy us cloth from the 'Gusta Fact'ry in checks and plaids for our dresses, but all the fiel'-hands clothes was made out of cloth what was wove on mistis' own loom. Sometime the po' white folks in the neighborhood would come an' ask to make they cloth on mistis' loom, and she always let 'em.

"Yes, ma'am, we had seamsters to make all the clothes for everybody, and mistis had a press-room, where all the clothes was put away when they was finished. When any body needed clothes mistis would go to the press-room an' get 'em.

"During the war mistis had one room all fixed up to take care of sick soldiers. They would come stragglin' in, all sick or shot, an' sometimes we had a room full of 'em. Mistis had one young boy to do nothin' but look after 'em and many's the night I got up and helt the candle for 'em to see the way to the room.

"Oh my Gawd, I saw plenty wounded soldiers. We was

right on the road to Brightsboro, and plenty of 'em pass by. That Confed'rate war was the terriblest, awfullest thing.

"Nobody but me knowed where mistis buried her gold money and finger rings and ear-rings and breat-pins. [TR: breast-pins?] I helt the candle then, too. Mistis and marster, (he was home then) an' me went down back of the grape arbor to the garden-house. Marster took up some planks, an' dug a hole like a grabe and buried a big iron box with all them things in it; then he put back the planks. Nobody ever found 'em, and after the war was over we went and got 'em.

"Yes, ma'am, everybody did they own work. De cook cooked, and the washer, she didn't iron no clothes. De ironer did that. De housemaid cleaned up, and nurse tended the chilrun. Then they was butlers and coachmen. Oh, they was a plenty of us to do eve'ything.

"We didn't have a stove, just a big fire place, and big oven on both sides, and long-handle spiders. When we was fixin' up to go to Camp Meeting to the White Oak Camp meeting grounds, they cooked chickens and roasted pigs, and put apples in they mouth and a lot of other food—good food too. De food peoples eat these days, you couldn't have got nobody to eat. Camp Meetin' was always in August and September. It was a good Methodis' meetin', and eve'ybody got religion. Sometimes a preacher would come to visit at the house, an' all the slaves was called an' he prayed for 'em. Sometimes the young ones would laugh, an' then marster would have 'em whipped.

"My young mistis had a sister older than her. She

married Mr. Artie Boyd, an' they had a big weddin' but she loved her home and her mother and father so much she wouldn't leave home. She just stayed on living there. When her baby come she died, and I tell you, ma'am, her fun'al was most like a weddin', with so many people an' so many flowers. All the people from the plantashun came to the house, an' the wimmen had they babies in they arms. One the ladies say, "How come they let all these niggers and babies come in the house?" But marster knowed all us loved mistis, and he call us in. Marse Artie he wrote a long letter an' all the things he got from mistis he give back to her fam'ly an' all his own things he give to his brother, an' then he died. Some say his heart strings just broke 'cause mistis died, and some say he took something.

"No, ma'am, I wasn't married till after freedom. I was married right here in 'Gusta by Mr. Wharton, the First Baptist Church preacher, an' I lived and worked here ever since."

[HW: Dist. 7
Ex-Slave #19]
Adella S. Dixon
District 7

BERRY CLAY
OLD SLAVE STORY
[MAY 8 1937]

# BERRY CLAY

Telfair County was the home of some colored people who never were slaves, but hired their services for wages just as the race does today. Berry Clay, half Indian, half white, was the son of Fitema Bob Britt, a full blood Indian, who died shortly after his son's birth. His mother later married William Clay, whose name was taken by the children as well as the mother. The family then moved to Macon.

Clay, next [TR: 'to the' scratched out] oldest of five children was 89 years old on August 5, 1936, and while he was never a slave, remembers many incidents that took place then. Not many years after his mother remarried, she became very ill and he recalls being lifted by his step-father to kiss her good bye as she lay dying. After her death, the family continued to live in South Macon where the father was employed as overseer for a crew at the Railroad yard.

This position often called for the punishment of slaves but he was too loyal to his color to assist in making their lives more unhappy. His method of carrying out orders and yet keeping a clear conscience was unique—the slave was taken to the woods where he was supposedly laid upon a log and severely beaten. Actually, he was made to stand to one side and to emit loud cries which were accompanied by hard blows on the log. The continuation of the two sounds gave any listener the impression that some one was severely beaten. It is said that Clay, the father, wore out several huge leather straps upon logs but that he was never known to strike a slave.

Mr. Wadley, by whom he was employed, was a well-known Macon citizen who served as President of the Central of Georgia Railroad for many years. A monument on Mulberry Street nearly opposite the Post Office is a constant reminder of the esteem in which he was held. His plantation was a huge one extending from the Railroad yard as far as the present site of Mercer University. A day of rest was given the slaves about once every three months in addition to the regular holidays which are observed today. On holidays, "frolics" at which square dances were the chief form of entertainment (by the music of a banjo or fiddle) were enjoyed. Ring games were played by the children. The refreshments usually consisted of ash cakes and barbecue. The ash cake was made by wrapping corn pones in oak leaves and burying the whole in hot ashes. When the leaves dried, the cake was usually done and was carefully moved to prevent its becoming soiled. [HW: A] skillful cook could produce cakes that were a golden brown and not at all ashy.

The membership of the local church was composed of slaves from several plantations. It was an old colored church with a white minister who preached the usual doctrine of the duty of a slave to his master. The form of service was the same as that of the white church. One unusual feature of the plantation was its Sunday School for the Negro children.

Courtships were very brief for as soon as a man or woman began to manifest interest in the opposite sex, the master busied himself to select a wife or husband and only in rare cases was the desire of the individual considered. When the selection was made, the master read the ceremony and gave the couple a home. He always requested, or rather demanded, that they be fruitful. A barren woman was separated from her husband and usually sold.

Very little money was handled by these people. The carriage drivers were more fortunate than the regular workers for they smuggled things to town when they drove the master and mistress and sold them while the family shopped or went visiting. At rare intervals, the field hands were able to earn small sums of money in this manner.

Food was provided by the owners and all families cooked for themselves whether they were many or one. The weekly allotments of meal, meat, etc., were supplemented through the use of vegetables which could always be obtained from the fields. On special days chicken or beef was given and each one had a sufficient amount for his needs. Hunting and fishing were recreations in which the slaves were not allowed to participate although they frequently went on secret excursions of this nature. All food stuff as well as cloth for garments was produced at home.

Clay is very superstitious, still believing in most of

the signs commonly believed in those days, because he has "watched them and found that they are true". He stated that the screeching of the owl may be stopped by placing a poker in the fire and allowing it to remain until it becomes red hot. The owl will then leave, but death will invariably follow its visit.

The attitudes of the two races in the South regarding the war were directly opposite. The whites beheld it as something horrible and dreaded the losses that would necessarily be theirs. Sons and fathers had property to be considered, but they were generous in their contributions to the soldiers. On the other hand, the slaves rejoiced as they looked forward to their freedom when the war was over. There were, however, a few who were devoted to their masters to the extent that they fought in their stead in the Confederate Army. Others remained at home and skillfully ran the plantation and protected the women and children until the end of the war.

When Sherman made his famous "March to Sea", one phalanx of his army wrought its destruction between this city and Griswoldville. A gun factory and government shoe factory were completely destroyed. Although the citizens gave the invaders everything they thought they desired, the rest was destroyed in most instances. They tried to ascertain the attitudes of the land owners toward his servants and when for any reason they presumed that one was cruel, their vengeance was expressed through the absolute destruction of his property. In nearly every instance smoke houses were raided and the contents either destroyed or given away. Barrels of syrup flowing through the yard was a common sight.

At the end of the war, the South was placed under military rule. The presence of the Yankee guardsmen had a psychological effect upon the Southerners and they were very humble.

Before the terrors of the war had subsided a new menace sprang up—the Klu Klux Klan. While its energy was usually directed against ex-slaves, a white man was sometimes a victim. One such occasion was recalled by Clay. The group planned to visit a man who for some reason became suspicious and prepared to outwit them if they came. He heated a huge pot of water and when a part of his door was crashed in he reached through the opening and poured gourds of boiling water upon his assailants. They retreated, [HW: and] while they were away, he made his way to Atlanta.

Another group which began its operations shortly after the close of the war was a military clan organized for the purpose of giving the ex-slaves a knowledge of drilling and war tactics. An order to disband was received from the "Black Horse Calvary" by the leader of the group. His life was threatened when he failed to obey so he prepared for a surprise visit. He fortified his house with twenty-five men on the inside and the same number outside. When the approaching calvarymen reached a certain point, the fifty hidden men fired at the same time. Seven members of the band were killed and many others wounded. There was no further interference from this group.

Clay and his father ran a grocery store just after Emancipation. He did not like this type of work and apprenticed himself to a painter to learn the trade. He is still considered an excellent painter though he does not receive much work.

He has always taken care of himself and never "ran about" at night. He boasts that his associates never included a dancing woman. As he has used tobacco for sixty-five years, he does not consider it a menace to health but states that worry will kill anyone and the man who wants to live a long time must form the habit of not worrying. His Indian blood—the high cheek bones, red skin and straight black hair now tinged with grey make this unmistakable—has probably played a large part in the length of his life.

[HW: Dist. 7
Ex-Slave #22]
Adella S. Dixon
District 7

PIERCE CODY
OLD SLAVE STORY
[HW: About 88]
[MAY 8 1937]

# PIERCE CODY

Pierce Cody was the eldest son of Elbert and Dorothy Cody. His father was born in Richmond, Virginia, his mother in Warren County. When the Emancipation Proclamation was signed, he, the eldest child in a large family, was in his early teens. This group lived on the place owned by Mr. Bob Cody, [HW: whose] family was a group of ardent believers in the Hardshell Baptist faith. So firm was their faith that a church of this denomination was provided for the slaves and each one required to become a member. A white minister invariably preached the then worn out doctrine of a slave's duty to his master, the reward of faithfulness and the usual admonition against stealing.

The members of this church were required to fast on one day of the week, the fast lasting all day until seven in the evening. The small boys, both white and colored, resenting the abstinence from food, usually secured a reserve supply which was cached during the week and secretly enjoyed on fast day. Fish were plentiful in all the streams and they sometimes sneaked away to the river and after enjoying the sport, cooked their catch on the banks of the stream.

Groups of ministers—30 to 40—then traveled from one plantation to another spreading the gospel, and were entertained as they traveled. On one occasion the group arrived at the Cody estate on fast day. The boys having been on one of their secret fishing trips had caught so many perch that they were not able to consume them on the banks, so had smuggled them to the kitchen, coaxed the cook to promise to prepare them, and had also sworn her to absolute secrecy regarding their origin. Although the kitchen was not directly connected with the "big house", the guests soon detected the aroma of fresh fish and requested that they be allowed to partake of this delicacy. When the boys, as well as the servants, heard this, they became panicky for they feared the wrath of the master. But the catch was so heartily relished that instead of the expected punishment, they were commended and allowed to fish on the next day of fasting.

As was characteristic of many others, the planter's home was near the center of a vast estate and in this instance had a tall lookout on the roof from which the watchman might see for miles around. The "quarters" were nearby and the care-free children who played in the large yard were closely watched as they were often stolen by speculators and later sold at auctions far away. The land was divided into many fields each of which was used to cultivate a particular product. Each field had its special crew and overseer.

Cody's father was [HW: one of the] feeders [HW: who] arose at least two hours before sunrise, to feed the stock. A large number of horses and more than two hundred head of cattle had to be fed by sunrise when they were to be turned into the pastures or driven to the field to begin the day's work. After sunrise, his father's duty [HW: as] foreman for plowers began. Other workers were hoe hands, additional foremen, cooks, weavers, spinners, seamstresses, tailors, shoemakers, etc. As everything used was grown and made on the estate there was plenty of work for all and in many instances [HW: slaves] learned trades which they liked and which furnished a livelihood when they were set free.

[HW: When he entered his teens] Cody's first duties began [HW: as] a plowhand who broke "newground." As all of this land was to be plowed, a lack of skill in making straight furrows did not matter, so beginners were preferably used. Shortly after he began plowing he was made foreman of one of the groups. Thus encouraged by his master's faith in his ability to do a man's work, he assumed a "grown up" attitude under the stimulus of his new responsibilities and was married shortly after.

At this time marriages resulted from brief courtships. After the consent of the girl was obtained, it was necessary to seek permission from the master, whether she lived on the same or an adjoining plantation. In the latter case, the marriage rites were performed by her master. The minister was not used in most instances—the ceremony [HW: being] read from a testament by the owner of the bride. Marriages were nearly always performed out of doors in the late afternoon. The bride's wedding dress was fashioned of cloth made on the plantation from a pattern of her own designing. Attendants at marriages were rare. After the ceremony, the guests danced far into the night by music from the fiddle and banjo. Refreshments consisting of ginger cakes, barbecue, etc., were served. Such a couple, belonging to two different masters, did not keep house. The [HW: husband] was allowed to visit his wife on Wednesday night and Saturday when he might remain through Sunday. All marriage unions were permanent and a barren wife was considered the only real cause for separation.

Church services for this group were held jointly with the white members, the two audiences being separated by a partition. Gradually, the colored members became dissatisfied with this type of service and withdrew to form a separate church. The desire for independence in worship must necessarily have been strong, to endure the inconveniences of the "brush arbor" churches that they resorted to. As a beginning, several trees were felled, and the brush and forked branches separated. Four heavy branches with forks formed the framework. Straight poles were laid across these to form a crude imitation of beams and the other framework of a building. The top and sides were formed of brush which was thickly placed so that it formed a solid wall. A hole left in one side formed a doorway from which beaten paths extended in all directions. Seats made from slabs obtained at local sawmills completed the furnishing. In inclement weather, it was not possible to conduct services here, but occasionally showers came in the midst of the service and the audience calmly hoisted umbrellas or papers and with such scant protection, the worship continued.

Sunday afternoons were quietly spent, visiting being the only means of recreation. One of the favorite stay at home pastimes was the inspection of heads. The pediculous condition made frequent treatment necessary for comfort. The young white men liked to visit the "quarters" and have the slaves search their heads. They would stretch full length upon the cabin floors and rest their heads upon a pillow. Usually they offered a gift of some sort if many of the tiny parasites were destroyed, so the clever picker who found a barren head simply reached into his own and produced a goodly number. There existed on this plantation an antagonistic feeling toward children (born of slave parents) with a beautiful suit of hair, and this type of hair was kept cropped very short.

Gossip, stealing, etc. was not tolerated. No one was ever encouraged to "tattle" on another. Locks were never used on any of the cabin doors or on the smokehouse. Food was there in abundance and each person was free to replenish his supply as necessary. Money was more or less a novelty as it was only given in 1¢ pieces at Christmas time. As food, clothing, and shelter were furnished, the absence was not particularly painful. Connected with nearly every home were those persons who lived "in the woods" in preference to doing the labor necessary to remain at their home. Each usually had a scythe and a bulldog for protection. As food became scarce, they sneaked to the quarters in the still of the night and coaxed some friend to get food for them from the smokehouse. Their supply obtained, they would leave again. This was not considered stealing.

Medical care was also free. Excellent physicians were maintained. It was not considered necessary to call a physician until home remedies—usually teas made of roots—had had no effect. Women in childbirth were cared for by grannies,—Old women whose knowledge was broad by experience, acted as practical nurses.

Several cooks were regularly maintained. Some cooked for the men who had no families, others for the members of the big house and guests. The menus varied little from day to day. A diet of bread—called "shortening bread,"—vegetables and smoked meat were usually consumed. Buttermilk was always plentiful. On Sundays "seconds" (flour) were added to the list and butter accompanied this. Chickens, fresh meat, etc., were holiday items and were seldom enjoyed at any other time.

Not only were the slaves required to work but the young men of the "big house" also had their duties. In the summer they went fishing. While this sport was enjoyed, it was done on an extremely large scale in order that everyone should have an adequate supply of fish. The streams abounded in all kinds of fish, and nets were used to obtain large quantities necessary. In winter hunting was engaged in for this same purpose. Rabbits, squirrels, etc., were the usual game, but in addition the trapping of wild hogs was frequently indulged in. The woods contained many of these animals which were exceptionally vicious. The hunters, however, trapped them in much the same way that rabbits are now caught, without injury to the flesh [TR: 'making the meat more delicious' marked out]. Deer were also plentiful and venison enjoyed during its season. Horned snakes were the greatest impediments to more abundant hunting.

Knowledge of the war was kept from the slaves until long after its beginning. Most of them had no idea what "war" meant and any news that might have been spread, fell on deaf ears. Gradually this knowledge was imparted by Yankee peddlers who came to the plantation to sell bed-ticking, etc. When the master discovered how this information was being given out, these peddlers were forbidden to go near the quarters. This rule was strictly enforced.

Eventually, the Confederate soldiers on their way to and from camp began to stop at the house. Food and everything available was given to them. Three of Mr. Cody's sons were killed in battle. As the Northern soldiers did not come near the home, the loss of property was practically negligible [TR: '—six cents being all' marked out].

When the Emancipation Proclamation was signed, the slaves were called to the "big house" in a group to receive the news that they were free. Both old and young danced and cheered when this information was given out. Many of the families remained there for a year or two until they were able to find desirable locations elsewhere.

Cody attributes his ability to reach a ripe old age to the excellent care he took of himself in his youth. He has used tobacco since he was a small boy and does not feel that it affects his health. Distilled liquor was plentiful in his young days and he always drank but never to an excess.

EX-SLAVE INTERVIEW

WILLIS COFER, Age 78
548 Findley Street
Athens, Georgia

Written by:
Grace McCune
Federal Writers' Project
Athens, Georgia

Edited by:
Sarah H. Hall
Athens, Ga.

and
Leila Harris
John N. Booth
Augusta, Georgia
[MAY 6 1938]

# WILLIS COFER

Willis was enjoying the warm sunshine of an April morning as he sat on his small porch. Apparently, he was pleased because someone actually wanted to hear him talk about himself. His rheumatism had been painful ever since that last bad cold had weakened him, but he felt sure the sunshine would "draw out all the kinks." Having observed the amenities in regard to health and weather, the old man proceeded with his story:

"Eden and Calline Cofer was my pa and ma and us all lived on de big old Cofer plantation 'bout five miles from Washin'ton, Wilkes. Pa b'longed to Marse Henry Cofer and ma and us chillun wuz de property of Marse Henry's father, Marse Joe Cofer.

"I wuz borned in 1860, and at one time I had three brudders, but Cato and John died. My oldest brudder, Ben Cofer, is still livin' and a-preachin' de Gospel somewhar up Nawth.

"Chilluns did have de bestes' good times on our plantation, 'cause Old Marster didn't 'low 'em to do no wuk 'til dey wuz 12 years old. Us jus' frolicked and played 'round de yard wid de white chilluns, but us sho' did evermore have to stay in dat yard. It wuz de cook's place to boss us when de other Niggers wuz off in de fields, and evvy time us tried to slip off, she cotch us and de way dat 'oman could burn us up wid a switch wuz a caution.

"Dere warn't no schools for us to go to, so us jes' played 'round. Our cook wuz all time feedin' us. Us had bread and milk for breakfas', and dinner wuz mos'ly peas and cornbread, den supper wuz milk and bread. Dere wuz so many chilluns dey fed us in a trough. Dey jes' poured de peas on de chunks of cornbread what dey had crumbled in de trough, and us had to mussel 'em out. Yessum, I said mussel. De only spoons us had wuz mussel shells what us got out of de branches. A little Nigger could put peas and cornbread away mighty fast wid a mussel shell.

"Boys jes' wore shirts what looked lak dresses 'til dey wuz 12 years old and big enough to wuk in de field. Den dey put 'em on pants made open in de back. Dem britches would look awful funny now, but dey wuz all us had den, and all de boys wuz mighty proud when dey got big enough to wear pants and go to wuk in de fields wid grown folkses. When a boy got to be a man enough to wear pants, he drawed rations and quit eatin' out of de trough.

"All de slave quarters wuz log cabins and little famblies had cabins wid jes' one room. Old Marster sho' did want to see lots of chilluns 'round de cabins and all de big famblies wuz 'lowed to live in two-room cabins. Beds for slaves wuz made by nailing frames, built out of oak or walnut planks to de sides of de cabins. Dey had two or three laigs to make 'em set right, and de mattresses wuz filled wid wheat straw. Dere warn't no sto'-bought stoves den, and all our cookin' wuz done in de fireplace. Pots wuz hung on iron cranes to bile and big pones of light bread wuz cooked in ovens on de hearth. Dat light bread and de biscuits made out of shorts wuz our Sunday bread and dey sho' wuz good, wid our home-made butter. Us had good old corn bread for our evvyday bread, and dere ain't nothin' lak corn bread and buttermilk to make healthy Niggers. Dere wouldn't be so many old sick Niggers now if dey et corn bread evvyday and let all dis wheat bread and sto'-bought, ready-made bread alone 'cept on Sunday.

"Dere wuz four or five acres in Marster's big old gyarden, but den it tuk a big place to raise enough for all de slaves and white folkses too in de same gyarden. Dere wuz jus' de one gyarden wid plenty of cabbage, collards, turnip greens, beans, corn, peas, onions, 'taters, and jus' evvything folkses laked in de way of gyarden sass. Marster never 'lowed but one smokehouse on his place. It wuz plumb full of meat, and evvy slave had his meat rations weighed out reg'lar. Dere wuz jes' one dairy house too whar de slaves got all de milk and butter dey needed.

Marster sho' did b'lieve in seeing dat his Niggers had a plenty to eat.

"Marster raised lots of chickens and de slaves raised chickens too if dey wanted to. Marster let 'em have land to wuk for deyselves, but dey had to wuk it atter dey come out of his fields. All dey made on dis land wuz deir own to sell and do what dey wanted to wid. Lots of 'em plowed and hoed by moonlight to make deir own crops.

"Us used to hear tell of big sales of slaves, when sometimes mammies would be sold away off from deir chilluns. It wuz awful, and dey would jes' cry and pray and beg to be 'lowed to stay together. Old Marster wouldn't do nothin' lak dat to us. He said it warn't right for de chilluns to be tuk away from deir mammies. At dem sales dey would put a Nigger on de scales and weigh him, and den de biddin' would start. If he wuz young and strong, de biddin' would start 'round $150 and de highest bidder got de Nigger. A good young breedin' 'oman brung $2,000 easy, 'cause all de Marsters wanted to see plenty of strong healthy chillun comin' on all de time. Cyarpenters and bricklayers and blacksmiths brung fancy prices from $3,000 to $5,000 sometimes. A Nigger what warn't no more'n jes' a good field hand brung 'bout $200.

"Dem bricklayers made all de bricks out of de red clay what dey had right dar on most all de plantations, and de blacksmith he had to make all de iron bars and cranes for de chimblies and fireplaces. He had to make de plow points too and keep de farm tools all fixed up. Sometimes at night dey slipped off de place to go out and wuk for money, a-fixin' chimblies and buildin' things, but dey better not let demselves git cotched.

"Mammy wove de cloth for our clothes and de white folkses had 'em made up. Quilts and all de bed-clothes wuz made out of homespun cloth.

"De fus' Sadday atter Easter wuz allus a holiday for de slaves. Us wuz proud of dat day 'cause dat wuz de onlies' day in de year a Nigger could do 'zactly what he pleased. Dey could go huntin', fishin' or visitin', but most of 'em used it to put in a good days wuk on de land what Marster 'lowed 'em to use for deyselves. Some of 'em come to Athens and help lay bricks on a new buildin' goin' up on Jackson Street. No Ma'am, I done forgot what buildin' it wuz.

"Us Niggers went to de white folkses churches. Mr. Louis Williams preached at de Baptist Church on de fust Sundays, and Meferdiss (Methodist) meetin's wuz on de second Sundays. Mr. Andy Bowden and Mr. Scott Cowan wuz two of de Meferdiss preachers. Me and pa jined de Baptis' Church. Ma wuz jes' a Meferdiss, but us all went to church together. Dey had de baptizin's at de pool and dere wuz sho' a lot of prayin' and shoutin' and singin' goin' on while de preacher done de dippin' of 'em. De onliest one of dem baptizin' songs I can ricollect now is, Whar de Healin' Water Flows. Dey waited 'til dey had a crowd ready to be baptized and den dey tuk a whole Sunday for it and had a big dinner on de ground at de church.

"De sho' 'nough big days wuz dem camp meetin' days. White folkses and Niggers all went to de same camp meetin's, and dey brung plenty 'long to eat—big old loafs of light bread what had been baked in de skillets. De night before dey sot it in de ovens to rise and by mawnin' it had done riz most to de top of de deep old pans. Dey piled red coals all 'round de ovens and when dat bread got done it wuz good 'nough for anybody. De tables wuz loaded wid barbecued pigs and lambs and all de fried chicken folkses could eat, and all sorts of pies and cakes wuz spread out wid de other goodies.

"Evvy plantation gen'ally had a barbecue and big dinner for Fourth of July, and when sev'ral white famblies went in together, dey did have high old times tryin' to see which one of 'em could git deir barbecue done and ready to eat fust. Dey jus' et and drunk all day. No Ma'am, us didn't know nuffin' 'bout what dey wuz celebratin' on Fourth of July, 'cept a big dinner and a good time.

"When slaves got married, de man had to ax de gal's ma and pa for her and den he had to ax de white folkses to 'low 'em to git married. De white preacher married 'em. Dey hold right hands and de preacher ax de man: 'Do you take dis gal to do de bes' you kin for her?' and if he say yes, den dey had to change hands and jump over de broomstick and dey wuz married. Our white folkses wuz all church folkses and didn't 'low no dancin' at weddin's but dey give 'em big suppers when deir slaves got married. If you married some gal on another place, you jus' got to see her on Wednesday and Sadday nights and all de chilluns b'longed to de gal's white folkses. You had to have a pass to go den, or de patterollers wuz sho' to git you. Dem patterollers evermore did beat up slaves if dey cotched 'em off dey own Marster's place 'thout no pass. If Niggers could out run 'em and git on deir home lines dey wuz safe.

"On our place when a slave died dey washed de corpse good wid plenty of hot water and soap and wropt it in a windin' sheet, den laid it out on de coolin' board and spread a snow white sheet over de whole business, 'til de coffin wuz made up. De windin' sheet wuz sorter lak a bed sheet made extra long. De coolin' board wuz made lak a ironin' board 'cept it had laigs. White folkses wuz laid out dat way same as Niggers. De coffins wuz made in a day. Dey tuk de measurin' stick and measured de head, de body, and de footses and made de coffin to fit dese measurements. If it wuz a man what died, dey put a suit of clothes on him before dey put him in de coffin. Dey buried de 'omans in da windin' sheets. When de Niggers got from de fields some of 'em went and dug a grave. Den dey put de coffin on de oxcart and carried it to de graveyard whar dey jus' had a burial dat day. Dey waited 'bout two months sometimes before dey preached de fun'ral sermon. For the fun'ral dey built a brush arbor in front of de white folkses church, and de white preacher preached de fun'ral sermon, and white folkses would come lissen to slave fun'rals. De song most sung at fun'rals wuz Hark from de Tomb. De reason dey had slave fun'rals so long atter de burial wuz to have 'em on Sunday or some other time when de crops had been laid by so de other slaves could be on hand.

"When white folkses died deir fun'rals wuz preached before dey wuz buried. Dat wuz de onliest diff'unce in de way dey buried de whites and de Niggers. Warn't nobody embalmed dem days and de white folkses wuz buried in a graveyard on de farm same as de Niggers wuz, and de same oxcart took 'em all to de graveyard.

"Our Marster done de overseein' at his place hisself, and he never had no hired overseer. Nobody never got a lickin' on our plantation lessen dey needed it bad, but when Marster did whup 'em dey knowed dey had been whupped. Dere warn't no fussin' and fightin' on our place and us all knowed better'n to take what didn't b'long to us, 'cause Old Marster sho' did git atter Niggers what stole. If one Nigger did kill another Nigger, dey tuk him and locked him in da jailhouse for 30 days to make his peace wid God. Evvy day de preacher would come read de Bible to him, and when de 30 days wuz up, den dey would hang him by de neck 'til he died. De man what done de hangin' read de Bible to de folkses what wuz gathered 'round dar while de murderer wuz a-dyin'.

"Its de devil makes folkses do bad, and dey all better change and serve God-a-Mighty, so as he kin save 'em before its too late. I b'lieve folkses 'haved better dem days dan dey does now. Marstar made 'em be good 'round his place.

"When us turned Marster's watch dogs loose at night, dey warn't nothin' could come 'round dat place. Dey had to be kept chained up in de daytime. Sometimes Marster let us take his dogs and go huntin' and dey wuz de best 'possum trailers 'round dem parts. When dey barked up a 'simmon tree, us allus found a 'possum or two in dat tree. Sometimes atter us cotched up lots of 'em, Marster let us have a 'possum supper. Baked wid plenty of butter and 'tatoes and sprinkled over wid red pepper, dey is mighty good eatments. My mouf's jus' a-waterin' 'cause I'm thinkin' 'bout 'possums.

"Yes Ma'am, us had corn shuckin's, and dey wuz big old times. Evvybody from plantations miles 'round would take time out to come. Sometimes de big piles of corn would make a line most a half a mile long, but when all de Niggers got at dat corn de shucks sho' would fly and it wouldn't be so long before all de wuk wuz done and dey would call us to supper. Dere wuz barbecue and chickens, jus' a plenty for all de Niggers, and corn bread made lak reg'lar light bread and sho' enough light bread too, and lots of 'tato pies and all sorts of good things.

"Atter da War wuz over, dey jus' turned de slaves loose widout nothin'. Some stayed on wid Old Marster and wukked for a little money and dey rations.

"Pa went down on the Hubbard place and wukked for 40 dollars a year and his rations. Ma made cloth for all de folkses 'round 'bout. Dey fotched deir thread and she wove de cloth for 50 cents a day. If us made a good crop, us wuz all right wid plenty of corn, peas, 'tatoes, cabbage, collards, turnip greens, all de hog meat us needed, and chickens too. Us started out widout nothin' and had to go in debt to de white folkses at fust but dat wuz soon paid off. I never had no chance to go to school and git book larnin'. All de time, us had to wuk in de fields.

"Ku Kluxers went 'round wid dem doughfaces on heaps atter de War. De Niggers got more beatin's from 'em dan dey had ever got from deir Old Marsters. If a Nigger sassed white folkses or kilt a hoss, dem Kluxers sho' did evermore beat him up. Dey never touched me for I stayed out of deir way, but dey whupped my pa one time for bein' off his place atter dark. When dey turned him loose, he couldn't hardly stand up. De Yankees jus' about broke up de Ku Kluxers, but day sho' wuz bad on Niggers while dey lasted.

"I wuz 'bout 21 years old when us married. Us never had no chillun and my wife done been daid for all dese long years, I don't know how many. I can't wuk and I jus' has to stay hyar wid my daid brother's chillun. Dey is mighty good to me, but I gits awful lonesome sometimes.

"No Ma'am, I ain't never seed but one ghost. Late one night, I wuz comin' by de graveyard and seed somethin' dat looked lak a dog 'ceppin' it warn't no dog. It wuz white and went in a grave. It skeered me so I made tracks gittin' 'way from dar in a hurry and I ain't never bean 'round no more graveyards at night.

"When I passes by de old graveyard on Jackson Street, I 'members lots of folkses whats buried dar, bofe white folkses and slaves too, for den white folkses put dey slaves whar dey aimed to be buried deyselves. Dat sho' used to be a fine graveyard.

"Us all gwine to git together someday when us all leaves dis old world. I'm ready to go; jus' a-waitin' for de Lord to call me home, and I ain't skeered to face de Lord who will judge us all de same, 'cause I done tried to do right, and I ain't 'fraid to die."

Uncle Willis was tired and sent a little boy to the store for milk. As the interviewer took her departure he said: "Good-bye Missy. God bless you. Jus' put yourself in de hands of de Lord, for dey ain't no better place to be."

PLANTATION LIFE

MARY COLBERT, Age 84
168 Pearl Street
Athens, Georgia

Written by:
Sadie B. Hornsby [HW: (White)]
Athens

Edited by:
Sarah H. Hall
Athens

and
John N. Booth
District Supervisor
Federal Writers' Project
Residencies 6 & 7
Augusta, Ga.

# MARY COLBERT

(NOTE: This is the first story we have had in which the client did not use any dialect. Mary Colbert's grammar was excellent. Her skin was almost white, and her hair was quite straight.

None of us know what a "deep" slave was. It may have the same meaning as outlandish Negro. The "outlandish Negroes" were those newly arrived Negroes who had just come in from any country outside of the United States of America, and were untrained. They were usually just from Africa. Sarah H. Hall)

With the thermometer registering 93 degrees in the shade on a particularly humid July day, the visitor trudged up one steep, rocky alley and down another, hesitantly negotiated shaky little bridges over several ravines, scrambled out of a ditch, and finally arrived at the address of Mary Colbert. It was the noon hour. A Negro man had tied his mule under an apple tree in one corner of Mary's yard. The animal was peacefully munching hay while his master enjoyed lunch from a battered tin bucket. Asked if Mary was at home, the man replied: "Yessum, jus' call her at de door."

A luxuriant Virginia creeper shaded the front porch of Mary's five-room frame house, where a rap on the front door brought the response: "Here I am, honey! Come right on through the house to the back porch." The aged mulatto woman was hanging out clothes on a line suspended between two peach trees. To the inquiry for Mary, she answered: "Yes, Honey, this is Mary. They say I am old, childish, and hellish; anyway, this is Mary."

"Dear, let's go in my parlor," she suggested in a cultured voice. "I wouldn't dare go out on the front porch wearing this dirty dress. It simply isn't my way of living." Mary is about five feet tall and wears her straight, snowy-white hair in a neat knot low on the back of her head. The sparkle in her bright brown eyes bespeaks a more youthful spirit than her wrinkled and almost white face would indicate. She was wearing a soiled print dress, brown cotton hose, and high-topped black shoes. In remarkably good English for one of her race she told that her daughter's family lives with her, "so that I won't be right by myself." Then she began her story:

"Honey, what is it you want me to tell you. Where was I born? Oh, my child! I was born right here in dear old hilly Athens. Yes, that's where I was born. Polly Crawford was my mother, and she belonged to Major William H. Crawford before he gave her to his son, Marse John Crawford. Now about my father, that is the dream. He died when I was just a little child. They said he was Sandy Thomas and that he was owned by Marster Obadiah Thomas, who lived in Oglethorpe County. All I can remember about my grandparents is this: When I found my grandma, Hannah Crawford, she was living on Major Crawford's plantation, where Crawford, Georgia, is now. Grandma was a little, bitty woman; so little that she wore a number one shoe. She was brought here from Virginia to be a field hand, but she was smart as a whip, and lived to be 118 years old. I used to tell my mother that I wished I was named Hannah for her, and so Mother called me Mary Hannah.

"I can't bring my grandfather to mind very clearly. I do remember that my mother took me to Penfield to see him, and told me if I wasn't a good little girl he would surely whip me. They called him 'Uncle Campfire', because he had such a fiery temper. For a living, after he got to be an old man, he made cheers (chairs), but for the life of me I don't know who he belonged to, because Major Crawford sold him before I was born.

"There were five of us children: Nat, Solomon, Susannah, Sarah, and myself. Marse John gave Solomon to his daughter, Miss Fannie, when she married Marse William H. Gerdine. Susannah belonged to Miss Rosa Golden, and Sarah and I belonged to the other Miss Fannie. She was Marse John's sister. Nat was Marse John's house boy, and our mother was his cook. We children just played around the yard until we were large enough to work.

"Yes, my dear, I was born in Marse John's back yard. He lived in a two-story frame house on Dougherty Street, back of Scudder's School. The two slave houses and the kitchen were set off from the house a little piece out in the yard. It was the style then to have the kitchen built separate from the dwelling house.

"Lord bless your life, Honey! We didn't live in log cabins, as you call them. There were two slave houses. The one Aggie lived in was two-story, the other one had just one story and they were both weatherboarded like Marse John's own house. The grown folks slept on beds made with tall oak posts. There were no metal springs then and the beds were corded instead. The straw-stuffed mattress ticks were made with plain and striped material, and pillows were filled with cotton. We children slept on trundle beds, which were pushed up under the big beds in the daytime, and pulled out for us to sleep on at night.

"No Ma'm, there was never any money given to me in slavery time. Remember, Dear, when the yankees came through here, I was only ten years old. Misses Fannie and Ann Crawford were Major Crawford's daughters, and they kept house for Marse John. That morning in May I was wearing a sleeveless apron, and they (Miss Fannie and Miss Ann) put a bag of gold and silver, and some old greenback Confederate money in my apron and told me to hold on to it. Miss Fannie and Miss Ann, both of them, patted me on the head and said: 'Now, be a good little girl and don't move.' On came the Blue Coats: they went all over the house searching everything with their guns and swords shining and flashing. I was so scared the sweat was running down my face in streams. Bless your life! When they came to the bedroom where I was standing by a bed, holding that money inside my apron, they didn't even glance at me the second time. Little did they think that little slave girl had the money they were hunting for. After the yankees were gone, I gave it all back to Miss Fannie, and she didn't give me the first penny. If any of the money was given to my mother she didn't tell me about it.

"I am going to tell you the truth about what we had to eat, so listen now. It was egg bread, biscuits, peas, potatoes—they they were called 'taters then—artichoke pickles, tea cakes, pies, and good old healthy lye hominy. There was plenty of meat served, but I was not allowed to eat that, as I was never a very strong child. I was a fool about stale bread, such as biscuit, cornbread, and light bread. Mother was a fine cook and her battercakes would just melt in your mouth. Of course, you know we had no stoves in those days and the cooking was done in open fireplaces, in ovens and pots. Oh yes! We had a garden. There was only one on the place and enough was raised in it to feed all of the people living there.

"I don't remember eating 'possums, rabbits, squirrels and fish until I went to Jackson, Mississippi, with Miss Rosa. There were plenty of those meats in Mississippi and I was then getting old enough and healthy enough to be allowed to eat them."

At this point, Mary insisted on serving lunch for her visitor, saying that she had lived with white people and knew how to cook. After a polite refusal, the story was continued:

"I was laughing at myself just the other day about those homespun dresses and sleeveless aprons I wore as a child. I reckon that was a sign you were coming to ask me about those things. I kept one of those dresses of mine until my own baby girl wore it out, and now I am sorry I let her wear it, for it would be so nice to have it to show you. We wore just a one piece costume in summer and had calico and muslin dresses for Sunday. Wintertime, I wore a balmoral petticoat, osnaburg drawers, and er-r-r. Well, Jacob! I never thought I would live to see the day I'd forget what our dresses were called. Anyway they were of woolen material in a checked design, and were made with a full skirt gathered on to a deep yoke. Uncle Patrick Hull—he was a deep slave belonging to Mr. A.L. Hull—made all the shoes for Marse John's slaves. We all wore brass-toed brogans.

"Oh, good! I should smile! A better man than Marse John never lived. Nobody better not beat his slaves. Marse John was the postmaster. He married Miss Sallie Eden, and everybody said she was mighty good, but I never knew her for she died when I was a baby. Marse John and his wife, Miss Sallie, had three children. They were: Miss Fannie, Miss Rosa and Marse Allie. Miss Annie Crawford, who teaches in the school here, is Marse Allie's daughter. She don't know me so well, but I know mighty well who she is. I think I have already told you that Misses Fannie and Rosa kept house for their brother, Marse John, after their mother died.

"Darling, please get this right: the plantation is a dream to me. If I should try to tell you about it, I am sure it would be only what my mother told me about it in the years long after the surrender. Whether the plantation was the property of Marse John or his father, William H. Crawford, I don't know, but I am sure there was an overseer, and I am quite sure it was a very large plantation. You know the town of Crawford was named for my white folks. The only thing I can be sure of, from my own memory, is of the things that took place here in Athens.

"Breakfast had to be served promptly at 7:30. When that 9:00 o'clock bell sounded at night, God bless your soul! You had to be in your house, and you had to be in bed by 10:00 o'clock. Marse John never punished but just two of his slaves that I can remember, but I have seen them get several good whippings. They were Ned and William, Aggie's and Lucy's boys, and Marse John cowhided them for misbehaving.

"There were jails during slavery time, but Marse John kept his slaves straight himself and did not allow any of them to be taken to jail. I have never seen slaves sold, but I have seen droves of them marching by, being taken to Watkinsville to be sold.

"No! No! Oh! No! You had better not dare let white people know that you could read, in those days. I remember one colored man, Alfred Evans, who used to read the Bible during slavery time. All the learning I have, I got after we were made free. There were two colored churches in Athens; one was Baptist and the other was Methodist. Yankee ladies came down from the North and taught us to read and write. I have often considered writing the history of my life and finally decided to undertake it, but I found that it was more of a job than I had expected it to be, and then too, I would have to tell too much, so I thought best to leave it alone.

"I went to church but very little during slavery time. However, I dearly loved to go to Sunday school, and never missed an opportunity of attending. One of our Sunday school songs was worded something like this:

> 'I want to be an angel,
> And with the angels stand.'

"My favorite song began:

> 'Around the Throne in Heaven,
> Ten Thousand children stand.'

"OO! Yes, I know how they buried folks in slavery time. For caskets they used straight, white pine boxes that they called coffins. They didn't have funerals like they do now. A preacher would say a few words at the grave and then he prayed, and after that everybody sang something like: 'I will arise and go to Jesus.' I was a singer in my younger days.

"All I remember 'bout Negroes going off to the North was when their masters took them along on trips to wait on them. Bless your life! That was one time when the ones that could read and write had the advantage. They were usually chosen to go along so if anything happened to the Marster on the trip, they could write back home. I never saw patrollers, but I heard that they used to beat up Negroes who were caught away from home without a pass. Marse John kept his slaves supplied with passes at all necessary times.

"Not all the slaves had to work on Saturday afternoons. This was their time of the week to get together and have a little fun around their quarters. Sunday mornings they went to church, as a rule, and on Sunday nights they visited each other and held prayer meetings in their homes. Don't get me wrong. They had to have passes to go visiting and attend those prayer meetings.

"Christmas time was a holiday season for slaves, and they had everything good you could want to eat. Listen, Child, I am telling you the truth. They even had pumpkin pie. Oh, yes! Santa Claus came to see slave children. Once I got too smart for my own good. Miss Fannie and Miss Ann had told us to go to bed early. They said if we weren't asleep when Santa Claus got there, he would go away and never come back. Well, that night I made up my mind to stay awake and see Santa Claus. Miss Fannie and Miss Ann slipped into our quarters right easy and quiet and were filling up stockings with candy, dolls, and everything you can imagine. While they were doing that, they turned around and saw me with my eyes wide open. Right there my Santa Claus ended. We didn't have any special observance of New Year's Day. It was the same as any other day.

"Mother said they had cornshuckings, quiltings, and cotton pickings on the plantation. She told me a good deal about the cornshuckings: about how they selected a general, whose job was to get up on top of the corn pile and holler at the top of his voice, leading the cornshucking song, while the others all shucked the corn and sang. After the corn was all shucked there were always fine eats. I can remember the quiltings myself. The women went from one house to another and quilted as many as 12 quilts in one night sometimes. After the quilts were all finished they had a big spread of good food too. Now it takes a whole month to quilt one quilt and nothing to eat.

"What games did we play? Let me see. Oh! yes, one of them was played to the rhyme:

> 'Chickimy, chickimy, Craney Crow
> I went to the well to wash my toe,
> When I got back my chicken was gone
> What time, Old Witch?'

"Then we would run and chase each other. Another game was played to the counting-out by the rhyme that started:

> 'Mollie, Mollie Bright, three-score and ten.'

"Honey, there is no use to ask me about Raw Head and Bloody Bones. When folks started talking about that, I always left the room. It is a shame how folks do frighten children trying to make them get quiet and go to sleep. I don't believe in ha'nts and ghosts. Since I have been grown, I have been around so many dead folks I have learned that the dead can't harm you; its the living that make the trouble.

"When his slaves were taken sick, Marse John always called in a doctor. An old woman, who was known as 'Aunt Fannie,' was set aside to nurse sick slaves. Dr. Joe Carlton was Marse John's doctor. What I am going to tell you is no fairy tale. Once I was so sick that Marse John called in Dr. Carlton, Dr. Richard M. Smith, Dr. Crawford Long, and Dr. James Long, before they found out what was wrong with me. I had inflammatory rheumatism and I wore out two and a half pairs of crutches before I could walk good again. Now, Dr. Crawford Long is a great and famous man in history, but it is sure true that he doctored on this old Negro many years ago.

"Honey, don't flatter me. Don't you know a little girl 10 years old can't remember everything that went on that far back. A few things they dosed the slaves with when they were sick was horehound tea, garlic mixed with whiskey, and the worm-few (vermifuge?) tea that they gave to Negro children for worms. That worm-few dose was given in April. Asafetida was used on us at all times and sage tea was considered a splendid medicine.

"When news came that Negroes had been freed there was a happy jubilee time. Marse John explained the new freedom to his slaves and we were glad and sorry too. My mother stayed with Marse John until he died. I was still a child and had never had to do anything more than play dolls, and keep the children in the yard. Lord, Honey! I had a fine time those days.

"It wasn't so long after the surrender before schools for Negroes were opened. It looked like they went wild trying to do just like their white folks had done. As for buying homes, I don't know where they would have gotten the money to pay for homes and land.

"At the time I married I was a washerwoman for the white folks. My first husband was Isaac Dixon, who came from some place in Alabama and had been owned by Dr. Lipscomb, the chancelor of the university. Dr. Lipscomb married us in the colored Methodist Church, and that night the church was crowded to overflowing. I wore a white dress made with a long train; that was the style then. After the ceremony, my mother served cake and wine at her house. Our six children were prettier than you, but only three of them lived to get grown. Our white friends named our children. My first husband died and then I married Jones Colbert, who belonged to Marse Fletcher Colbert of Madison County. We just went around to the preacher's house and got married. Jones was an old man when I married him. He was a preacher. He is dead now and so are all my children except one. I have one grandson, and this is the shameful part about him; his mother won't married when he was born, but of course she married later.

"Now I am going to tell you the truth as I see it. Abraham Lincoln was an instrument of God sent to set us free, for it was God's will that we should be freed. I never did hitch my mind on Jeff Davis; like the children of Israel, he had his time to rule. Booker T. Washington! Well, now I didn't give him a thought. He had to do his part. His mistress had taught him to read.

"Why did I join the church? Well, when the white folks sent their help off to Mississippi trying to keep them slaves, my sister and I went with Miss Rosa Crawford to Jackson. Before I left home my mother gave me an alabaster doll and told me to be a good girl and pray every night. Well, I never saw so many slave-houses in my life as I saw in Mississippi. Every night when I heard a colored man named Ben praying in his room that made me think of what my mother had told me and I grew more and more homesick for her. Finally one night I crept into Uncle Ben's room and asked him to tell me about God, and he did. After that, every night I went into his room and we prayed together. Yes, Honey, I found God in Jackson, Mississippi, and I joined the church just as soon as I could after I got back to my mother and dear old Athens.

"Yes, Honey, I was raised and loved by my own white folks and, when I grew to be old enough and large enough, I worked for them. I have been with, or worked for, white folks all my life and, just let me tell you, I had the best white folks in the world, but it was by God's plan that the Negroes were set free."

[HW: Dist. 1
Ex. Slave #21
(with Photograph)]
[HW: "JOHN COLE"]

Subject: A SLAVE REMEMBERS
District: No. 1 W.P.A
Editor: Edward Ficklen
Supervisor: Joseph E. Jaffee
[MAY 8 1937]

# JOHN COLE

## A SLAVE REMEMBERS

The front door of a little vine-clad cottage on Billups Street, in Athens, Georgia quaked open and John Cole, ex-slave confronted a "gov'mint man."

Yes, he was the son of Lucius Cole and Betsy Cole, was in his 86th year, and remembered the time "way back" when other gov'mint men with their strange ways had descended on Athens.

And far beyond that, back to the time when they had tried him out as a scullion boy in the big town house where his mother was the cook, but it seemed that the trays always escaped his clumsy young hands.

So "Marse Henry" had put him on the 200 acre Oglethorpe plantation as apprentice to training of the farm horses whose large unmanageableness he found more manageable than the dainty china of the banker's house. He simply had followed more after his father, the carriage driver than his mother, the cook.

Of course, all fifteen of the hands worked from sun-up to sun-down, but his aunt was the plantation cook, and it was not so bad there.

The night brought no counsel, but it brought better. Stretch cow-hides over cheese-boxes and you had tambourines. Saw bones from off a cow, knock them together, and call it [HW: a drum]. Or use broom-straws, on fiddle-strings, and you had your entire orchestra.

Grow older, and get by the gates with a pass (you had to have a pass or the paddle-rollers would get you,) and you had you a woman. If the woman wasn't willing, a good, hard-working hand could always get the master to make the girl marry him—whether or no, willy-nilly.

If a hand were noted for raising up strong black bucks, bucks that would never "let the monkey get them" while in the high-noon hoeing, he would be sent out as a species of circuit-rider to the other plantations—to plantations where there was over-plus of "worthless young nigger gals". There he would be "married off" again—time and again. This was thrifty and saved any actual purchase of new stock.

Always on Saturday afternoon you would have till "first dark" for base-ball, and from first dark till Sunday-go-to meeting for drinking and dancing. Sunday you could go to the colored church (with benefit of white clergy) or you could go to the white church just like real class except you sat in the rear.

No, it was not a bad life.

You usually weren't sick, but if you were sick, it afforded you the luxury of tea. Turpentine and caster oil composed the entire materia medica. Turpentine was used for sore throats, cuts and bruises. Castor oil was used for everything else except a major fracture which called for the master sending in a doctor to the quarters.

Yes, the gov'mint men with the blue uniforms and the shiny brass buttons had descended from the North on Athens—descended in spite of the double-barrelled cannon that the little master and the little master's men had tried on them. The blue clad invaders had come in despite of the quick breast-works, and the new-fangled cannon, and Bob Toombs boast that he "could beat the damn Yankees with corn-stalks before breakfast". (If only they had fought that way—if only they had [HW: not] needed grape-shot had enough to invent cannon mouths that spoke at the same time and were meant to mow down men with a long chain—if only they had not been able to fight long after Bull Run, and after breakfast!)

Yes, the Yankees had come over the classic hills of Athens (Athens that had so many hills that she would have been named Rome except for her first land-grant college,) had left, and had come again to stay, and to bring freedom to John Cole and his kind.

This was six months after Lee and his palandins had laid down the sword—the gallant, the unstained (but, alas, claimed Meade's batteries) the unconstitutional sword. Six months had gone and freedom had come.

But John Cole, slave of Henry Hull, the banker, found that his freedom was the freedom of "the big oak"— Athens famed tree-that-owns-itself. He was free, but he had no way to go anywhere. He was rooted in the soil and would stay fast rooted. He worked on with his master for 20 years, without pay.

Did he believe, back in slavery time in "signs" and in "sayings"—that the itching foot meant the journey to new lands—that the hound's midnight threnody meant murder?

No, when he was a young buck and had managed the bad horses, he had had no such beliefs. No, he was not superstitious. If the foot itched something ought to be put on it (or taken off it)—and as to the hounds yelping, nobody ever knew what dark-time foolishness a hound-dog might be up to.

But he was old, now. Death always comes in the afternoon. He does believe in things that have been proved. He does believe that a squinch-owl's screeching ("V-o-o-o-d-o-o! W-h-o-o-o? Y-ou-u!") is a sure sign of death. Lowing of a cow in afternoon Georgia meadows means death mighty close. If death come down to a house, better stop clock and put white cloth on mirrors. No loud talking permitted. Better for any nigger to bow low down to death....

To what factors did he attribute his long life, queried the gov'mint man.

Long living came from leaving off smoking and drinking.

Would he have a nickle cigar?

He would.

Yes, he was feeling quite tol'able, thank you. But he believed now in the owl and the cow and the clock.

In the morning-time one lives, but death always come in the afternoon. Better for any nigger, anywhere, to bow low down to death.

United States. Work Projects Administration

## PLANTATION LIFE AS VIEWED BY EX-SLAVE

JULIA COLE, Age 78
169 Yonah Avenue
Athens, Georgia

Written by:
Corry Fowler
Athens

Edited by:
Sarah H. Hall
Athens

Leila Harris
Augusta

and
John N. Booth
District Supervisor
Federal Writers' Project
Residencies 6 & 7

# JULIA COLE

A knock on the door of the comfortable little frame house which Julia Cole shares with her daughter, Rosa, brought the response, "Who dat?" Soon Rosa appeared. "Come in Honey and have a cheer," was her greeting and she added that Julia had "stepped across de street to visit 'round a little." Soon the neighborhood was echoing and reverberating as the call, "Tell Aunt Julia somebody wants to see her at her house," was repeated from cabin to cabin. A few moments later Julia walked in. Yellowish gingercake in color, and of rather dumpy figure, she presented a clean, neat appearance.

She and her daughter, who cooks for a dentist's family, take much pride in their attractively furnished home. Julia was of pleasant manner and seemed anxious to tell all that she could. It is doubtful if Rosa made much progress with her ironing in an adjoining room, for every few minutes she came to the door to remind her mother of some incident that she had heard her tell before.

Julia began her story by saying: "I was born in Monroe, Georgia and b'longed to Marster John Grant. My Mamma was Mittie Johnson, and she died de year 'fore de war ended. I don't 'member my Pa. Mamma had four chillun. Richard and Thomas Grant was my brothers, but me and my sister Hattie was Johnsons. Marse John had a big plantation and a heap of slaves. Dey was rich, his folks was. Dey is de folks dat give Grant's Park to Atlanta.

"Dey called my grandpa, 'Uncle Abram.' Atter he had wukked hard in de field all day, he would jus' lay down on a bench at night and sleep widout pullin' off his clothes. Us had home-made beds in de cabins widout no paint on 'em. Evvything slaves had was home-made, jus' wooden-legged things. Even de coffins was made at home out of pine wood. Now me, I didn't sleep in de cabin much. I slept on a little trundle bed up at de big house. In de daytime my bed was pushed back up under one of de big beds.

"Marse John's son, Marse Willie Grant, blowed de bugle in de mornin's by 4 o'clock to git de slaves up in time to be in de fields by daybreak. When slaves got too old to wuk, dey took keer of de chillun in a house down below de kitchen. Mamma wukked in de field when she was able. Nobody on our place had to wuk in de fields on Sadday evenin's. Dat was de time de 'omans washed deir clothes and cleaned up.

"Chillun didn't have much to do. Us loved to hunt for turkey nests 'cause dey give us a teacake for evvy turkey egg us fetched in. Chillun et in de yard at de big house, whar dey give us plenty of meat and cornbread wid good vegetables for dinner. For breakfast and supper, us had mostly buttermilk and cornbread. On Sundays us had bread made from wheat flour and sopped good old syrup wid it. Sometimes Marse John would give us 'mission to kill little pigs at night and broil 'em over de coals in our yards, and how us did enjoy 'em! I ain't never suffered for nothin' in all my life, 'cause de Grants was mighty good white folks. De old White home on Prince Avenue was deir summer home. When dey built it, woods was all 'round and dere warn't many houses in dat section.

"Us had plenty of clothes made out of homespun checks, and Marse John give us brass-toed shoes. Our dresses was well sewed and made wid belts to 'em. Nobody went 'bout half naked on our plantation lak some of de old folks f'um other farms talks 'bout. Us had good well-made clothes, even if dey was made out of common cloth.

"Nobody on our plantation run away to de North, and de paddyrollers didn't git nobody at our place neither. Marse John was too good to evvybody for his slaves to want to cut up and run 'way and do things to make de paddyrollers hunt 'em down. Dey didn't have no jails 'cause dey didn't need none on our place. Sometimes Marse John made a colored man named Uncle Jim Cooper give 'em a good whuppin' when dey needed it.

"When us was sick, dey give us herbs and things of dat sort. In de springtime, dey give us jerusalem oak seed in syrup for nine mornin's and by den us was allus rid of de worms. Dey 'tended to slave chillun so good and dutiful dat dere warn't many of 'em died, and I don't never 'member no doctor comin' to my Mamma's house.

"Old Missus used to teach us in da blue back speller, and when I didn't know my lesson she made me run f'um de house to de gyarden gate for punishment. De more words I missed; de more times I had to run. Us had our own church services on de plantation under homemade brush arbors, and our colored preacher was Uncle Charles Cooper.

"Once some sojers come by our place lookin' for Marse John. He had done hid in de loft of de meat house and told evvybody on de place dey better not tell whar he was. Dey didn't find Marse John, but dey did find his son, Marse Willie, and dey tuk him 'long wid 'em. Marse Willie was de only chile dat Marster and Missus had and it nearly killed 'em for him to be tuk 'way from 'em. When Mr. Lincoln's general got to our place he was a-ridin' a big red hoss dat sho' was a grand animal. Dem sojers went in de smokehouses and stores evvywhar and tuk what dey wanted.

"Not long 'fore de war ended, my Mamma tuk a 'lapse f'um measles and died. 'Fore she died, she sont for Marse John and told him what she wanted done, and he done jus' what she axed. She give him my brothers, Richard and Thomas, and told him to take dem two boys and to make men out of 'em by makin' 'em wuk hard. I jus' lak to have died when my Mamma died. Dey carried her to de graveyard and put her down in de grave and I jus' couldn't help it; I jumped right down in dat grave wid her, and dey had to take me out. My brothers said I was plum crazy dat day.

"Atter de war was over, Marster moved his family to Atlanta on Peachtree Street. His grandson dat was born dat year died not long ago. Dey didn't have no farm in Atlanta and so dey didn't need all deir old servants. My sister Hattie was a baby and Auntie tuk her to Atlanta wid de Grants.

"I don't know what 'come of de others on Marster's farm. I had to git in a covered wagon and come wid my Uncle Jordan Johnson to Athens. I didn't want to leave, and I hid down under our things in de wagon when dey made me come. When us crossed de river, I was sho' us was 'bout to git drownded. One time atter dat us tuk a trip to Madison to see de old breastplates (breastworks) dar.

"My brother Tom got to be captain of a colored troop dat went to de Philippine Islands. Over dar de sojers kilt a big snake and et it all but de head. He had dat thing stuffed and brought it home. Atter he left de army, he got a job in de Atlanta Post Office whar he wukked 'til he was 'tired.

"I was hired out to de Marks family and stayed dar for years and dat was a mighty good place to be hired out. I was married twice. Me and Crit Clayton married at home. I ain't never seed nothin' lak dat pretty flowerdy weddin' dress dat I wore and I had de prettiest hat and things dat I ever seed. My next husband was Andrew Cole—He was Rosa's Pa. I forgits de name of de white preacher dat married us when us went to his house and axed him to. Four of our seven chillun is still livin'.

"Dey tells me our old big house near Monroe is standin' yit, and I sho' do wish I could see it once more 'fore I die, but since I broke my hip a few years ago I jus' don't ride in dem automobiles. No Ma'am, I don't limp. De Lord was good to heal my hip and I ain't takin' no chances on breakin' no more of my bones."

EX-SLAVE INTERVIEW

MARTHA COLQUITT, Age 85
190 Lyndon Avenue
Athens, Georgia

Written by:
Mrs. Sarah H. Hall
Federal Writers' Project
Athens, Georgia

Edited by:
John N. Booth
District Supervisor
Federal Writers' Project
Residencies 6 & 7
Augusta, Georgia

# MARTHA COLQUITT

The aged Negress leaned heavily on her cane as she shuffled about her tiny porch in the waning sunlight of a cold January day. An airplane writing an advertising slogan in letters of smoke high in the sky was receiving but indifferent attention from Aunt Martha. Sha shivered and occasionally leaned against a post until a paroxysm of coughing subsided. "What would you have thought of that if it had suddenly appeared in the sky when you were a child?" she was asked. "It would have scared me plum to death," was the response. "I didn't come out here just to see dat," she continued, "I didn't have nothin' to make no fire wid, and I had to git out in de sunshine 'cause it wuz too cold to stay in de house. It sho' is mighty bad to have to go to bed wid cold feet and cough all night long."

Her visitor could not resist the impulse to say, "Let's make a trade, Aunt Martha! If I give you a little money will you buy wood; then while you enjoy the fire will you think back over your life and tell me about your experiences when I come back tomorrow?" "Bless de Lord! I sho' will be glad to tell you de truf 'bout anything I can 'member," was her quick reply as she reached for the money.

## [TR: Return Visit]

The next day Aunt Martha was in bed, slowly eating a bowl of potlicker and turnip greens into which cornbread had been crumbled.

"My ches' hurt so bad I couldn't git up today," was her greeting, "but set right dar by my bed and I can talk all right, long as I don't have to walk 'bout none. Walkin' makes me cough."

Soon the bowl was empty and when she had wiped her mouth with the sleeve of her nightgown, Aunt Martha began:

"When I wuz born, my ma b'longed to Marse Billie Glenn and us lived on his big plantation way down below Lexin'ton. My pa wuz Anderson Mitchell. He come from Milledgeville and b'longed to Mr. D. Smith. The Smithies lived close by Marse Billie's place. My ma wuz Healon Mitchell. I don't know what her last name wuz 'fore she married. She wuz born in Virginny, and her and my grandma wuz sold and brought to Georgia when ma wuz a baby. Grandma never did see none of her other chillun or her husband no more, and us never did hear nothin' 'bout 'em.

"Ma had four chillun. Lucy wuz my onlies' sister. Mr. Davenport bought her and she growed up at his place, what wuz called 'De Glade.' It wuz a big fine place at Point Peter, Georgia. Lucy married a Taylor.

"My brother, Isaac, wuz raised at Mr. Hamilton's place at Point Peter. After he growed up, he worked in Atlanta and bought him a home dar. He got in a fight wid a man what had done stobbed his mule, and de man hurt Isaac so bad he went crazy and died in de 'sylum at Milledgeville, but dey took him back and buried him in Atlanta.

"My other brother wuz Anderson Mitchell, and after freedom come he got work in Athens at de compress. His boss man moved to Augusta and took Anderson wid him to work in de compress dar. One day somethin' blowed up and he wuz scalded so bad it paralyzed him. Dey brought him back here, but he soon died.

"Ma's house was right on de edge of Marse Billie's yard, 'cause she was de cook. Grandma lived in de same house wid ma and us chillun, and she worked in de loom house and wove cloth all de time. She wove de checkidy cloth for de slaves clo'es, and she made flannel cloth too, leaseways, it wuz part flannel. She made heaps of kinds of cloth.

"Our beds had big home-made posties and frames, and us used ropes for springs. Grandma brought her feather bed wid her from Virginny, and she used to piece up a heap of quilts outen our ole clo'es and any kind of scraps she could get a holt of. I don't know what de others had in dey cabins 'cause ma didn't 'low her chillun to visit 'round de other folkses none.

"Ma's chillun all had vittals from de white folkses kitchen. After Marse Billie's fambly done et and left de table, de cook wuz s'posed to take what wuz left to feed de house niggers and her own chillun, and us did have sho' 'nuff good vittals. All de other slave folks had day rations weighed out to 'em every week and dey cooked in dey own cabins. When de wheat wuz ground at de mill it made white flour, and shorts, and seconds. Most of de shorts wuz weighed out in rations for de slave folks. Now and den at Christmas and special times dey got a little white flour. Dey liked cornbread for reg'lar eatin'. Dey wuz always lots of hogs on Marse Billie's plantation, and his colored folkses had plenty of side meat. Slaves never had no time to hunt in de day time, but dey sho' could catch lots of 'possums at night, and dey knowed how to git catfish at night too.

"'Cross de road from de Big 'Ouse, Marse Billie had a big gyarden, and he seed dat his help had plenty of somethin' good to bile. Dey won't no separate gyardens. Dey didn't have no time to work no gyardens of dey own.

"In summertime us chillun wore just one piece of clo'es. It wuz a sack apron. In winter grandma made us yarn underskirts and yarn drawers buttoned down over our knees. Ma made our home-knit stockings. Dey called our brass toed shoes 'brogans.' I don't speck you ever seed a brass toed shoe!

"Our Big 'Ouse sho' wuz one grand fine place. Why, it

must have been as big as de Mill Stone Baptist Church! It wuz all painted white wid green blinds and had a big old high porch dat went nigh all 'round de house.

"If I ever did hear what Marse Billie's wife wuz named, I done plum clear forgot. Us called her 'Mist'ess' long as she lived and I don't recollect hearin' her called nothin' else. Marster and Mist'ess never had no little chillun whilst I was dar. Miss Lizzie wuz dey youngest child and she wuz most grown when I wuz born.

"Marse Billie's overseer lived in a four-room house up de road a piece from the Big 'Ouse. Nobody thought 'bout none of Marse Billie's overseers as pore white folkses. Every overseer he ever had wuz decent and 'spectable. Course dey won't in de same class wid Marse Billie's fambly, but dey was all right. Dey wuz four or five homes nigh our plantation, but all of 'em b'longed to rich white folkses. If dey wuz any pore white folkses 'round dar, us chillun never heared nothin' of 'em.

"I don't know just how many slaves Marse Billie had, but dey sho' was a drove of 'em. Sometimes he had 'em all git together in de back yard at de Big 'Ouse, and dey just filled up de yard.

"De overseer blowed a horn to wake 'em up just 'fore day, so as everybody could cook, eat, and git out to de fields by sunrise. Dey quit nigh sundown, in time for 'em to feed de stock, do de milkin', tend to bringin' in de wood, and all sorts of other little jobs dat had to be done 'fore it got too dark to see. Dey never wuz no work done at night on our plantation.

"If any of Marse Billie's help wuz whipped, I never

knowed nothin' 'bout it. Dey used to say dat if any of 'em didn't work right de overseer would take 'em to de workshop. Us chillun never did know what happened when dey took 'em to de workshop. It wuz too fur away for us to hear what happened dar. De workshop was a big lone shed off to itself, whar dey had da blacksmith place, and whar harness wuz mended, and all sorts of fixin' done to de tools and things.

"Us never heared of no jail. Marse Billie bossed his place and us never knowed 'bout no trouble. De workshop wuz de nighest thing to a jail or a court dat anybody on our plantation knowed anything 'bout. Us never seed nobody in chains 'til long atter de War, when us wuz livin' in Lexin'ton, and Mr. Jim Smith come through dar wid some colored folkses all chained up, but us never did know how come dey wuz chained.

"No slave never runned away fron Marse Billie's plantation. Dey never even wanted to try. Dey wuz always 'fraid dey might not be able to take as good keer of deyselves as Marse Billie did for 'em, and dey didn't know what would happen to 'em off de plantation.

"I heared 'em talkin' 'bout paterollers, but I never did see one. Folkses said dey would git you and beat you if dey cotch you off de plantation whar you b'longed 'thout no pass. If any of Marse Billie's slaves got cotched by de paterollers, I never knowed nothin' 'bout it.

"I never heared of no trouble twixt de white folkses and dey colored folkses. Grandma and ma never 'lowed us to go to no other cabins, and us didn't hear 'bout no talk what wuz goin' on 'mongst de others. At night ma always spinned and knit, and grandma, she sewed, makin' clo'es for us chillun. Dey done it 'cause dey wanted to. Dey wuz workin' for deyselves den. Dey won't made to work at night. On Sadday night, ma bathed all her chillun. I don't know what de other famblies done den. Slaves wuz 'lowed to frolic Sadday night, if dey b'haved deyselves. On Sunday nights dey most always had prayer meetings.

"On Christmas mornin' all of us would come up to de yard back of de Big 'Ouse and Marse Billie and de overseer handed out presents for all. Dey wuz a little dram and cake too. Us chillun got dolls, and dresses, and aprons. Them stuffed rag dolls wuz de prettiest things! On New Year's day all de mens would come up to de Big 'Ouse early in de morning and would work lively as dey could a-cuttin' wood and doing all sorts of little jobs 'til de dinner bell rung. Den Marse Billie would come out and tell 'em dey wuz startin' de New Year right a-workin' lively and fast. Den he would say dat dey would be fed good and looked atter good, long as dey worked good. He give 'em a good taste of dram and cake all 'round, and let 'em go back to dey cabins for dinner, and dey could have de rest of de day to frolic.

"Dem cornshuckin's us used to have sho' wuz a sight. Corn would be piled up high as dis house, and de folkses would dance 'round and holler and whoop. Ma 'lowed us chillun to watch 'em 'bout a half hour; den made us come back inside our cabin, 'cause dey always give de corn shuckin' folkses some dram, and things would git mighty lively and rough by de time all de corn wuz shucked.

"On bright moonshiny nights folkses would invite de neighbors to come for cotton pickin's. After the cotton wuz picked dey would eat barbecue, and dance and have a big time.

"I never seed but one weddin' 'fore freedom come, and dat wuz when Marse Billie's daughter, Miss Lizzie Glenn, married Mr. Deadwyler. Dey had everything at dat weddin'. Yes, Ma'am, just everything. Miss Lizzie had on a white silk dress a-trailin' so far behind her dat it took two ladies to tote her train. Her veil wuz floatin' all 'bout her, and she wuz just de prettiest thing I ever did see in my whole life. A long time atter dat, Mr. Deadwyler, he died, and left Miss Lizzie wid two chillun, and she married Mr. Roan.

"I never seed no slave marriage. Ma went to 'em sometimes, but she never 'lowed us to go, 'cause she said us wuz too little. Marse Billie sont atter his own preacher, and de couple would come up to de Big 'Ouse and stand in de parlor door to be married 'fore Marster and Mist'ess. Den de colored folkses would go back down to da cabins and have a weddin' supper and frolic and dance. Dat's what ma told me 'bout 'em.

"Us used to play lots, but us never did have no special name for our playin'. 'Swingin' the Corner,' wuz when us all jined hands in a low row, and de leader would begin to run 'round in circles, and at de other end of de line dey would soon be runnin' so fast dey wuz most flyin'.

"Us all de time heared folkses talkin' 'bout voodoo, but my grandma wuz powerful 'ligious, and her and ma told us chillun voodoo wuz a no 'count doin' of de devil, and Christians wuz never to pay it no 'tention. Us wuz to be happy in de Lord, and let voodoo and de devil alone. None of us liked to hear scritch owls holler, 'cause everybody thought it meant somebody in dat house wuz goin' to die if a scritch owl lit on your chimney and hollered, so us would stir up de fire to make the smoke drive him away. I always runned out and tried to see 'em, but old as I is, nigh 86, I ain't never seed no scritch owl.

"Yes, Ma'am, I sho' does b'lieve in ha'nts, 'cause I done heared one and I seed it too, leasewise I seed its light. It wuz 'bout 30 years ago, and us had just moved in a house whar a white fambly had moved out. The ma had died a few days atter a little baby wuz born, and de baby had died too. One night I heared a strange sound like somebody movin' 'round in de house, and pretty soon a dim light comes a-movin' into my room real slow and atter goin' 'round de room it went out of sight in de closet.

"Next day I went to see de white folkses what had lived dar 'fore us moved in, and de husband tole me not to worry, dat it wuz his wife's ha'nt. He said she wuz huntin' for some money she had hid in de house, 'cause she wanted her chillun what wuz still livin' to have it. I went back home and 'most tore dat house down lookin' for dat money. Long as us lived dar I would see dat light now and den at night, and I always hoped it would lead me to de money but it never did.

"When folkses got sick, Marse Billie had 'em looked atter. Mist'ess would come every day to see 'bout 'em, and if she thought dey wuz bad off, she sont atter Dr. Davenport. Dr. Davenport come dar so much 'til he courted and married Marse Billie's daughter, Miss Martha Glenn. I wuz named for Miss Martha. Dey sho' did take special good keer of de mammies and de babies. Dey had a separate house for 'em, and a granny 'oman who didn't have nothin' else to do but look atter colored babies and mammies. De granny 'oman took de place of a doctor when de babies wuz born, but if she found a mammy in a bad fix she would ax Mist'ess to send for Dr. Davenport.

"Us didn't have no separate church for colored folkses. De white folkses had a big Baptist church dey called Mill Stone Church down at Goosepond, a good ways down de road from Marse Billie's plantation. It sho' wuz a pretty sight to see, dat church, all painted white and set in a big oak grove. Colored folkses had dey place in de gallery. Dey won't 'lowed to jine de church on Sunday, but dey had reg'lar Sadday afternoons for de slaves to come and 'fess dey faith, and jine de church. Us didn't know dey wuz no other church but de Baptist. All de baptizin' wuz done on Sunday by de white preacher. First he would baptize de white folkses in de pool back of de church and den he would baptize de slaves in de same pool.

"My grandma wuz a powerful Christian 'oman, and she did love to sing and shout. Dat's how come Marse Billie had her locked up in de loom room when de Yankee mens come to our plantation. Grandma would git to shoutin' so loud she would make so much fuss nobody in de church could hear de preacher and she would wander off from de gallery and go downstairs and try to go down de white folkses aisles to git to de altar whar de preacher wuz, and dey wuz always lockin' her up for 'sturbin' worship, but dey never could break her from dat shoutin' and wanderin' 'round de meetin' house, atter she got old.

"Dem Yankee sojers rode up in de Big 'Ouse yard and 'gun to ax me questions 'bout whar Marse Billy wuz, and whar everything on de place wuz kept, but I wuz too skeered to say nuthin'. Everything wuz quiet and still as could be, 'cept for Grandma a-singin' and a-shoutin' up in de loom house all by herself. One of dem Yankees tried the door and he axed me how come it wuz locked. I told him it wuz 'cause grandma had 'sturbed de Baptist meetin' wid her shoutin'. Dem mens grabbed de axe from de woodpile and busted de door down. Dey went in and got grandma. Dey axed her 'bout how come she wuz locked up, and she told 'em de same thing I had told 'em. Dey axed her if she wuz hongry, and she said she wuz. Den dey took dat axe and busted down de smokehouse door and told her she wuz free now and to help herself to anything she wanted, 'cause everything on de plantation wuz to b'long to de slaves dat had worked dar. Dey took grandma to de kitchen and told ma to give her some of de white folkses dinner. Ma said 'But de white folkses ain't et yet.' 'Go right on,' de Yankees said, 'and give it to her, de best in de pot, and if dey's anything left when she gets through, maybe us will let de white folkses have some of it.'

"Dem brash mens strutted on through de kitchen into de house and dey didn't see nobody else down stairs. Upstairs dey didn't even have de manners to knock at Mist'ess' door. Dey just walked right on in whar my sister, Lucy, wuz combin' Mist'ess' long pretty hair. They told Lucy she wuz free now and not to do no more work for Mist'ess. Den all of 'em grabbed dey big old rough hands into Mist'ess' hair, and dey made her walk down stairs and out in de yard, and all de time dey wuz a-pullin' and jerkin' at her long hair, tryin' to make her point out to 'em whar Marse Billie had done had his horses and cattle hid out. Us chilluns wuz a-cryin' and takin' on 'cause us loved Mist'ess and us didn't want nobody to bother her. Dey made out like dey wuz goin' to kill her if she didn't tell 'em what dey wanted to know, but atter a while dey let her alone.

"Atter dey had told all de slaves dey could find on de place not to do no more work, and to go help deyselves to anything dey wanted in de smokehouse, and 'bout de Big 'Ouse and plantation, dey rode on off, and us never seed no more of 'em. Atter de Yankees wuz done gone off Grandma 'gun to fuss: 'How, dem sojers wuz tellin' us what ain't so, 'cause ain't nobody got no right to take what belongs to Marster and Mist'ess.' And Ma jined in: 'Sho' it ain't no truf in what dem Yankees wuz a-sayin'', and us went right on living' just like us always done 'til Marse Billie called us together and told us de war wuz over and us wuz free to go whar us wanted to go, and us could charge wages for our work.

"When freedom comed my pa wanted us to move off right away over to Mr. Smithies' place so our family could be together, but us stayed on wid Marse Billie de rest of dat year. Den pa and ma moved to Lexin'ton, whar pa digged walls and ditches and made right good pay. Ma took all four of us chillun and run a good farm. Us got along fine.

"'Fore de War, all work stopped on de plantation for de funeral of a slave. Grandma didn't think chillun ought to see funerals, so de first one I ever seed, wuz when ma died two years atter de War wuz done over. A jackleg colored preacher talked, but he didn't have sense 'nuff to preach a sho' 'nuff sermon.

"Us heared a heap 'bout dem Ku Kluxers, but none of my folks never even seed any of 'em. Dey wuz s'posed to have done lots of beatin' of colored folks, but nobody knowed who dem Ku Kluxers wuz.

"A long time atter de War I got married to Traverse

Colquitt. De weddin' took place at my sister's house, and us sho' did have a big weddin' and a fine dinner afterwards. Den next day my husband carried me to whar he wuz born, and his ma give us another big fine dinner. She had a table longer dan this room, and it wuz just loaded with all sorts of good things. De white folkses dat my husband had used to work for had sent some of de good vittals.

"Most of my life atter de War wuz spent in Lexin'ton. Does you know anythin' 'bout Mr. John Bacon dat used to run de only hotel dar den? Well, I worked for him for many a year. His daughter, Miss Mamie Bacon, lives here in Athens and she is old and feeble like me. She lives 'bout four blocks from here, and whenever I'se able to walk dat far, I goes to see her to talk 'bout old times, and to git her to 'vise me how to git along. I sho'ly does love Miss Mamie.

"My husband died 'bout a year ago. Us had eight boys and two girls, but dey ain't but four of our chillun livin' now. Least, I thinks dey is all four alive. Two of my sons lives somewhar in Alabama, and one son stays in New York. My only livin' daughter lives wid me here, pore thing! Since she seed one of her chillun killed last year, she ain't had no mind a t'all. I'se tryin' to look atter her and de other child. Her husband done been dead a long time. My neighbors helps me, by bringin' me a little to eat, when dey knows I ain't got nothin' in de house to cook. De storekeeper lets me have a little credit, but I owe her so much now dat I'se 'shamed to ax her to let me have anythin' else. De white folkses on Prince Avenue is right good to let me have dey clo'es to wash, and de young gals in the neighborhood helps me to do de washin'. I sho' is hopin' de old age pension will soon git started comin' to me. Some dat I know, has been gittin' dey old age pensions two or three months. I done signed up for mine twict, so maybe it will 'gin to come 'fore I is done plum wore out."

When her visitor was ready to leave, Martha hobbled to the door and bade her an affectionate farewell. "Goodbye, Lady! I prays for you every night. May de good Lord bless you."

## PLANTATION LIFE AS VIEWED BY AN EX-SLAVE

MINNIE DAVIS, Age 78
237 Billups St.
Athens, Ga.

Written By:
Mrs. Sadie B. Hornsby
Athens, Georgia

Edited By:
Mrs. Sarah H. Hall
Athens, Georgia

and
John N. Booth
WPA Residencies 6 & 7

August 29, 1938

# MINNIE DAVIS

The bareness of Minnie Davis' yard was relieved by a single rosebush, and her small house might best be described as a "tumble-down shack." An unsteady wooden box served as a step to the fragment of porch before the front door.

"Good mornin', Mam," was the greeting of a Negro man who hastened to answer the visitor's knock at the door. "Yes Mam, Miss Minnie's at home." He turned, tapped on the door of one of the four rooms adjoining the hall, and called: "Miss Minnie, a white lady wants to see you." Minnie hobbled to the door and invited the visitor to her bedroom, where a suite of handsome walnut furniture reflected the period when marble tops were standard parts of dressers and washstands. A low chair, an old table, and a rusty heater completed the furnishings of the room.

Age and ill health have not dealt kindly with Minnie, and her short-cut, kinky hair is almost white, but her eyes and face retain a remarkably youthful appearance. She is a small thin woman of gingercake color and, despite the sweltering heat, she wore a pink flannel nightgown, faded and dingy, and a pair of high top black shoes, so badly run over that she hobbled along on the sides of them. Minnie is well educated, and she taught school for so long that her speech is remarkably free of dialect.

When the nature of the visit was explained, Minnie said: "A white woman has been here several times before, but I was sick and didn't understand clearly what she wanted me to tell her." She then explained that she did not care to talk for publication at all. She said she was hungry and had nothing at all in the house to eat. Her nephew, Ed, an ex-postman lived with her, she explained, and he would go for food if there was any money. She might feel like talking a little if she had a little something to eat. The interviewer provided the cash and Ed soon returned with a pint of milk and some cinnamon rolls. After her repast, Minnie began to talk, giving the impression that every word was carefully weighed before it was uttered.

"I was born in Greene County near Penfield, Georgia," she said. "Aggie Crawford was my mother and she was married to Jim Young. My only sister was Mariah, and my three brothers were Ned, John, and Jim. Ned was a mulatto. I know who his father was, but of course you won't ask me that. I wouldn't want to expose my own mother or the man who was Ned's father. I was quite a small child during the war period, and I can tell you very little of that time, except the things my mother told me when I grew old enough to remember. My mother belonged to the Crawford family in Greene County, but when I knew anything we were living in Athens and were the slaves of Marster John Crawford.

"As children we played around the yard; those of us who were old enough had odd jobs to do. The unceiled house that my father and mother shared with three other families was weatherboarded and had a chimney made of sticks and dirt. There was a bed in each corner of the room and from one to three children slept in the bed with their parents: the rest of the children slept on the floor. The tall old home-made wooden beds had very much the appearance of beds used now, except that cords were used instead of the metal springs that came into use later. Our osnaburg mattress ticks were filled with straw. I'm quite sure there were no pillows. There was also a two-story house on the lot for slaves." She was asked what she called her father and mother during slavery time, and her reply was: "I have always said father and mother because I liked it better, and the Bible teaches us to say that.

"Grandmother Dilsey and grandfather Levi Crawford lived in Lexington. I saw my grandmother one time, but I don't know what she did at the white folks' house. Grandfather was a carpenter.

"I never got any money in slavery time. If the slaves ever got any, it was when the Yankees came through here. At that time the white people gave their money to the slaves for safekeeping, and after the Yankees went on it was returned to the white owners.

"My mother was the cook and looked after the house. Oh, yes indeed, we had good food to eat. Bread, milk, meat, collard greens, turnips, and potatoes. I would say we had just everything that was grown in the garden and on the plantations to eat at that time. The cooking was done in the kitchen in the yard. The fireplace was as wide as the end of this room, and a long iron bar extended from one end to the other. The great cooking pots were suspended over the coals from this bar by means of pot hooks. Heavy iron skillets with thick lids were much used for baking, and they had ovens of various sizes. I have seen my mother bake beautiful biscuits and cakes in those old skillets, and they were ideal for roasting meats. Mother's batter cakes would just melt in your mouth and she could bake and fry the most delicious fish. There was no certain thing that I liked to eat more than anything else in those days. I was young and had a keen appetite for all good things. Miss Fannie and Miss Susan often made candy and it was so good I could have eaten all they made, had they given it to me. My father hired his time out; he made and sold gingercakes on the railroad.

"In the summertime we wore homespun dresses made with a full skirt gathered onto a tight-fitting waist. In the wintertime the dresses were made of checked woolen material called linsey cloth. For underwear, we wore balmoral petticoats and osnaburg drawers. We went barefooted most of the time. I remember one particular time when the ground was frozen and I went about without any shoes, but it didn't bother me. Barefooted children seldom had bad colds in winter. We wore just anything on Sunday, but we had to look nice and clean.

"Marster John Crawford, son of the distinguished William H. Crawford, was my owner. Indeed, he was good to us. I'll tell you after awhile about the time he wouldn't let the town marshal whip my mother. They told me his wife was a fine woman and that she was as good to her slaves as she could be. She died very young in life and Marse John's sisters, Miss Fannie and Miss Susan, kept house for him after that. Marse John's three children were Miss Fannie, Miss Rosa, and Marse Allie. Miss Rosa married Marse Tom Golden, and Miss Fannie married a Gerdine; I've forgotten his first name.

"Marse John may have had an overseer on one of his plantations, but I don't remember. I do know he didn't have a carriage driver for he didn't have a carriage. I don't believe I can describe the peculiar shape of his fine eight-room house. It was on Dougherty Street, right back of Scudder's School. The Crawfords were considered very uppity people and their slaves were uppish too. Marse John didn't have many slaves and they had to get up and get going early every morning. Marse John was postmaster of Athens and had to be in his office by eight o'clock every morning so he ordered that his breakfast be served regularly at seven-thirty.

"No Mam, our white folks didn't teach their slaves to read and write because it was against the law. However, they did read the Bible to us, and the slaves that were smart enough, were asked to repeat the verses they had learned from hearing Miss Fannie, Miss Sue, and Marse John read. The Crawford children were caught teaching my mother to read and write, but they were made to stop.

Mother was quick to learn and she never gave up. She would steal the newspapers and read up about the war, and she kept the other slaves posted as to how the war was progressing. She knew when the war was over, almost as soon as Marse John did.

"I don't recall any certain reason why the slaves were punished; they needed it, I'm sure of that. Some folks need to be punished now. Miss Sue, as we called her, whipped the slaves for misbehavior. I remember one time there was quite a commotion. The town marshal came to our house to whip my mother. It had been told that she had been writing letters, asking people to buy whiskey from her, but Marse John wouldn't let the marshal touch her. There was a jail, but I don't recall that any of Marse John's slaves were ever put in there. I was told that his slaves were, as a rule, well behaved and that they gave him no trouble.

"Yes Mam, we went to church, that is, those of us who cared to go did. There wasn't any separate church for colored people in Athens, that I can remember. We went to church and Sunday School at the First Presbyterian Church, where the slaves were allowed to sit in the gallery. I recall that Dr. Hoyt used to pray that the Lord would drive the Yankees back. He said that 'Niggers were born to be slaves.' My mother said that all the time he was praying out loud like that, she was praying to herself: 'Oh, Lord, please send the Yankees on and let them set us free.' I wasn't enough of a singer to have a favorite song, and I was too happy playing with the Crawford children to be interested in going to baptizings and funerals.

"I did go to my father's funeral. When he was taken sick Dr. Holt attended his case, and it was not long before he told Marse John that Father would never get well. When he died Mother hollered and screamed something terrible. Miss Sue told her not to cry because, 'the Lord knows best.' 'Yes, Miss Sue,' answered Mother, 'but you have never loved a man to lose.' With that, they both cried. When anyone died in those days, the people sat up all night and didn't go to bed until the funeral was over. Now, no real sympathy is shown.

"I don't believe any of Marse John's slaves ever went to the war. He was good to them and everyone of them loved him. I heard of patterollers chasing slaves and whipping them if they were caught away from home without a pass, and sometimes they locked them up. However, nothing of the kind ever happened to any of Marse John's slaves. He was a highly respected citizen and everyone in Athens knew better than to touch his Negroes.

"After the work for the day was finished at the big house, the slaves went to their quarters to weave cloth and sew, but when ten o'clock came and the bell sounded, everything had to be quiet. Slaves on our place worked Saturday afternoons the same as any other day. On Saturday nights the young folks and a few of the older folks danced. Some of them got passes from Marse John so they could visit around. They popped corn, pulled candy, or just sat around and talked. Those of us who desired went to Sunday School and church on Sundays; others stayed at home and did their washing and ironing, and there was always plenty of that to be done.

"Christmas was a grand time at Marse John's. We had everything good to eat under the sun at that time and, as my mother was the cook, I was sure of getting my share of the good things. Miss Fannie and Miss Sue played Santa Claus to slave children. I was sorry when Mary got too smart and peeped to see what it was all about, for after that they just came to our house and handed us the things that would have come as Santa Claus.

"New Year's Day was no different from other days, except that Marse John gave the grown folks whiskey to drink that day like he did on Christmas morning. They couldn't risk giving slaves much whiskey because it made them mean, and then they would fight the white folks. They had to be mighty careful about things like that in order to keep down uprisings.

"My mother went to cornshuckings, cotton pickings, and quiltings. They must have had wonderful times, to hear her tell it. She said that after the corn was shucked, cotton picked, or quilts quilted, they always gave them plenty of good things to eat and drink and let them aloose to enjoy themselves for the balance of the night. Those things took place at harvest time, and everyone looked forward to having a good time at that season. Mother said that Marse John was particular with his slaves, and wouldn't let them go just anywhere to these things.

"About the only game I can remember playing as a child was a doll game. The Crawford children would use me for the doll, and then when my turn came to play mamma and claim one of them for my doll, Miss Fanny or Miss Sue would appear and then I would have to be a doll for them. I didn't mind, for I dearly loved them all.

"Now about Raw Head and Bloody Bones; I am going to tell you, Miss, my Marster's people were cultured and refined, and they wouldn't allow such things told to their own children or to their slaves' children. They didn't want anything said or done to frighten any little children, and if a nurse or anyone else was caught doing such a thing, that person was punished for it. With the heritage of training like that I could hardly be expected to believe in such things.

"Marse John was grand to sick slaves. He always sent for Dr. Moore, who would make his examination and write out his prescription. When he left his parting word was usually 'Give him a sound thrashing and he will get better.' Of course he didn't mean that; it was his little joke. Dr. Holt, Dr. Crawford Long, and Dr. Jones Long were sometimes called in for consultation on particularly serious cases. We didn't like Dr. Moore and usually begged for one of the other doctors. I don't think my white folks used teas made of herbs, leaves or roots; they may have, but I don't remember it. However, I do know that we wore little sacks of asafetida around our necks to keep off diseases, and the white folks wore it too.

"On the day we learned of the surrender, the Negroes rallied around the liberty flag pole that they set up near where the city hall is now. All day long they cut up and there was a song they sung that day that went something like this:

> 'We rally around the flag pole of liberty,
> The Union forever, Hurrah! Boys Hurrah!'

"Next morning when the Negroes got up the white folks had cut that pole down. We were mortally afraid of the Yankees when they appeared here a short time after the surrender. We were afraid of the Ku Klux Klan riders too. The Negroes did act so bad; there were lots of killings going on for a long time after the war was supposed to be over.

"Mother was glad and sorry too that she was free. Marse John had been so good to all his slaves that none of them really wanted to leave him. We stayed on a while, then mother left and rented a room. She worked hard and bought a house as soon as she could; others did the same. There were very few slaves that had any money at all to begin on.

"Immediately following the surrender northern people opened Knox Institute. One of my teachers was Miss Dora Brooks, a white woman from the North. The principal was a white man, he was Mr. Sortur. After I graduated from Knox Institute, I went to the Atlanta University four years, then came back to Athens and taught school here forty years. I taught whatever grade they assigned me to each year, never any certain grade from year to year. First and last, I've taught from first grade through high school. I would be teaching now if it were not for my bad health. I receive a teacher's pension, but have never applied for an old age pension.

"My husband was Samuel B. Davis, publisher of the Athens Clipper. I published this newspaper myself for a short while after his death, then sold it. We didn't have a big wedding, just a very simple one at my mother's house. I was married in a nice white dress, but it was nothing fancy. Our two children were born dead. Once I had a nice home, beautifully furnished. All I have left of it is this old house and my good bedroom suite. The rest of my possessions have gotten away from me during my continued illness.

"I often think of Abraham Lincoln; he did a good deed for my race. Jeff Davis was a good man and, no doubt, he thought he was doing the right thing. Booker T. Washington was a man of brilliant mind, but he was radically wrong in many of his views pertaining to education of the black race. He lectured here once, but I didn't bother to hear him speak.

"Yes Mam, indeed I had rather be free. Oh! religion is glorious. If God has set you free from the bonds and penalties of sin, I think you ought to live up to your Lord's commands. I dearly love to go to church and hear the preacher tell of God. It gives me strength to live until He is ready for me to go.

"Now, Miss, I hope I have told you what you wanted to know, but I must admit the things that took place way back there are rather vague in my mind. I'm an old woman and my mind is not as clear as it once was. Next week, if I am strong enough to make the trip, I am going to spend the day with Mary Colbert, and go over the old times you and I have discussed. She remembers them better than I do, because she is older."

Whitley
[HW: Unedited
Atlanta]
E. Driskell

EX-SLAVE MOSE DAVIS
[APR 8 1937]

# MOSE DAVIS

In one of Atlanta's many alleys lives Mose Davis, an ex-slave who was born on a very large plantation 12 miles from Perry, Georgia. His master was Colonel Davis, a very rich old man, who owned a large number of slaves in addition to his vast property holdings. Mose Davis says that all the buildings on this plantation were whitewashed, the lime having been secured from a corner of the plantation known as "the lime sink". Colonel Davis had a large family and so he had to have a large house to accommodate these members. The mansion, as it was called, was a great big three-storied affair surrounded by a thick growth of cedar trees.

Mose's parents, Jennie and January Davis, had always been the property of the Davis family, naturally he and his two brothers and two sisters never knew any other master than "The Old Colonel".

Mr. Davis says that the first thing he remembers of his parents is being whipped by his mother who had tied him to the bed to prevent his running away. His first recollection of his father is seeing him take a drink of whiskey from a five gallon jug. When asked if this was'nt against the plantation rules "Uncle Mose" replied: "The Colonel was one of the biggest devils you ever seen—he's the one that started my daddy to drinking. Sometimes he used to come to our house to git a drink hisself".

Mose's Father was the family coachman. "All that he had to do was to drive the master and his family and to take care of the two big grey horses that he drove. Compared to my mother and the other slaves he had an easy time," said Uncle Mose, shaking his head and smiling: "My daddy was so crazy about the white folks and the horses he drove until I believe he thought more of them than he did of me. One day while I was in the stable with him one of the horses tried to kick me and when I started to hit him Daddy cussed me and threatned to beat me."

His mother, brothers, and sisters, were all field hands, but there was never any work required of Mose, who was play-mate and companion to Manning, the youngest of Colonel Davis' five sons. These two spent most of the time fishing and hunting. Manning had a pony and buggy and whenever he went to town he always took Mose along.

Field hands were roused, every morning by the overseer who rang the large bell near the slave quarters. Women [TR: and] young children were permitted to remain at home until 9 o'clock to prepare breakfast. At 9 o'clock these women had to start to the fields where they worked along with the others until sundown. The one break in the day's work was the noon dinner hour. Field hands planted and tended cotton, corn, and the other produce grown on the plantation until harvest time when everybody picked cotton. Slaves usually worked harder during the picking season than at any other time. After harvest, the only remaining work was cleaning out fence corners, splitting rails building fences and numerous other minor tasks. In hot weather, the only work was shelling corn. There was no Sunday work other than caring for the stock.

On this plantation there were quite a few skilled slaves mostly blacksmiths, carpenters, masons, plasterers, and a cobbler. One of Mose's brothers was a carpenter.

All slaves too old for field work remained at home where some took care of the young children, while others worked in the loom houses helping make the cloth and the clothing used on the plantation. Since no work was required at night, this time was utilized by doing personal work such as the washing and the repairing of clothing, etc.

On the Fourth of July or at Christmas Colonel Davis always had a festival for all his slaves. Barbecue was served and there was much singing and dancing. These frolics were made merrier by the presence of guests from other plantations. Music was furnished by some of the slaves who also furnished music at the mansion whenever the Col. or some of the members of his family had a party. There was also a celebration after the crops had been gathered.

Although there was only one distribution of clothing per year nobody suffered from the lack of clothes because this one lot had enough to last a year if properly cared for. The children wore one piece garments, a cross between a dress and a slightly lengthened shirt, made of homespun or crocus material [TR note: "crocus" is a coarse, loosely woven material like burlap]. No shoes were given them until winter and then they got the cast-offs of the grown ups. The men all wore pants made of material known as "ausenberg". The shirts and under wear were made of another cotton material. Dresses for the women were of striped homespun. All shoes were made on the premises of the heaviest leather, clumsely fashioned and Uncle Mose says that slaves like his father who worked in the mansion, were given much better clothing. His father received of "The Colonel" and his grown sons many discarded clothes. One of the greatest thrills of Mose's boyhood was receiving first pair of "ausenberg" pants. As his mother had already taught him to knit (by using four needles at one time) all that he had to do was to go to his hiding place and get the socks that he had made.

None of the clothing worn by the slaves on this particular plantation was bought. Everything was made by the slaves, even to the dye that was used.

Asked if there was sufficient food for all slaves, Uncle Mose said "I never heard any complaints." At the end of each week every family was given some fat meat, black molasses, meal and flour in quantity varying with the size of the family. At certain intervals during the week, they were given vegetables. Here too, as in everything else, Mose's father was more fortunate than the others, since he took all his meals at the mansion where he ate the same food served to the master and his family. The only difference between Week-day and Sunday diet was that biscuits were served on Sundays. The children were given only one biscuit each. In addition to the other bread was considered a delicacy. All food stuff was grown on the plantation.

The slave quarters were located a short distance below the mansion. The cabins one-roomed weatherboard structures were arranged so as to form a semi-circle. There was a wide tree-lined road leading from the master's home to these cabins.

Furnishings of each cabin consisted of one or two benches, a bed, and a few cooking utensils. These were very crude, especially the beds. Some of them had four posts while the ends of others were nailed to the walls. All lumber used in their construction was very heavy and rough. Bed springs were unheard of—wooden slats being used for this purpose. The mattresses were large ausenberg bags stuffed to capacity with hay, straw, or leaves. Uncle Mose told about one of the slaves, named Ike, whose entire family slept on bare pine straw. His children were among the fattest on the plantation and when Colonel Davis tried to make him put this straw in a bag he refused claiming that the pine needles kept his children healthy.

The floors and chimneys on the Davis Plantation were made of wood and brick instead of dirt and mud as was the case on many of the other surrounding plantations. One window (with shutters instead of window panes) served the purpose of ventilation and light. At night pine knots or candles gave light. The little cooking that the slaves did at home was all done at the open fireplace.

Near the living quarters was a house known as the "chillun house." All children too young for field work stayed at this house in the care of the older slave women. There was no hospital building on the premises. The sick had to remain in their individual cabins where they too were cared for by slaves too old for field work.

Only one family lived in a cabin. Mose's mother and father each had a separate cabin. He did not explain the reason for this but said that he was made to live in his father's cabin. Whenever he could, (usually when his father was away with the Colonel for a day or two) he stayed in his mothers cabin. "The only difference between the houses we lived in during slavery and those that some of us live in now who said is that we had more room there than we have now." He says that even the community cook house was larger than some of the living quarters of today. All cabins were white washed the same as the other buildings on the plantation, and the occupants were required to keep the interiors and the surrounding clean at all times. The overseer's cabin was located a short distance away from the slave cabins, so that it would be easier for him to keep check on his charges.

There was little if any sickness but Colonel Davis employed a doctor who visited the plantation each week. On other occasions the overseer administered such remedies as castor oil, turpentine, etc., and the slaves had remedies of their own. For stomach ache they used a tea made of Jimson weeds. Another medicine was heart leaf tea. Manual and religious training were the only types allowed on the plantation. Trades like carpentry, blacksmithing, etc. were learned from the white mechanics sometimes employed by Colonel Davis. All slaves were required to attend church and a special building was known as "Davis' Chapel." A Negro preacher officiated and no white people were present. Uncle Mose doesn't know what was preached as he and Manning always slipped into town on Sundays to see the girls. Uncle Mose says he and Manning were together so much that occasionally they even slept in the same bed,—sometimes in Manning's house and sometimes at his own house.

A pool for baptism was filled with well water. The colored pastor performed all baptisms and marriages.

Book learning was prohibited in any form. Sometimes Mose tried to persuade Manning to teach him to read and write but Manning always refused. Mose's cousin who was taught to read and write forged Colonel Davis' name to a check and drew the money from the bank before the hand writing was discovered. For this act he was given a sound whipping and assigned to hard labor by the master, "And", said Uncle Mose, "he didn't even have the pleasure of spending one penny". When asked if his cousin was arrested and placed in jail he replied that the jails were not for the slaves, as their punishment was usually left to their individual masters. When his cousin was whipped this was an exception to "The Colonel's rule"; he was entirely against any form of whipping. His usual method of punishment was to cut off individual privileges for a limited amount of time (in proportion to the nature of the offense), along with an assignment of extra heavy work.

The fame of the "Paddle-Rollers" was widespread among the slaves, but none of Colonel Davis' servants attempted to run away or leave the plantation often without the required pass (if they did they were never caught).

There was very little talk on the plantation about the actual beginning of the Civil War. Slaves was very guarded in their talk as they feared the master's wrath. Uncle Mose thought little or nothing about the War and had even less to say.

When the Yankee soldiers came to the plantation they drove wagons to the smoke house and took all the meat away. "The funny part about it was that "The Colonel" had taken shelter in this particular house when he saw the Yankees coming," said Uncle Mose. "He didn't have time to hide any of his other belongings." When the soldiers had left, The Colonel looked around and said to Manning and Mose: "Just like I get that, I guess I can get some more."

Uncle Mose says that when freedom was declared, his father came rushing to their cabin waving his arms like a windmill, shouting: "Boy we is free—you can go and git yourself a job 'cause I ain't goin' to hitch up no more horses". Some of the slaves remained on the plantation where they worked for wages until their deaths. His father was one of them and after his death, his mother moved to another plantation to live with another son. Meanwhile Mose started traveling from place to place as soon as he was told that he was free to go as he pleased. He paid one visit to the plantation where he learned of his father's death. He then asked Manning, who was operating the plantation, for the ox that had belonged to his father and when Manning refused to part with this animal, he made a secret visit back, that night, and took the animal away. He has not been back since.

At this time Mr. Davis stretched himself, saying: "Well, I guess that's about as straight as I can get it—Wish that I could tell you some more but I can't." Smiling broadly, he bade the interviewer a pleasant good-bye.

EX-SLAVE INTERVIEW

IKE DERRICOTTE, Age 78
554 Hancock Avenue
Athens, Georgia

Written by:
Miss Grace McCune
Athens

Edited by:
Mrs. Sarah H. Hall
Athens

and
John N. Booth
District Supervisor
Federal Writers' Project
Residencies 6 & 7
Augusta, Georgia

August 19, 1938

*[TR: One page of this interview was repeated in typescript; where there was a discrepancy, the clearer version was used.]*

# IKE DERRICOTTE

Ike Derricotte's brown-painted, frame bungalow, well back from the street, faces a wide grassy yard where tall pecan trees provide summer shade and winter nuts.

A mulatto woman answered the knock at the front door. Her long, straight, white hair was neatly arranged in a low-pinned coil at the back of her head. Her print frock and white shoes were immaculate. "Yes Mam, Ike is at home," was the answer to the inquiry for her husband. "Jus' have a seat on de porch here 'cause it's so much cooler dan inside de house, and I'll call Ike. He's jus' piddlin' 'round de back yard dis mornin'."

Almost at once a tall, well-built man of gingercake color appeared. He wore an old black cap, blue work shirt, blue wool trousers, and black shoes. "Howdy-do, Miss! Did you want to see me?" was his greeting. His eyes sparkled when he learned that we wished to record the story of his life. "Yes Mam, I'll be glad to tell you what I kin," he promised, "and Miss, I'll jus' bet I kin tell you somepin dat very few folks kin say 'bout dem old days. I was born right here on dis same street, and I'm still livin' on it, but dis house and lot ain't my birthplace. When I was born, dis section was mostly in woods. Jus' look at it now; houses has been built up and down both sides of what was den jus' de big road. Times has changed in lots of ways since dem days.

"My mother's name was Myra, and she was a laundry 'oman owned by Mr. Stevens Thomas. Mr. Thomas was one of de biggest merchants in Athens dem days. He owned de square between Thomas Street and Wall Street, and it s'tended back to Clayton Street.

"William Derricotte was my father, and he belonged to Col. Robert Thomas. My father spent most of his time beautifyin' de yards 'round de big house, and in dese days and times he would be called a landscape gardener. Dey jus' called 'em yard boys den. Atter Pa and Ma was married, Marster Stevens sold Ma to Marster Robert, so dat dey could be together. Mr. Robert Thomas' place was right up dis same old street, whar de Y.W.C.A. is now, and right dar is whar I was born. Dat was in 1860, a long time ago; and lots of things has happened since den. Lots of people has moved away and lots more has died out, 'til dere ain't many of de folks left here dat lived in Athens den. De Thomases, Dorseys, and Phinizys was some of de oldest families here.

"I was too little to know much about de war but, little as I was, dere's one thing dat's still as fresh in my memory now as den, and dat's how people watched and waited to hear dat old Georgia train come in. Not many folks was able to take de papers den, and de news in 'em was from one to two weeks old when dey got here. All de men dat was able to fight was off at de front and de folks at home was anxious for news. De way dat old train brought 'em de news was lak dis: if de southern troops was in de front, den dat old whistle jus' blowed continuously, but if it was bad news, den it was jus' one short, sharp blast. In dat way, from de time it got in hearin', evvybody could tell by de whistle if de news was good or bad and, believe me, evvybody sho' did listen to dat train.

"Times was hard durin' de war but from what I've heared de folks dat was old folks den say, dey warn't near as bad here as in lots of other places. Yes Mam! Sho' I kin 'member dem Yankees comin' here, but dat was atter de war was done over. Dey camped right here on Hancock Avenue. Whar dey camped was mostly woods den, and deir camp reached nearly all de way to whar Milledge Avenue is now. Us chillun was scared to death of dem soldiers and stayed out of deir way all us could. My Marster, Mr. Stevens Thomas, hid all of his family's silver and other valuables dat could be put out of sight, for dem Yankees jus' went 'round takin' whatever dey wanted. Dey stole all kinds of food out of de homes, went into de smokehouses and got hams, and cotched up de chickens. Dey jus' reached out and tuk what dey wanted and laughed about it lak dey hadn't been stealin'.

"Dem Yankees brought de smallpox here wid 'em and give it to all de Athens folks, and dat was somepin awful. Folks jus' died out wid it so bad. Dey built a hospital what dey called de 'pest house' out whar de stockade is now. It was rough and small but I reckon it helped some. It warn't near large enough for all de folks dat was sick wid smallpox at one time, and so dey finally got to whar dey used it jus' for de colored folks, 'cause it seemed dat smallpox went harder wid dem dan wid de white folks.

"When de war ended us didn't leave Mr. Stevens Thomas. Ma kept on cookin' and wukin' 'round de house, and Pa wuked lots for other folks, larned to do brickwork, build walls, and things lak dat. Atter he got to be a brickmason he allus had plenty to do.

"Marbles was de favorite game of de chillun dem days but us never got to play much lak chillun does dese days, 'cause times was so hard right atter de war dat as soon as chillun got big enough dey had to go to wuk. Some of our very best times was at de old swimmin' hole. Us dammed up dat little crick right back of whar de Seaboard Depot is now and it made a fine pool to swim in. It was cool for it was shady off down dar in de woods, and us spent many a hour dar on days as hot as dis one is. When dey missed us at home, dat was de fust place dey thought of when dey come to hunt us. I had some mighty good times in dat crick and I couldn't begin to count de duckin's I got dar and de whuppin's my Ma and Pa give me for stayin' so long.

"De biggest time in all de year was de Commencement Day; evvybody got busy and fixed up for dat. My Marster allus had lots of company at commencement times, and us had de most good things to eat. Out in town dey was 'pared for it too. Tables was all along de sidewalks whar you could buy any kind of 'freshments you wanted. Course dere warn't as many kinds of 'freshments den as dey has now, but dere was allus plenty of de strong sort. One time durin' commencement week, Ma give me a whole quarter to spend. I was de happiest and de richest boy in dis town; jus' had more money to spend dan anybody, and I walked de streets from one table to another tryin' to see whar I was gwine to spend all dat money." Here, Ike laughed heartily. "Miss," he said, "you jus' never could guess what I spent all dat money for. I bought a whole quarter's worth of ginger-cakes and lit out for de swimmin' hole. Us chillun had a fine time down at de swimmin' hole dat day. De Cobbs and Lumpkins owned all dat land in dar 'round our swimmin' hole den. Dey owned from de Catholic Church straight through to College Avenue.

"I mighty well 'member de fust wuk I ever done. I was still jus' a little fellow when Miss Belle Brumby told Ma she wanted me for a butler boy and dat she would pay me $2.50 a month. I jus' jumped up and down and begged her to let me wuk for Miss Belle. Why, I jus' knowed I would git rich right away, 'cause $2.50 was a mighty lot of money." Ike laughed as he said: "How many boys would wuk for dat pay for a week now, let alone a whole month? Ma did let me wuk for Miss Belle and I was happy, but I know my Mist'ess had a time wid me 'cause, when I got on dat white coat dey let me wear to wait on de table, I knowed more dan evvybody else put together and dere couldn't nobody tell me how to keep de flies off de table.

Miss Belle is one fine 'oman, dey jua' don't come no finer and no better.

"When I was fourteen my Pa hired me out to be a shoemaker. De shop whar I was 'prenticed was down on Broad Street, jus' about whar de Bernstein Furniture Store is now. Dat old buildin' was tore down long years ago and evvything 'long dar is changed now. De Athens Hardware Store is de only Broad Street business of dem days dat has stood in de same place and endured through all dese years.

"When I went to wuk for Mr. Joe Barry in his shoe shop on Jackson Street, right in back of whar Mr. Lee Morris' store is now, I felt lak I had got to be a real sho' 'nough important shoemaker. I wuked for him 'bout 12 or 14 years. He was a good man to wuk for and he was de only shoemaker I ever knowed to git rich at his trade; he really did make money in dat shop. I've been a shoemaker ever since 1874, but I never have been able to git far ahead. In spite of all our trouble for 85 years atter de war, it seems to me dat times was much better den dan dey is now. Course, folks didn't make as much den as dey does now. Carpenters, bricklayers, shoemakers, in fact 'most any kind of laborers who got from $1.00 to $1.50 a day thought dey had fine wages den. Boys was paid from $2.50 to $5.00 a month. Cooks got $5.00 to $6.00 a month, and of course, dey got deir meals whar dey wuked. Sometimes odds and ends of old clothes was give to 'em, and dey got along very well, even if most of 'em did have families and big families at dat. Folks could live on less den 'cause things was cheaper. You could git meal for 50¢ a bushel; side meat was 5¢ to 6¢ a pound; and you could git a 25-pound sack of flour for 50¢. Wood was 50¢ a load. House rent was so cheap dat you didn't have to pay over $3.00 a month for a 2 or 3 room house, and lots of times you got it cheaper. Most evvybody wore clothes made out of homespun cloth and jeans, and dey didn't know nothin' 'bout ready-made, store-bought clothes. Dem clothes what dey made at home didn't cost very much. Livin' was cheap, but folks lived mighty well in dem days.

"Us has been married more dan 50 years and dey has all been happy years. Us has had our troubles and hard luck, but dey come to evvybody. De Lord has been mighty good to us, 'specially in lettin' us be together so long. It was what you might call a case of love at fust sight wid us. I was visitin' down at Camak, Georgia at Christmastime. She lived at Sparta, and was spendin' Christmas at Camak too, but I didn't see her 'til I was 'bout to leave for Athens. I jus' thought I never could go 'way atter I fust seed her, but I did, and I didn't git to see her again for 12 long months. Us writ to one another all dat year and got married at Christmastime, one year from de time us fust met.

"Us has still got dat old pen I used when I writ and axed her to marry me; I'd lak to show it to you. 'Scuse me please whilst I goes in de house to git it." Soon Ike returned. "Ain't it a sight?" he proudly exclaimed as he displayed the relic. "I made it up myself in December 1886 and it got her consent to marry me, so I'se kept it ever since. My wife and me wouldn't part wid it for nothin'." The wooden pen staff is very smooth as though from long usage except at the tip end, where it appears to have been gnawed. It looks very much as though Ike may have chewed on it as he wrote that all important letter. The iron pen point, much too large to fit the standard grooves of the ordinary pen staff, was placed on the staff and tightly wrapped. After 52 years of service the pen point and its staff are still in good condition. Ike has the Prince Albert coat that he wore on his wedding day and he insists that it looks and fits as well now as it did on the occasion of his marriage. "I'm keepin' de coat and pen for our chillun," he declared.

Before resuming the conversation, Ike went back in the house to put the treasured pen away. In a few moments he returned. "God has been good to us," he said, "for He let us have all nine of our chillun 'til dey was grown up. Us wuked mighty hard to raise 'em and give all of 'em a good education. Dat was somepin us couldn't have when us was growin' up and I'm thankful to be able to say dat us was able to send 'em all to college. Four of our chillun has gone on ahead to de next world, and de five dat's left is scattered from place to place; none of 'em is wid us now, but dey don't forgit us. Dey writes to us and visits us often and us goes to see dem. One son is goin' mighty well as a lawyer in Washin'ton, D.C., and our baby lives in New York City. It's been 'bout 3 years now since my daughter Juliette died atter a automobile wreck near Dalton, Georgia. Did you know 'bout Juliette? She give her life to wuk for de Y.W.C.A., and she went all over de world tryin' to make things better for de young women of our race. Somebody writ a memorial book 'bout her. I wish dere was a copy of dat book here for you to see, but it was borrowed from us and it ain't been returned.

"Did you know I had jus' come back from Washin'ton, whar I visited dat lawyer son of mine? He sends for me nearly evvy summer and I enjoy visitin' dar, but

I wouldn't lak to live up dar 'cause dem folks ain't lak our own southern people. I must say dey is mighty nice and good to me when I goes dar though. Once when I was dar somebody told me dat if I wanted to have a good time I mustn't let nobody know I was a Georgian 'cause dey said dat de northerners don't lak our State. De rest of de time I was dar on dat visit I tuk partic'lar pleasure in tellin' evvybody how proud I was of my State and my home.

"Dat reminds me of Miss Sally Hodgson. She was in de North, and one evenin' she was tryin' to tell de folks up dar dat de southern people warn't as bad as some of de Yankees had said dey was, and dat de white folks down South didn't mistreat de colored folks. Miss Sally said dat de very next mornin' de papers up dar was full of news 'bout de lynchin' of 8 Negroes in one night at Watkinsville. If you had knowed Miss Sally, you would know how funny dat was," Ike laughed. "She said atter dat dere warn't no way she could convince dem folks up dar dat Georgia was a good place to live in.

"Us had some good friends in de North and sometimes dey comes down here to see us. One of my wife's friends, a 'oman wid a lot of education has jus' gone back to Philadelphia atter a visit here in our home. Us travels a good deal and us has found dat de world ain't so large but dat us is allus runnin' up against somebody dat us knows wherever us goes.

"Sometimes when you is in a strange place it's mighty handy to find somebody you have knowed a long time ago. I 'member one time when I was visitin' in Washin'ton and wanted to git a glimpse of de President. I didn't say nothin' to nobody 'bout what was on my mind, but atter my son went to his wuk in de mornin' I slipped off to de capitol widout tellin' nobody whar I was gwine. I found a waitin' room outside de President's office and I made up my mind I would set dar 'til de President had to go out for dinner or to go home for supper. I never thought about he might have a side door he could come and go from widout usin' de door to de waitin' room. Atter I had set dar in dat waitin' room de best part of two days watchin' for de President, somebody said: 'Howdy, Uncle Ike! What is you doin' here in de President's waitin' room?' I looked up and dar stood Albon Holsey. He had growed up in Athens. He was de boy dey 'signed to wait on President Taft when he was at Miss Maggie Welch's home for a day and night in January 'fore he was inaugurated. I bet Albon is still got dat $5.00 Mr. Taft give him de mornin' he left Athens, but he don't need to spend it now 'cause folks say he got rich off of his chain of stores for colored folks, and anyhow he's got a fine job dese days. Well, I s'plained to Albon dat I was jus' waitin' to git a peep at de President whenever he happened to pass through dat room. Albon he smiled sort of wise-like. He tuk out one of his cyards and writ sompin on it, and axed a lady to take it right in to de President. She warn't gone 2 minutes 'fore she come back and said: 'De President will see Mr. Holsey and his friend now.' I was wuss skeered dan I has ever been at any other time in my life. Us walked in and I was 'fraid de President could hear my knees knockin' together, and my heart was beatin' so fast and loud it seemed to me lak it was 'bout to bust. De President spoke to us and when he found out dat I was from Athens, he axed me lots of questions. He said dat he was interested in Athens. Soon Albon said us must be goin' and when us got out of dar I was right weak, but I was might proud and happy to think de President had tuk time to talk pleasant lak wid a pore old Negro shoemaker.

"Another time in Washin'ton a friend of my son's tuk me to a club one night whar some of de richest of our race is members. Dat night I met a man who had went to school wid de Mr. Teddy Roosevelt dat was President atter Mr. McKinley; den I met another Negro dat had been a classmate of President Hoover and one dat went to school wid President Franklin D. Roosevelt. It's right strange how dey all heads for Washin'ton, D.C. to stay.

"Athens has allus been a real quiet town, and dere never was no real serious trouble here 'tween de races, not even when Matt Davis and Pink Morton was Postmasters here. People was allus predictin' trouble 'bout dat, but de folks here was too level-headed for dat. Dey knowed dey could straighten out deir own troubles widout havin' to fly off de handle in a race riot, and so dey 'tended to deir own business' and de races got along all right through it all.

"Atter all, Athens is a good place to live in. Here us has de best neighbors in de world; dey's allus ready to look atter one another in times of sickness and trouble. Wid de kind of good, Christian folks dat lives here, Athens is bound to go ahead."

United States. Work Projects Administration

## PLANTATION LIFE

BENNY DILLARD, Age 80
Cor. Broad and Derby Streets
Athens, Ga.

Written by:
Grace McCune [HW: (white)]
Athens

Edited by: Sarah H. Hall
Athens

and
John N. Booth
District Supervisor
Federal Writers' Project
Residencies 6 & 7
Augusta, Ga.

# BENNY DILLARD

Benny's rocky little yard is gay with flowers and a flourishing rose vine shades the small porch at the front of his ramshackle two-room cabin. The old Negro was busily engaged at washing his clothes. He is of medium size, darker than gingerbread in color, and his clothing on this day consisted of a faded blue shirt, pants adorned with many patches, and brogans. A frayed sun hat covered the gray hair that is "gittin' mighty thin on de top of my haid."

Benny was singing as he worked and his quavering old voice kept tune and rhythm to a remarkable degree as he carefully and distinctly pronounced:

> "Jesus will fix it for you,
> Just let Him have His way
> He knows just how to do,
> Jesus will fix it for you."

Almost in the same breath he began another song:

> "All my sisters gone,
> Mammy and Daddy too
> Whar would I be if it warn't
> For my Lord and Marster."

About this time he looked up and saw his visitor. Off came the old sun hat as he said: "'Scuse me, Missy, I didn't know nobody was listenin' to dem old songs. I loves to sing 'em when I gits lonesome and blue. But won't you come up on my porch and have a cheer in de shade? Dere's a good breeze on dat little porch." Having placed a chair for the visitor and made himself comfortable on a crude bench, Benny began his story:

"Missy, de good Lord gives and he takes away, and us old darkies is a-passin' out of dis world. Dat was why I was a-singin'. One of my bestest friends done passed on to Glory dis very mornin'. I knows I'se goin' to miss old Randal Clayton 'cause both of us warn't no good but for to set and talk 'bout old times." Tears rolled down his face as he told of his friend, and the visitor, fearful that he was too much overcome by grief to be able to give a good story, suggested that another engagement be made to record his reminiscences, but he objected. "Lawsy, Missy!" he protested. "Please don't go now, for dem old times is on my mind today and I would so love to talk 'bout 'em now, if you don't mind. If I talks too much, jus' tell me, 'cause I'se mighty apt to do dat when onct I gits started.

"My Mammy and Daddy, dey warn't from dis part of de country. My Mammy said dat not long atter she got to America from a trip on de water dat took nigh 6 months to make, dey brung her from Virginny and sold her down here in Georgy when she was jus' 'bout 16 years old. De onliest name she had when she got to Georgy was Nancy. I don't know whar my Daddy come from. Him and Mammy was both sold to Marse Isaac Dillard and he tuk 'em to live on his place in Elbert County, close to de place dey calls Goose Pond. Dey lived at home on dat big old plantation. By dat, I means dat Marse Isaac growed evvything needed to feed and clothe his folks 'cept de little sugar, coffee, and salt dey used. I don't 'member so much 'bout times 'fore de big war 'cause I warn't but 6 years old when us was made free. Tellin' de slaves dey was free didn't make much diff'unce on our place, for most of 'em stayed right on dar and wukked wid Old Marster jus' lak dey allus done. Dat plantation was jus' lak a little town, it was so big and it had evvything us wanted and needed.

"Slaves lived in log cabins what had red mud daubed in de cracks 'twixt de logs. De roofs was made out of boards what had so many cracks 'twixt 'em, atter a few rains made 'em swink (shrink), dat us could lay in bed and see de stars through dem big holes. Even if us did have leaky houses, folkses didn't git sick half as much as dey does now. Our homemade beds was made out of rough planks nailed to high poles; leastways de poles was high for de headpieces, and a little lower for de footpieces. For most of dem beds, planks was nailed to de wall for one long side and dere was two laigs to make it stand straight on de other long side. Dey never seed no metal springs dem days but jus' wove cords back and forth, up and down and across, to lay de mattress on. I never seed no sto'-bought bed 'til atter I was married. Bedticks was made out of homespun cloth stuffed wid wheatstraw, and sometimes dey slept on rye or oatstraw. Pillows was stuffed wid hay what had a little cotton mixed in it sometimes. Atter a long day of wuk in de fields, nobody bothered 'bout what was inside dem pillows. Dey slept mighty good lak dey was. Dey fixed planks to slide across de inside of de holes dey cut out for windows. De doors swung on pegs what tuk de place of de iron hinges dey uses dese days. Dem old stack chimblies was made out of sticks and red mud.

"De fireplaces was a heap bigger dan dey has now, for all de cookin' was done in open fireplaces den. 'Taters and cornpone was roasted in de ashes and most of de other victuals was biled in de big old pots what swung on cranes over de coals. Dey had long-handled fryin' pans and heavy iron skillets wid big, thick, tight-fittin' lids, and ovens of all sizes to bake in. All of dem things was used right dar in de fireplace. Dere never was no better tastin' somepin t'eat dan dat cooked in dem old cookthings in open fireplaces.

"Chillun never had no wuk to do. Dey jus' et and frolicked around gittin' into evvything dey could find. Dey never got no lickin's 'less dey was mighty bad, 'cause our Marster said he warn't gwine to 'low no beatin' on his Niggers 'cept what he done his own self, and dat was pow'ful little. In hot weather chillun played on de crick and de best game of all was to play lak it was big meetin' time. White chillun loved to play dar too wid de little slave chillun. Us would have make-believe preachin' and baptizin' and de way us would sing was a sight. One of dem songs us chillun loved de best went lak dis:

> 'Why does you thirst
> By de livin' stream?
> And den pine away
> And den go to die.
>
> 'Why does you search
> For all dese earthly things?
> When you all can
> Drink at de livin' spring,
> And den can live.'

"When us started playin' lak us was baptizin' 'em, us th'owed all us could ketch right in de crick, clothes and all, and ducked 'em. Whilst us was doin' dat, us was singin':

> 'Git on board, git on board
> For de land of many mansions,
> Same old train dat carried
> My Mammy to de Promised Land.'

"One day our Marster hid in de trees and watched us 'cause Mist'ess had done been fussin' down 'bout chillun all comin' in soaked to de hide. He waited 'til he seed all de preachin' and baptizin', den he hollered for us to stop and he tuk de ones what was doin' all de baptizin' and made 'em pray and sing, den he ducked 'em good in de water and made us all go up to de house to show Mist'ess how come so many of dem pore chillun had done been gittin' wet so much. Us got a tannin' den dat Marster 'lowed would help us to git sho' 'nough 'ligion.

"De wooden bowls what slave chillun et out of was made out of sweetgum trees. Us et wid mussel shells 'stid of spoons. Dem mussel shells was all right. Us could use 'em to git up plenty of bread and milk, or cornpone soaked wid peas and pot likker. Dey never let chillun have no meat 'til dey was big enough to wuk in de fields. Us had biscuit once a week, dat was Sunday breakfast, and dem biscuits was cakebread to us. De fust bought meat us chillun ever seed was a slab of side-meat Daddy got from de sto' atter us had done left de plantation, and us was skeered to eat it 'cause it warn't lak what us had been used to.

"Chillun jus' wore one piece of clothes in summertime and dey all went bar'foots. De gals' summer gyarment was a plain, sleeveless apron dress, and de boys wore skimpy little shirts and nothin' else. Dey mixed cow-hair wid de cotton when dey wove de cloth to make our winter clothes out of, and I'm a-tellin' you Missy, dat cow-hair cloth sho' could scratch, but it was good and warm and Marster seed to it dat us had all de clothes us needed. De 'omans made all de cloth used on de place; dey cyarded, spun, and den wove it. Mammy was de weaver; dat was all she done, jus' wove cloth. Dey dyed it wid red mud and ink balls, and sich lak.

"Marster never lakked to git up real early hisself in slavery time, so he had one man what got de Niggers up out of bed so early dat dey had done et breakfast and was in de field when daylight come. Atter de war was over and evvybody was free, all de Niggers used to jus' piddle and play 'round evvy mornin' whilst dey was waitin' for Marster to come. Dem and de mules would be jus' a-standin' still and when de word was passed dat Marster had done got up all of 'em would start off wid a rush, jus' a-hollerin': 'Whoa, dar! Gee haw!' jus' lak dey had done been wukkin' hard all mornin'. One day Marster cotch 'em at it, and he didn't say a word 'til time come to pay off, and he tuk out for all de time dey had lost.

"Sometimes slaves run away and hid out in caves. Dey would pile up rocks and sticks and pine limbs to hide de caves, and sometimes dey would stay hid out for weeks, and de other Niggers would slip 'em somepin t'eat at night. Dere warn't many what run off on our place, 'cause our Marster was so good to all of 'em dat dere warn't nothin' to run from.

"Marster made all his wuk tools at home. Plowsheers was made out of wood trimmed to de right shape and fastened to a iron point. When dey was plowin' in de young cotton, dey nailed a board on one side of de plow to rake de dirt back up 'round de cotton plants.

"Marster's gin was turned by a mule. Dat big old gin wheel had wooden cogs what made de gin wuk when de old mule went 'round and 'round hitched to dat wheel. Dat old cotton press was a sight. Fust dey cut down a big old tree and trimmed off de limbs and made grooves in it for planks to fit in. It was stood up wid a big weight on top of it, over de cotton what was to be pressed. It was wukked by a wheel what was turned by a mule, jus' lak de one what turned de gin. A old mule pulled de pole what turned de syrup mill too. Missy, dem old mules done deir part 'long side de Niggers dem days, and Marster seed dat his mules had good keer too. When dem mules had done turned de mill 'til de juice was squez out of de sugarcane stalks, dey strained dat juice and biled it down 'til it was jus' de finest tastin' syrup you ever did see. Marster's mill whar he ground his wheat and corn was down on de crick, so de water could turn de big old wheel.

"Dem old cornshuckin's was sho' 'nough big times, 'cause us raised so much corn dat it tuk several days to shuck it all. Us had to have two generals. Dey chose sides and den dey got up on top of de biggest piles of corn and kept de slaves a-singin' fast so dey would wuk fast. De fust crowd what finished got de prize. Dere ain't much I can 'member of words to dem old cornshuckin' songs. One general would start off singin': 'Shuck up dis corn, shuck up dis corn, 'cause us is gwine home,' and de other general would be a-shoutin': 'Make dem shucks fly, make dem shucks fly, us is gwine to go home.' Over and over dey kept on singin' dem lines. Come nighttime Marster would have big bonfires built up and set out torches for 'em to see how to wuk, and evvy time he passed 'round dat jug of corn likker shucks would fly some faster. When all de corn was done shucked and de big supper had been et, dere was wrastlin' matches and dancin' and all sorts of frolickin'.

"'Til dey could git a colored preacher, slaves had to go to church wid deir white folks. Missy, I 'members yit, de fust preacher I ever heared. He was a white man, Preacher Gibson dey called him, and his sermons made you mind what you was 'bout 'cause he preached straight from de Bible. Dat day when I fust heared him his text was: 'If you gits lost in sin, den you is lost from God's word, and will have to be borned again.' Dat's de trufe, Missy, it sho' is. Young folks dese days is headed plumb straight for 'struction, 'cause dey won't listen to de Gospel. If dey don't change from de way dey is goin' now de old debbil is gwine to ketch 'em sho. All of us had better mind what us is 'bout, for 'ligion most times now is by our own minds and thoughts, and somebody else is apt to follow de 'ligion he sees in us. De Bible says to teach young folks de way dey should go, and dey won't depart from deir raisin'. You sho' can't raise 'em right by jus' teachin' 'em dese days; it evermore do take plenty of layin' on of dat rod. I would jus' lak to see how dese young folks would lak it if dey had to ride for miles and miles in a oxcart, or else walk it, to git to 'tend church. Dere wouldn't be many of de ones I knows 'round here would git dar. Us used to have four steers hitched to our old cart, and it was slow-goin', but us got dar.

"Atter us got our own churches us still had to have white preachers for a long time and den us was 'lowed to have colored preachers. When somebody wanted to jine our church us 'zamined 'em, and if us didn't think dey was done ready to be tuk in de church, dey was told to wait and pray 'til dey had done seed de light. Anybody can jine up wid de church now, Missy, and it ain't right de way dey lets 'em come in widout 'zaminin' 'em. De good Lord sho' don't lak dat way of handlin' His church business. One of dem cand-i-dates was a mean Nigger and our preacher and deacons wouldn't let him in our church. Den he went over to another church and told 'em dat he had talked wid de Lord 'bout how us wouldn't let him jine up wid us, and he 'lowed dat de Lord said to him: 'Dat's all right. I done been tryin' to jine up in dat church for 15 years myself, and can't git in, so you go on and jine another church.' Dat other church let dat bad Nigger in and it warn't long 'fore dey had to turn him out, 'cause he warn't fittin' to be in no church.

"Our preacher used to give us parables. One of 'em

was lak dis: 'I'se seed good cotton growin' in de grass.' He 'splained it dat dere was some good in de wust sinners. Another of his parables was: 'If you can't keep up wid de man at de foot, how is you gwine to keep up wid de higher-up folks?' Dat meant if you can't sarve God here below, how is you gwine to git along wid him if you gits to Heben? Our preacher told us to sarve both our marsters. De fust Marster was God, he said, and de other one was our white marster.

"I ain't never been inside no courtroom and don't never 'spect to be dar, 'cause, missy, I don't mind nobody's business but my own, and dat's all I can do.

"No Mam, I don't never git much sick. I had a bad old haid cold last winter, but I stopped dat wid coal oil and by breathin' in smoke from scorched leather. Light'ood splinter tea is helpful when I has a chist cold. Salts ain't de best thing for old folks to be doctored wid. I takes common cookin' soda sweetened wid a little sugar. Dem is old-time doses from way back in de old days, and I still use 'em all.

"Durin' of de war time, soda and salt was both hard to git. Dey biled down de dirt from under old smokehouses to git salt, and soda was made out of burnt corncobs. You would be s'prised to see what good cookin' could be done wid dat old corncob soda.

"Us wukked for Mr. Green Hubbard de fust year us left de old plantation, but he wouldn't pay us so us left him and rented some land to farm. Den I went to wuk for Mr. Stephens and stayed wid him 25 years. He was one of de owners of de Georgy Railroad and I used to drive for him when he went to 'Gusty (Augusta) to dem board meetin's. He had one of dem old-time gins what run by mule power, and us sho' did gin a heap of cotton. Lots of times he had us to haul it all de way to 'Gusty on dem wagons. Mr. Stephens' place was at Crawford, Georgy.

"Me and my gal runned away to git married. If you please, Mam, come inside and look at her pitcher. Ain't she a fine lookin' gal? Well, she was jus' as good as she looks. I keeps her pitcher hangin' right over my bed so as I can look at her all de time." The small room was tidy and clean. In one corner a narrow, single bed, neatly made, stood beneath the picture of Benny's wife, Mary. The picture showed a young woman dressed in white in the style of the period when tight waists and enormous puffed sleeves were in vogue. An old washstand supporting a huge mirror, a small table, evidently used as a dining table, two chairs, a small cupboard filled with dishes, and a small, wood-burning stove completed the furnishings of the room. Back on the porch again, Benny resumed the story of his marriage.

"Her daddy wouldn't 'gree for us to git married 'cause he wanted her to stay on and wuk for him. She warn't but seventeen. My boss-man let us use his hoss and buggy and, Missy, dat fast hoss is what saved de day for us. When I got to whar I was to meet her, I seed her runnin' down de road wid her daddy atter her fast as he could go on foot. I snatched her up in dat buggy and it seemed lak dat hoss knowed us was in a hurry 'cause he sho' did run. Squire Jimmie Green married us and when us got back to my boss-man's house her daddy had done got dar and was a-raisin' cane. Boss Stephens, he come out and told her daddy to git on 'way from dar and let us 'lone, 'cause us was done married and dere warn't nothin' could be done 'bout it. Us had a hard time gittin' started housekeepin', 'cause my daddy couldn't holp us none. Our bed was one of dem home-made ones nailed to de side of de house. Us lived together 43 years 'fore de Lord tuk her home to Heben 15 years ago. Dem 43 years was all of 'em happy years. Since she's been gone I'se mighty lonesome, but it won't be long now 'til I see her, for I'se ready to go whenever de Good Lord calls me."

[HW: Atlanta
Dist. 5
Driskell]

THE EXPERIENCE OF GEORGE EASON IN SLAVERY TIME
[MAY 8 1937]

# GEORGE EASON

Mr. George Eason was born in Forsyth, Ga., on the plantation of Mr. Jack Ormond. In addition to himself there were six other children, one of whom was his twin brother. He and his brother were the oldest members of this group of children. His mother, who was the master's cook, had always belonged to the Ormond family while his father belonged to another family, having been sold while he (George) was still a baby.

It so happened that Mr. Ormond was a wealthy planter and in addition to the plantation that he owned in the country, he also maintained a large mansion in the town.

The first few years of his life were spent in town where he helped his mother in the kitchen by attending to the fire, getting water, etc. He was also required to look after the master's horse. Unlike most other slave owners who allowed their house servants to sleep in the mansion, Mr. Ormond had several cabins built a short distance in the rear of his house to accommodate those who were employed in the house. This house group consisted of the cook, seamstress, maid, butler, and the wash woman. Mr.

Eason and those persons who held the above positions always had good food because they got practically the same thing that was served to the master and his family. They all had good clothing—the women's dresses being made of calico, and the butler's suits of good grade cloth, the particular kind of which Mr. Eason knows nothing about. He himself wore a one-piece garment made of crocus.

Mr. Eason was about 7 or 8 years of age when he was first sent to work in the field. It was then that his troubles began. He says that he was made to get up each morning at sun-up and that after going to the field he had to toil there all day until the sun went down. He and his fellow slaves had to work in all types of weather, good as well as bad. Although the master or the overseer were not as cruel as some he had heard of they tolerated no looseness of work and in case a person was suspected of loafing the whip was applied freely. Although he was never whipped, he has heard the whip being applied to his mother any number of times. It hurt him, he says, because he had to stand back unable to render any assistance whatever. (This happened before he was sent to the plantation.) When his mother got these whippings she always ran off afterwards and hid in the woods which were nearby. At night she would slip to the cabin to get food and while there would caution him and the other children not to tell the master that they had seen her. The master's wife who was very mean was always the cause of her receiving these lashings.

Some nights after he and the other slaves had left the field they were required to do extra work such as ginning cotton and shelling peas and corn, etc. The young women were required to work that in some respects was as hard as that the men did, while the older women usually did lighter work. When the time came to pick the cotton all hands were converted into pickers. Night was the only time that they had to do their washing and to cultivate the small gardens they were allowed to have.

During the months when there was little field work to do they were kept busy repairing fences, etc. on the farm. Every day was considered a working day except Sunday, Thanksgiving and Christmas. They were not allowed to celebrate on these days as were the slaves on other nearby plantations.

Clothing on the Ormond plantation was usually insufficient to satisfy the needs of the slave. Each year one issue was given each slave. For the men this issue consisted of 1 pair of brogan shoes, several homespun shirts, a few pairs of knitted socks, and two or three pairs of pants. The brogans were made of such hard leather until the wearers' feet were usually blistered before the shoes were "broken in." The women, in addition to a pair of shoes and some cotton stockings were given several homespun dresses. On one occasion Mr. Eason says that he wore his shoes out before time for an issue of clothing. It was so cold until the skin on his feet cracked, causing the blood to flow. In spite of this his master would give him no more shoes. All clothing was made on the plantation except the shoes.

Those women who were too old for field work did the sewing in addition to other duties to be described later.

Indigo was cultivated for dyeing purposes and in some instances a dye was made by boiling walnut leaves and walnut hulls in water. In addition to her duties as cook, Mr. Eason's mother had to also weave part of the cloth. He told of how he had to sit up at night and help her and how she would "crack" him on the head for being too slow at times.

The amount of food given each slave was also inadequate as a general rule. At the end of each week they all went to a certain spot on the plantation where each was given 1 peck of meal, 1 gal. of syrup, and 3 pounds of meat. They often suffered from that particular stomach ailment commonly known as hunger. At such times raids were made on the smokehouse. This was considered as stealing by the master and the overseer but to them it was merely taking that which they had worked for. At other times they increased their food by hunting and fishing. Possums and coons were the usual game from such a hunting expedition. All meals usually consisted of grits, bacon, syrup, corn bread and vegetables. On Sundays and holidays the meals varied to the extent that they were allowed to have biscuits which they called "cake bread." The slaves made coffee by parching corn meal, okra seed or Irish potatoes. When sufficiently parched any one of the above named would make a vile type of coffee. Syrup was used for all sweetening purposes. The produce from the gardens which the master allowed them could only be used for home consumption and under no circumstances could any of it be sold.

The cabins that the slaves occupied were located on one section of the plantation known as the "quarters." These dwellings were crude one-roomed structures usually made from logs. In order to keep the weather out mud was used to close the openings between the logs. In most instances the furnishing of a cabin was complete after a bed, a bench (both of which were made by the slave) and a few cooking utensils had been placed in it. As there were no stoves for slave use all cooking was done at the fireplace, which, like the chimney, was made of mud and stones. One or two openings served the purpose of windows, and shutters were used instead of glass. The mattresses on which they slept were made from hay, grass or straw. When a light was needed a tallow candle or a pine knot was lighted.

Absolute cleanliness was required at all times and the floors, if they were made of wood, had to be swept and scrubbed often. In addition to the private dwellings there was one large house where all children not old enough to go to the field were kept. One or two of the older women took charge of them, seeing that they had a sufficient amount of corn bread, vegetables and milk each day. All were fed from a trough like little pigs.

These old women were also responsible for the care of the sick. When asked if a doctor was employed, Mr. Eason replied that one had to be mighty sick to have the services of a doctor. The usual treatment for sick slaves was castor oil, which was given in large doses, salts and a type of pill known as "hippocat." (ipecac)

Although they were not permitted any formal type of learning religious worship it was not denied them. Each Sunday Mr. Ormond required that all his slaves attend church. All went to the white church where they sat in back and listened to the sermon of a white preacher. Mr. Eason says that the slaves believed in all kinds of and every conceivable type of signs. Their superstitions usually had to do with methods of conjure.

A preacher was never used to perform a wedding ceremony on the Ormond plantation. After the man told the master about the woman of his choice and she had been called and had agreed to the plan, all that was necessary was for the couple to join hands and jump over a broom which had been placed on the ground.

Mr. Ormond permitted few if any celebrations or frolics to take place on his farm. When he did grant this privilege his slaves were permitted to invite their friends who of course had to get a "pass" from their respective masters. They, too, were required to secure a pass from Mr. Ormond if they wanted to visit off the premises. If caught by the "Paddle Rollers" (Patrollers) without this pass they were soundly whipped and then taken to their master.

At the beginning of the Civil War all the slaves talked among themselves concerning the possible outcome of the war. However, they never let the master or the overseer hear them because it meant a whipping.

When Sherman and his army marched through they burned all the gin houses on the Ormond plantation and took all the available live stock. Mr. Ormond took a few prized possessions and a few slaves (one of whom was Mr. Eason) and fled to Augusta, Ga.

After freedom was declared he was still held in bondage and hired out by the day. Once he ran away but was found and brought back. In 1867 the remaining members of the Ormond family moved to Atlanta, bringing him along with them. After most of them had died he was finally permitted to go or stay as he pleased.

Immediately after freedom had been declared he had the good fortune to find his father. However, he never got a chance to spend any time with him as the Ormonds refused to release him.

Says Mr. Eason: "Slavery had a good point in that we slaves always felt that somebody was going to take care of us." He says that he has heard some wish for the good old days but as for himself he prefers things to remain as they are at present.

United States. Work Projects Administration

## PLANTATION LIFE AS VIEWED BY EX-SLAVE

CALLIE ELDER, Age 78
640 W. Hancock Avenue
Athens, Georgia

Written by:
Sadie B. Hornsby
Athens

Edited by:
Sarah H. Hall
Athens

Leila Harris
Augusta

and
John N. Booth
District Supervisor
Federal Writers' Project
Residencies 6 & 7
[JUN 6 1938]

# CALLIE ELDER

Callie lives with her daughter, Cornelia, in a 6-room house near the crest of a hill. Their abode is a short distance from the street and is reached by steep stone steps. In response to the call for Callie, a tall mulatto woman appeared. Her crudely fashioned blue dress was of a coarse cotton fabric and her dingy head rag had long lost its original color. Straight black hair, streaked with gray, and high cheek bones gave the impression that in her ancestry of mixed races, Indian characteristics predominate. Her constant use of snuff causes frequent expectoration and her favorite pastime seems to be the endeavor to attain an incredible degree of accuracy in landing each mouthful of the amber fluid at the greatest possible distance. As she was about to begin conversation, a little yellow boy about five years old ran into the room and Callie said: "'Scuse me please, I can't talk 'til I gits my grandboy off so he won't be late to school at Little Knox. Set down in dat dar cheer and I'll be right back."

Soon Callie returned and it was evident that her curiosity was aroused. When the interviewer explained the purpose of the visit, she exclaimed: "Lordy! Miss, what is de government gwine do next? For de God's truth, I never knowed I would have to tell nobody what happened back in dem days, so its jus' done slipped out of my mind.

"Anyhow, I warn't even born in Clarke County. I was born in Floyd County, up nigh Rome, Georgia, on Marse Billy Neal's plantation. Ann and Washin'ton Neal was my Mammy and Pappy. No Ma'am, no preacher never married 'em. Marse Billy Neal, he owned bofe of 'em and atter my Pappy axed him could he marry Mammy, Marse Billy made 'em go up to de hall of de big house and jump backwards over a broom.

"Dere was six of us chillun: me and Frances, Beulah, Thomas, Felix, and Scott. Dere was mighty little wuk done by chillun in slav'ry days. I jus' played 'round and kicked up my heels wid de rest of de chillun. When us played our hidin' game, us sung somepin' lak dis:

> 'Mollie, Mollie Bright
> Three score and ten,
> Can I git dere by candlelight?
> Yes, if your laigs is long enough!'

"Sometimes us played what us called de 'Crow' game. Us spread our fingers out, side by side and counted 'em out wid a rhyme. De one de last word of de rhyme fell on had to be de crow. I didn't love to be counted out and made de crow, but it was a heap of fun to count de others out. Since I been knee high to a grasshopper, I ain't never done nothin' but wuk 'round white folks' houses.

"Our log cabins what us lived in was daubed inside and out wid mud to keep out bad weather. Our beds was held together by cords what was twisted evvy which way. You had to be mighty careful tightenin' dem cords or de beds was liable to fall down. Us slept on wheat straw mattresses and had plenty of good warm quilts for kiver.

"Grown folks was fed cornbread and meat wid plenty of vegetables in de week days and on Sunday mornin's dey give 'em wheat bread, what was somethin' slaves didn't see no more 'til de next Sunday mornin'. 'Bout four o'clock on summer afternoons, dey sot a big old wooden bowl full of cornbread crumbs out in de yard and poured in buttermilk or potliquor 'til de crumbs was kivered. Den dey let de chillun gather 'round it and eat 'til de bowl was empty. In winter chillun was fed inside de house.

"'Possums, Oh, mussy me! My grandpa hunted 'possums at night and fetched in two and three at a time. Don't say nothin' 'bout dem rabbits for dere warn't no end to 'em. Rabbits stewed, rabbits fried, and rabbits dried, smoked, and cured lak hog meat! I et so many rabbits when I was young I can't stand to look at 'em now but I could eat 'possums and gnaw de bones all day long. Marse Billy let grandpa go fishin' and he was all time bringin' back a passel of minnows and other fishes. Us rubbed 'em down wid lard and salt and pepper, den rolled 'em in cornmeal and baked 'em. I never seed no fried meat 'til I was a big strappin' gal. Dere was one big gyarden whar dey raised 'nough vegetables for all de white folks and slaves too. All de bilin' was done in pots swung on cranes over coals in de fireplace.

"Our clothes was made new for us in de fall out of cloth wove in looms right dar on de plantation. Top clothes was dyed wid hick'ry bark. De full skirts was gathered to tight fittin' waisties. Underskirts was made de same way. De dresses had done wore thin 'nough for hot weather by de time winter was gone so us wore dem same clothes straight on through de summer, only us left off de underskirts den. Slave chillun didn't never wear no shoes. Our foots cracked open 'til dey looked lak goose foots. Us wore de same on Sunday as evvy day, 'cept dat our clothes was clean, and stiff wid meal starch when us got into 'em on Sunday mornin's.

"Marse Billie Neal was our owner and Miss Peggy was his old 'oman. Dey was jus' as good to us as dey could be. Deir two chillun was Marse Tom and Marse Mid. De car'iage driver never had much to do but drive Marse Billy and Miss Peggy 'round and, course he had to see dat de hosses and car'iage was kept clean and shiny. I don't 'member if he tuk de chillun 'round. Chillun didn't stand de show dey does now.

"Oh, no Ma'am, I sho' can't tell nothin' t'all 'bout how big dat old plantation was, but it was one whoppin' big place. Dere was too many slaves on dat plantation for me to count. De overseer got 'em up by 4:00 o'clock and de mens had to be in de fields by sunrise. De 'omans went out 'bout 8:00 o'clock. Dey stopped wuk at sundown and by de time dey et and done de chores for de day it was 10:00 o'clock 'fore dey hit de bed. De cabins was built in a circle and de overseer went de rounds evvy night to see if de slaves was in bed.

"Yes Ma'am, dey whupped de Niggers. My Pappy and grandpa was de wust ones 'bout gittin' licked. Evvy time Pappy runned away Marse Billy sicked dem hounds on his heels and dey was sho' to ketch him and fetch him back. Dey had to keep knives from Pappy or when dem dogs cotch him he would jus' cut 'em up so dey would die. When dey got him back to de house, dey would buckle him down over a barrel and larrup him wid a plaited whup. 'Omans warn't whupped much. My grandpa York was so bad 'bout runnin' 'way Marse Billy made him wear long old horns. One Sunday Marse Billy went by our church to see if all his Niggers was dar what was sposen to be dar. And dere grandpa was a-sottin' wid dem horns on his head. Marse Billy told him he could take de horns off his head whilst he was in de meetin' house. At dat grandpa dropped dem horns, and lit a rag to de woods and it tuk de dogs days to find him.

"If one slave kilt another, Marse Billy made de overseer tie dat dead Nigger to de one what kilt him, and de killer had to drag de corpse 'round 'til he died too. De murderers never lived long a-draggin' dem daid ones 'round. Dat jus' pyorely skeered 'em to death. Dere was a guard house on de farm, whar de wust Niggers was kept, and while dey was in dat guard house, dey warn't fed but once a day. It warn't nothin' unusual for Marse Billy to sell slaves, but he never sold his best Niggers. De ones he sold was allus dem he couldn't git no wuk out of.

"Not a Nigger could read or write on Marse Billy's plantation. Dey was all too dumb to larn. Dere was a shackly sort of church house on our plantation and on Sundays atter de Niggers had cleaned deyselfs up, if dey told Marse Billy dey wanted to go to church, he sent 'em on. All I knows 'bout baptizin's is dey jus' tuk 'em to de river and plunged 'em in. Dey sung somepin' 'bout: 'Gwine to de River for to be Baptized.' Us had prayer meetin's on Wednesday nights sometimes.

"Oh, Mussy! Don't ax me 'bout fun'rals. I got de misery in my laigs and I feels too bad dis mornin' to let myself even think 'bout fun'rals. Back den when slave folks died dey jus' put 'em in home-made pine coffins what dey throwed in a wagon and tuk 'em to de graveyard. At dem buryin's, dey used to sing:

> 'Am I born to die
> To let dis body down.'

"None of our Niggers ever runned away to de North. Dey was too busy runnin' off to de woods. Jus' to tell de truth dem Niggers on our place was so dumb dey didn't even take in 'bout no North. Dey didn't even know what de war was 'bout 'til it was all over. I don't know whar to start 'bout dem patterollers. Dey was de devil turned a-loose. Dere was a song 'bout 'Run Nigger run, de patteroller git you!' and dey sho' would too, I want to tell you.

"What de slaves done on Saddy night? Dey done anything dey was big 'nough to do. Dere warn't no frolickin' 'cept on Sadday night. Niggers on our place wukked all day Sadday 'cept once a month. Some of de slaves would slip off and stay half a day and de overseer wouldn't miss 'em 'cause dere was so many in de field. It was jus' too bad for any Nigger what got cotched at dat trick. Sadday night, slaves was 'lowed to git together and frolic and cut de buck.

"Christmas Day Marse Billy called us to de big house and give us a little fresh meat and sweet bread, dat was cake. Christmas warn't much diff'unt f'um other times. Jus' more t'eat. Us jus' had dat one day off, and New Year's Day was used as a holiday too.

"Oh, dem cornshuckin's! All day 'fore a cornshuckin' dey hauled corn and put it in great piles as high as dis here house. Us sung all de time us was shuckin' corn. Dere was a lot of dem old shuckin' songs. De one us sung most was: 'Whooper John and Calline all night.' Marse Billy, he give 'em coffee and whiskey all night and dat made 'em git rough and rowdy. Den de shucks did fly. Us had one more grand feast when de last ear of corn had done been shucked. Dere warn't nothin' lackin'.

"Cotton pickin's warn't planned for fun and frolic lak cornshuckin's. If Marse Billy got behind in his crops, he jus' sent us back to de fields at night when de moon was bright and sometimes us picked cotton all night long. Marster give de 'oman what picked de most cotton a day off, and de man what picked de most had de same privilege.

"Old Aunt Martha what nussed de chillun while deir Mammies wukked in de field was de quiltin' manager. It warn't nothin' for 'omans to quilt three quilts in one night. Dem quilts had to be finished 'fore dey stopped t'eat a bit of de quiltin' feast. Marse Billy 'vided dem quilts out 'mongst de Niggers what needed 'em most.

"Dem blue and white beads what de grown 'omans wore was jus' to look pretty. Dey never meant nothin' else. Mammy would skeer us down 'bout Rawhead and Bloody Bones. Us was all time a-lookin' for him, but he never got dar. What skeered us most was painters (panthers) a-howlin' close to our cabins at night. You could hear 'em most any night. When Mammy wanted to make us behave all she had to say was: 'I hears dem painters comin'!' Dat made us jus' shake all over and git mighty still and quiet. De mens tried to run dem painters down, but dey never did ketch one.

"One of de cabins was allus ha'nted atter some of de slaves got kilt in it whilst dey was fightin'. Nobody never could live in dat cabin no more atter dat widout ha'nts gittin' atter 'em. De wust of 'em was a 'oman ha'nt what you could hear sweepin' up leaves in de yard and all dat time you might be lookin' hard and not see a leaf move. In dat cabin you could all time hear ha'nts movin' cheers and knockin' on de wall. Some of dem ha'nts would p'int a gun in your face if you met 'em in de dark. Dem ha'nts was too much for me.

"Our white folks was good as dey knowed how to be when us got sick. I don't 'member dat dey ever had a doctor for de slaves, but dey give us all kinds of home-brewed teas. Pinetops, mullein and fat light'ood splinters was biled together and de tea was our cure for diff'unt ailments. Scurvy grass tea mixed wid honey was good for stomach troubles, but you sho' couldn't take much of it at a time. It was de movin'est medicine! Round our necks us wore asafetida sacks tied on strings soaked in turpentine. Dat was to keep diseases off of us.

"What does I 'member 'bout de war? Well, it was fit to

fetch our freedom. Marse Billy had a fine stallion. When de sojers was comin', he sont Pappy to de woods wid dat stallion and some gold and told him not to let dem yankees find 'em. Dat stallion kept squealin' 'til de yankees found him, and dey tuk him and de gold too. Grandma was a churnin' away out on de back porch and she had a ten dollar gold piece what she didn't want dem sojers to steal, so she drapped it in de churn. Dem yankees poured dat buttermilk out right dar on de porch floor and got grandma's money. Marse Billy hid hisself in a den wid some more money and other things and dey didn't find him. Dey tuk what dey wanted of what dey found and give de rest to de slaves. Atter de sojers left, de Niggers give it all back to Marster 'cause he had allus been so good to 'em.

"Us stayed on wid Marse Billy for sev'ral years atter de war. He paid us $10 a month and he 'lowanced out de rations to us evvy week; most allus on Monday 'cause Sundays us had 'nough company to eat it all at one time. He give us three pounds of fat meat, a peck of meal, a peck of flour, 25¢ worth of sugar, and a pound of coffee. Dat had to last a whole week.

"I didn't take in nothin' 'bout Abraham Lincoln, Jefferson Davis and dat dar Booker T. Washin'ton man, but I heared folks say dey was all right.

"What is you talkin' 'bout Miss? I didn't need to have no big weddin' when I married Lige Elder. It was a big 'nough thing to git a man lak what I got. What did I want to have a big weddin' for when all I was atter was my man? Us had done been married 25 years 'fore us had no chillun. Dis here Cornelia what I lives wid was our first chile. She ain't got no chillun. Isaac, my boy, has got four chillun. My old man died 'bout two years ago.

"I j'ined de church 'cause I was happy and wanted de world to know I had done got 'ligion. I think evvybody ought to git 'ligion. God says if us do right he will give us all a home in His Heaven.

"I'd rather have de days as dey is now in some ways. But one thing I does lak to do is eat and us had a plenty of good eatin' den and never had to worry none 'bout whar it was a-comin' f'um. Miss, ain't you through axin' me questions yet? I'm tired of talkin'. I done let de fire go out under my washpot twice. Dem white folks ain't gwine to lak it if dey has to wait for deir clothes, and dis misery in my laigs, it sho' does hurt me bad dis mornin'."

MARTHA EVERETTE, EX-SLAVE
Hawkinsville, Georgia

(Interviewed By Elizabeth Watson—1936)
[JUL 20 1937]

# MARTHA EVERETTE

Born in Pulaski County about 1848, the daughter of Isaac and Amanda Lathrop, Martha Everette has lived all her life near where she was born.

Prior to freedom, her first job was "toting in wood", from which she was soon "promoted" to waiting on the table, house cleaning, etc. She make no claims to have ever "graduated" as a cook, as so many old before-the-war Negresses do.

"Aunt" Martha's owner was a kind man: he never whipped the slaves, but the overseer "burnt 'em up sometimes." And her mother was a "whipper, too"—a woman that "fanned" her children religiously, so to speak, not overlooking Martha. All the Watson slaves attended the (White) Baptist church at Blue Springs.

Rations were distributed on Sunday morning of each week, and the slaves had plenty to eat. The slaves were also allowed to fish, thus often adding variety to their regular fare.

Negro women were taught to sew by the overseers' wives, and most of the slaves' clothes were made from cloth woven on the plantation. The Yankees visited the

Lathrop plantation in '65, asked for food, received it, and marched on without molesting anything or any body. Truly, these were well-behaved Yankees!

"Aunt" Martha says that she remembers quite well when the Yankees captured Jefferson Davis. She and other slave children were in the "big house" yard when they heard drums beating, and soon saw the Yankees pass with Mr. Davis.

"Aunt" Martha, now old and decrepit, lives with one of her sons, who takes care of her. This son is a gardener and a carpenter and, being thrifty, fares much better than many Negroes of his generation.

[HW: Dist. 5
Ex-Slave #30]
By E. Driskell
Typed by A.M. Whitley
1-29-37

FIRST COPY OF ARTICLE ENTITLED:
"AN INTERVIEW WITH LEWIS FAVOR," EX-SLAVE
[MAY 8 1937]

*[TR: informant also referred to as Favors in this document.]*

# LEWIS FAVOR

Among Atlanta's few remaining ex-slaves is one Lewis Favors. When he fully understood this worker's reasons for approaching him he consented to tell what he had seen and experienced as a slave. Chewing slowly on a large wad of tobacco he began his account in the following manner: "I was born in Merriweather County in 1855 near the present location of Greenville, Georgia. Besides my mother there were eight of us children and I was elder than all of them with one exception. Our owner was Mrs. Favors, but she was known to everybody as the "Widow Favors." My father was owned by a Mr. Darden who had a plantation in this same county. When the "Widow's" husband died he left her about one-hundred acres of land and a large sum of money and so she was considered as being rich. She didn't have many slaves of her own and so her son (also a plantation owner) used to send some of his slaves over occasionally to help cultivate her crops, which consisted of cotton, corn, and all kinds of vegetables."

In regard to her treatment of the slaves that she held Mr. Favors says: "She wasn't so tight and then she was pretty tight too."

Those slaves who were field hands were in the field and at work by the time it was light enough to see. They plowed, hoed, and then later in the season gathered the crops. After the harvesting was over the fences were repaired and rails were split. In rainy weather nobody had to work out of doors, instead they shelled the peas and corn and sometimes ginned the cotton. At night the women were required to spin and to weave. In the winter season no work was required at night unless they had not spun as much thread as was required. At such times they had to work at night until the amount set had been reached.

Mr. Favor's mother was the cook for the "Widow Favors" and her two neices who lived with her. The Favors had paid the owner of a hotel Four hundred dollars to have the hotel cook teach her (Mr. Favors mother) to prepare all kinds of fancy dishes. His father was a field hand on the Darden plantation. In addition to this he repaired all the shoes when this was necessary.

As a child Mr. Favors was not very strong physically and because of this the "Widow" made him her pet. He never had to do any work other than that of waiting on the mistress while she ate her meals. Even in this he had to get up at four o'clock in the morning and help his mother in the kitchen. Sometimes he would sweep the yards if he felt like doing so. When he grew older he was given the task of picking the seed out of the cotton at night.

On Sundays all the servants were free to do as they pleased, that is, with the exception of Mr. Favors, his mother, and the two women who serve as maids to the "Widow's" two neices. At other times if a task was done before the day was over with they were given the remaining time to do as they pleased. However, everybody had a one week holiday at Christmas.

Mr. Favors made the following statement in regard to the clothing: "Everybody wore the homespun cotton clothes that were made on the plantation by the slave women. The women wore striped ausenberg dresses while the men wore ausenberg pants and shirts that had been made into one garment. My clothes were always better than the other little fellows, who ran around in their shirttails because I was always in the house of the "Widow." They used red clay to do the dyeing with. In the winter time cracked feet were common. The grown people wore heavy shoes called brogans while I wore the cast-off shoes of the white ladies. We all wrapped our feet in bagging sacks to help them to keep warm. We were given one complete outfit of clothes each year and these had to last until the time for the next issue."

Sheets for the beds were also made out of homespun material while the heavier cover such as the quilts, etc., were made from the dresses and the other clothing that was no longer fit for wear.

As a general rule all of the slaves on this plantation had enough food to keep them well and healthy. At the end of each week the field hands were given enough food to last them seven days. For most of them the week's supply consisted of three and one-half pounds of pork or fat meat, one peck of meal, flour, and black molasses. The only meals that they had to prepare from the above mentioned articles were breakfast and supper. Dinner was cooked in the plantation kitchen by one of the women who was too old for work in the fields. For this particular meal the slaves had some different type of vegetable each day along with the fat meat, corn bread, and the pot liquor which was served every day. They were allowed to come in from the fields to the house to be served. Breakfast usually consisted of fat meat, molasses, and corn bread while supper consisted of pot-liquor, bread, and milk. The only variation from this diet was on Sunday when all were allowed to have bisquits instead of corn bread. Mr. Favors was asked what happened if anyone's food was all eaten before it was time for the weekly issue and he answered: "It was just too bad for them 'cause they would have to do the best they could until the time came to get more." When such a thing happened to anyone the others usually helped as far as their limited supplies would permit.

Mr. Favors says that he, his mother, and the two maids ate the same kind of food that the "Widow," and her nieces were served. After he had seen to the wants of all at the table he had to take a seat at the table beside his owner where he ate with her and the others seated there.

There were two one-roomed cabins located directly behind the four-roomed house of the "Widow," the entire lot of them were built out of logs. These two cabins were for the use of those servants who worked in the house of their owner. At one end of each cabin there was a wide fireplace which was made of sticks, stones, and dried mud. Instead of windows there were only one or two small holes cut in the back wall of the cabin. The beds were made out of heavy planks and were called "Georgia Looms," by the slaves. Wooden slats were used in the place of bed springs while the mattresses were merely large bags that had been stuffed to capacity with hay, wheat straw, or leaves. The only other furnishings in each of these cabins were several benches and a few cooking utensils. Mr. Favors says: "We didn't have plank floors like these on some of the other plantations; the plain bare ground served as our floor." As he made this statement he reminded this worker that he meant his mother and some of the other house servants lived in these cabins. He himself always lived in the house with the "Widow Favors," who had provided a comfortable bed along with a small chair for his use. These slaves who worked in the fields lived in several cabins that were somewhat nearer to their fields than the other two cabins mentioned above.

The remaining buildings on the Favors' plantation were the smokehouse and the cook house where in addition to the cooking the younger children were cared for by another old person. The woman who cared for these children had to also help with the cooking.

Whenever any of the slaves were sick the doctor was called if conditions warranted it, otherwise a dose of castor oil was prescribed. Mr. Favors stated that after freedom was declared the white people for whom they worked gave them hog-feet oil and sometimes beef-oil both of which had the same effect as castor oil. If any were too ill to work in the field one of the others was required to remain at the cabin or at some other convenient place so as to be able to attend to the wants of these so indisposed.

When Mr. Favors was asked if the servants on this plantation ever had the chance to learn how to read or to write he answered: "They was all afraid to even try because they would cut these off," and he held up his right hand and pointed to his thumb and forefinger. At any rate the "Widow," nieces taught him to read a few months before the slaves were set free.

On Sunday all were required to attend the white church in town. They sat in the back of the church as the white minister preached and directed the following text at them: "Don't steal your master's chickens or his eggs and your backs won't be whipped." In the afternoon of this same day when the colored minister was allowed to preach the slaves heard this text: "Obey your masters and your mistresses and your backs won't be whipped." All of the marriages ware performed by the colored preacher who read a text from the Bible and then pronounced the couple being married as man and wife.

Although nobody was ever sold on the Favors plantation Mr. Favors has witnessed the selling of others on the auction block. He says that the block resembled a flight of steps. The young children and those women who had babies too young to be separated from them were placed on the bottom step, those in their early teens on the next, the young men and women on the next, and the middle-aged and old ones on the last one. Prices decreased as the auctioneer went from the bottom step to the top one, that is, the younger a slave was the more money he brought if he was sold.

Sometimes there were slaves who were punished by the overseer because they had broken some rule. Mr. Favors says that at such times a cowhide whip was used and the number of lashes that the overseer gave depended on the slave owner's instructions. He has seen others whipped and at such times he began praying. The only punishment that he ever received was as a little boy and then a switch was used instead of the whip. If the "Patter-Roller" caught a slave out in the streets without a pass from his master they proceeded to give the luckless fellow five lashes with a whip called the cat-o-nine-tails. They gave six lashes if the slave was caught out at night regardless of whether he had a pass or not.

As none of the slaves held by the "Widow" or her son ever attempted to run away there was no punishment for this. However, he has heard that on other plantations blood hounds were used to trail those who ran away and if they were caught a severe beating was administered.

Sometime after the civil war had begun the "Widow Favors" packed as many of her belongings as possible and fled to LaGrange, Georgia. He and his mother along with several other slaves (one of whom was an old man) were taken along. He never heard any of the white people say anything about the war or its possible results. At one time a battle was being fought a few miles distant and they all saw the cannon balls fall on the plantation. This was when the journey to LaGrange was decided upon. Before leaving the "Widow" had the slaves to bury all the meat, flour, and other food on the plantation so that the Yankee soldiers would not get it. Mr. Favors was given about two thousand dollars in gold currency to keep and protect for his owner. At various intervals he had to take this money to the "Widow". so that she might count it. Another one of the slaves was given the son's gold watch to keep on his person until the Yanks left the vicinity.

Before freedom was declared Mr. Favors says that he prayed all of the time because he never wanted to be whipped with the cowhide, like others he had seen. Further he says that it was a happy day for him when he was told that he could do as he pleased because he realized then that he could do some of the things that he had always wanted to do.

When freedom was declared for the slaves the Favors family freed slaves valued at one-hundred and fifty thousand dollars. The live stock that they sold represented a like sum. Mr. Favors and his mother remained with the "Widow," who gave him his board in return for his services and paid his mother twenty-five dollars per year for hers as cook.

"Even after the war things were pretty tough for us" stated Mr. Favors. "The plantation owners refused to pay more than thirty or forty cents to a person for a days work in the fields. Some of them would not allow an ex-slave to walk in the streets in front of their homes but made them take to the out-of-the-way paths through the woods to reach their various destinations. At other times white men cut the clothes from the backs of the ex-slaves when they were well dressed. If they didn't beg hard enough when thus accosted they might even be cut to death!" After the first three years following the war conditions were somewhat better, he continued.

Mr. Favors says that his old age is due to the fact that he has always taken good care of himself and because he has always refrained from those habits that are known to tear a person's health down.

[HW: Dist. 6
Ex-Slave #28]

THE STORY OF AUNT MARY FERGUSON, EX-SLAVE
1928 Oak Street
Columbus, Georgia
December 18, 1936

# MARY FERGUSON

"Aunt" Mary Ferguson, née Mary Little, née Mary Shorter, was born somewhere in Maryland; the exact locality being designated by her simply as "the eastern shore" of that state. She was born the chattel of a planter named Shorter, so her first name, of course, was Mary Shorter.

For many years she has resided with a daughter and a granddaughter, at 1928 Oak Avenue, Columbus, Georgia.

"Aunt" Mary was about thirteen years old when, in 1860, she was sold and brought South. The story of which, as told in her own words is as follows:

"In 1860 I wuz a happy chile. I had a good ma an a good paw; one older bruther an one older suster, an a little bruther an a baby suster, too. All my fambly wucked in de fields, 'ceptin me an de two little uns, which I stayed at home to mind. (mind—care for).

"It wuz durin' cotton chopping time dat year (1860), a day I'll never fergit, when de speckulataws bought me. We come home from de fiel' 'bout haf atter 'leven dat day an cooked a good dinner, I hopin her. O, I never has forgot dat last dinner wid my fokes! But, some-ow, I had felt, all de mawnin, lak sumpin was gwineter happin'. I could jes feel it in my bones! An' sho nough, bout de middle of the even', up rid my young Marster on his hoss, an' up driv two strange white mens in a buggy. Dey hitch dere hosses an' cum in de house, which skeered me. Den one o' de strangers said, 'git yo clothers, Mary; we has bought you frum Mr. Shorter." I c'menced cryin' an' beggin' Mr. Shorter to not let 'em take me away. But he say, 'yes, Mary, I has sole yer, an' yer must go wid em.'

"Den dese strange mens, whose names I ain't never knowed, tuk me an' put me in de buggy an' driv off wid me, me hollerin' at de top o' my voice an' callin' my Ma! Den dem speckulataws begin to sing loud—jes to drown out my hollerin.'

"Us passed de very fiel whar paw an' all my fokes wuz wuckin, an' I calt out as loud as I could an', as long as I could see 'em, 'good-bye, Ma!' 'good-bye, Ma!' But she never heared me. Naw, nah, daz white mens wuz singin' so loud Ma could'n hear me! An' she could'n see me, caze dey had me pushed down out o' sight on de floe o' de buggy.

"I ain't never seed nor heared tell o' my Ma an' Paw, an' bruthers, an' susters from dat day to dis.

"My new owners tuck me to Baltymore, whar dey had herded tergether two two-hoss wagon loads o' Niggers. All o' us Niggers wuz den shipped on a boat to Savannah, an' frum dar us wuz put on de cyars an' sont to Macon.

"In Macon, us wuz sold out, and Doctor (W.R.) Little,

of Talbotton, bought me at oxion (auction) an' tuck me home wid 'im. Den I wuz known as Mary Little, instid of Mary Shorter."

In the continuation of her narrative, "Aunt" Mary said that the Littles trained her to be a nurse. Before the war ended, she was inherited by Mr. Gus (the late Hon. W.A.) Little.

She remembers that all the "quality", young white men who went to the war from Talbotton took Negro men-servants (slaves) along with them. These were usually called body-servants, and it was a body-servant's duty to cook, wash, and do general valet service for his master. In a pinch, he was also supposed to raid a hen roost, or otherwise rustle food for his "white fokes".

According to "Aunt" Mary, the Little Negroes were very religious and given to much loud praying and singing, which often so disturbed Dr. Little that he gave orders for them to stop it, and also ordered that all lights in the slave quarters be out at 9 o'clock each night.

"So us tuck to slippin' off to a big gully in de pastur to sing and pray whar de white fokes couldn' hear us.

"My fust baby wuz bawned in 1862, during de secon' year o' de war. I has had several husbants, my las' un, he died 'bout seventeen years ago.

"I ain't never seed but one hant in my life, an' I didn' know it wuz a hant 'til Aunt Peggy (an old slave woman) tole me so. Dis hant was in de shape o' a duck, an' it followed me one day frum de big house kitchen ter de hawg pen whar I wuz gwine ter slop de hawgs. When I got back, I said, 'Aunt Peggy, dar's a strange duck done tuck up wid us!' And she say, 'hush, chile, dat's a hant!' I been seein' 'im fur severrel years! An' dat sholy skeert me!"

When asked if she had ever been whipped when a slave, "Aunt" Mary replied, "Yes, and thank God fur it, fur ole Miss taught me to be hones' an' not to steal." She admitted that being whipped for stealing made her an honest woman.

"Aunt" Mary's oldest child is now a man of 74. Her hair is as white as cotton and her eye sight is dim, but she is still mentally alert. She says that colored people are naturally religious and that they learned all their "devilment" from the Whites. She deplores the wickedness into which the world has drifted, but thanks God that slavery ended when it did.

She has never had any particular love for the Yankees, and thinks that they treated the Southern white folks "most scandalously" after the war, yet feels that she owes them a debt of gratitude for freeing her people. She admits that her awful hatred of slavery was born of her sad experience as a girl when she was so unceremoniously separated from her loved ones, as previously told. She is also of the firm opinion the those "speculataws" who brought her from Maryland to Georgia in 1860 are "brilin in hell fur dey sin" of seperating her from her people.

Must Jesus bear the cross alone
and all the world go free?
No, there is a cross for every one;
there's a cross for me;
This consecrated cross I shall bear til
death shall set me free,
And then go home, my crown to wear;
there is a crown for me.

Sung for interviewer by Mary Ferguson, ex-slave, December 18, 1936.

**FOLKLORE INTERVIEW**

CARRIE NANCY FRYER
415 Mill Street
Augusta, Georgia

Written by:
Miss Maude Barragan
Federal Writers' Project
Residency #13
Augusta, Georgia

# CARRIE NANCY FRYER

An angular, red-skinned old Negro women was treading heavily down the dusty sidewalk, leaning on a gnarled stick and talking to a little black girl. A "sundown" hat shaded a bony face of typical Indian cast and her red skin was stretched so tight over high cheek bones that few wrinkles showed.

"Auntie," she was asked, "have you time to tell me something about slavery times?" "No'm, I sorry," she answered, "but I gwine to see a sick lady now, and I gots to 'tend to somepin'." "May I come back to see you at your house?" "Yas'm, any time you wants. I live in de lil' house on de canal, it has a ellum tree in front. I riz it from sapling. I name dat lil' tree 'Nancy' so when I gone, folks kin come by and bow and say 'Howdy, Nancy.'"

She seated herself on a stone step and spread her many skirts of gray chambray, hand-sewed with big white stitches. An old woman came by, her shining black face puckered with anxiety, dressed in a starched white uniform and a battered black hat, well brushed.

"Morning, Nancy," she said. "You look mighty peak-ked dis morning."

"Hunh!" grunted Nancy, "I oughter. I bin to see de mayor. I say 'Mr. Mayor, here I is. I ain' got nuttin' to eat—it ain' right for a woman my age to beg food. Now what yer gwine do 'bout it?' De mayor say: 'Auntie, you go right down to de welfare office at de Court House and tell de lady I sont you to git somepin' to eat.' I done dat—dey promise to send a lady, but I ain' see no lady yit." A heavy sigh rolled out. "I didn' lef' skin of meat in my house or a piece of cornpone. But I didn' take nuttin' to heart 'cause de Lord is my helper."

The old woman sighed too. "Yeah, Nancy, das de way dey does. I ain' gwine keep nasty house for nobody. But white people's funny. Dey think if you got clean house and bleachin' sheets you mus' have somepin' to eat in-side." She clenched her fist, and her voice rose. "I tells you right now—I gwine keep my house neat jus' like I bin taught, ef I never gits no somepin' t'eat and ain' got cornpone in de oven."

"A poor creeter come to my house today to beg for somepin' to eat," said Nancy, "I ain' got nuttin' and I tell her so. She say she gwine to de court-house too."

"T'won't do no good," answered the other woman. "Come over here, Nancy. I wants to talk to you."

With a dignified excuse, Nancy creaked to her long length and moved deliberately to the edge of the sidewalk. Whisperings followed, the voices of the two old women rising in their excitement.

"I ain' gwine into somepin' I don't know nuttin' about."

"Nobody gwine 'swade me either."

"My husband didn' put no composin' on me. If I don't git but one meal a day, I ain' gwine dirty. I didn' have mouthful t'eat in my house."

The interested eavesdropper decided that the welfare office had talked social security to the women instead of direct relief, and they were worried and suspicious about the matter. The old black woman was getting angrier and angrier.

"If any of 'em lookin' for me to have nasty old tore-up house, I ain' gwine did it. You dunno when sickness come. When my boy got his leg broke up, soon as dey could, dey put him off on me. Miz' Powell say: 'Steve, if you don't be good to your ma, de Lord gwine take your blessing from you.' Dey paid Steve $137.00, Nancy, and he ain't gimmie a nickle! He spent it on a woman in Edgefield. But my gal is diffunt. If she ain' got but one mouthful she gwine give me half."

Nancy nodded: "Dat like my gal too."

The old woman took up her complaint again: "Um got daughter. When you walk in her house, you think dey is a white person's house. When I was workin and able, I put down as many bleachin' sheets as any white 'oman."

Nancy's ponderous sigh rolled out. She was very "peaked" indeed on this hot September morning. "If sister got a hoecake of bread, she gwine give it to me. Ain' nobody else to help now—de Lord done come along and got ev'y one of my mother's chillun but me."

Seeing that present necessities were too important to permit an interview, the visitor said: "Nancy, I'll see you tomorrow." A preoccupied goodbye followed the interviewer, and the excited conversation rose again.

Three days later Nancy was found on the cluttered back porch of her house by the canal. She was moving heavily about, picking up behind a white boy and her bright-faced grandchild. Her face was still worried, but her manner was warm and friendly.

"I knowed you'd be comin'," she said, smiling, "but I looked for you yesterday." She sat down and settled herself for conversation, her long hands, still nice looking in spite of rheumatism, moving nervously over her gray chambray lap. "Dis las' gone August I was 72 years old," she began, "my sister say I older dan dat, but I know I born las' year of de war. I was born on governor Pickens' place, de Grove place fur out, and my mother was Lizbeth Cohen. Must have was my father a Indian, he brighter dan me, but redder. I kin' member Miss Dooshka Pickens, de one what went to Europe. Dey put all de lil' chillun in a row for her to look at, and she sittin' up on her lil' pony lookin' at us chillun. She was a pretty thing, yeah, I knowed her well. After de war my mother and father rented land, paid de rent. We liveded well. I would go to school three months when we first gether all de krep (crop). We had a colored teacher in de Baptist Church where dey taught school. De name was Spring Grove.

"My father died and mother, she moved over in

Ca-lina on General Butler's place. She work in de fields. I wouldn' go to school but three months in de year. When I growed up I work for Colonel Doctor McKie in de house. He de fines' doctor I ever knowed. I got married to General Butler's place where my mother was. I done had six chillun before I come to Augusta. I nused to work for Dr. Sam Litchenstein, 17 years. He moved to Louisville and dat thow me out anything to do. He tried to git me to go down dere wid him but I fell in bad health. Den my daughter and dis yere grandchild, I couldn' bear to leave dem. I cried when Dr. Sam lef', he was good to me. I nused to carry dis grandchild to his house wid me all de time."

As Nancy's plantation recollections seemed vague, she was prompted to talk about remedies and cures and on these her mind worked with speed and decision.

"I had high blood pressure so bad I couldn' walk right. My head nused to spin, laying down all night, couldn' res. One night I doze off in my sleep and a lady's spirit come to me. Her and my mother was two friends, her name was Cyndie Gardenigh. She say: 'Honey, in de morning when you git up, you git you some jimpson weed and put it wid cookin' salt and bind it on your head.' I done det. I nused to have long hair to my shoulder. Jimpson weed done cut my hair off, but it cured my blood pressure. Mus' did kill 'em!"

Asked how she treated her rheumatism, Nancy replied:

"Git a pint glass wid a pint of kerosene in it, and a block of camphor. Cut up de camphor and mix it round in de kerosene. Pat it on when de pain come. When I got up dis morning, dis yere hand I couldn' move, and now it feel a heap better. Lord, I done work so hard thoo' life, and all done tuk from me!"

A moment's silence brought shadows to Nancy's face. A twinge in her knee reminded her of rheumatism cures. She rubbed the painful spot and resumed: "You know what I am wearin' on my leg now? I made me two lil' bags and put a Irish potato in it, and when it drawed up jus' as hard as a log it done me good. But you got to steal two Irish potatoes, and put around both legs jus' below de knee. I jus' be leanin' back stiff all de time, couldn' walk. A old white man told me about dat. He see me walkin' along crooked and he say: 'Auntie, what's de matter?' I told him. He say: 'Now, I'll tell you what cure me. I was off in a furn (foreign) country, and a man say; me walking cripple, and he told me to steal two Irish potatoes and wear 'em, and when dey git hard you burn 'em up.' I specked I bin crooked up all kind of fashion if I ain't done dat: I always bind a piece of brass around my leg. Das' good like gold."

The eager grandchild was hanging over Nancy's shoulder, listening and smiling. The white boy edged up, and Nancy laughed. "Hunh! I spects dese chillun kin 'member tomorrow every word I tells you today. Dey knows everything." Her bony arm encircled the Negro child. "Jooroosalom oak—we got some and give it to dis lil' thing for worms. She went off in a trance and never come out until 2 o'clock nex' day. I think we got de wrong thing and give her root instead of seed. I never fool wid it no more it skeered me so. Thought we had killed de child."

Nancy was asked what her methods were in raising children.

"Bin so long I mos' forgot," she said. "All my babies growed straight 'cause I swep' 'em 9 times for 9 mornings from de knees down on out, dataway, and bathed 'em wid pot liquor and dish water. I ain' nused no root cep' sassafax roots to make tea outten das good to purge your blood in de spring of de year. Drinkin' water from a horse trough, I hearn' tell das good for whoopin' cough and all lika-dat."

"Dat daughter of mine, she had a wen on her neck big as a apple. An old lady come to me. 'I come to git my child today,' she say, 'a lady died dis morning and I wants to take her dere.' Well I didn' want my child gwine to de death house but she take her. De corpse ain' cold yit. She put her 9 times across, nine times straight, and dat child was cured. Yas'm, she got jus' as pretty face now! Ain' no use talkin', she straighten my child, her and de Lord! De wen went and jus' pass away. You got to do it before de corpse git cold, jus' after de breaf' pass out of de body."

"I done mark three of my chillun. Yas'm, I ruin't three of 'em. I was een de country and I was gwine thoo' de orchard, and de cherries was scarce. I looked up in de man's cherry tree, and one tree was full of fruit. Dey jus' as pretty! I say: 'Jim, please sir, give me one of dem cherries.' Jim say: 'No!' I stood dere wishin' for dem cherries, scratchin' my wrist, and my child born wid cherry on his wrist, right where I scratch! I took de baby and showed him to old man Jim, and he cry and pray over dat cherry and told me to forgive him and he never would do it no more. But he done it den."

"I live in de country. I come to town where a white man was down here on McKinne Street makin' dat soft white candy. I stood up and wished for it. It did look so pretty and I wanted some so bad and I didn' have no money. I was cryin', scratchin' my forehead over my right eye near de hair. He didn' give me none. When my gal born, she had white mark right on her forehead in de place I scratched."

"My sister-in-law made me ruin't my other child. Twas an old man coming along. He was ruptured. He had on a white ap'on, and she bus' out laughin' and say: 'Look at dat!' I jus' young gal, ain' be thinkin' and I bus' out laughin' too, he did look funny. I ruin't my boy. He was in de same fix and when I look at him I feel so bad, and think 'dat didn' have to be.'"

"Dis kin happen: anybody see another person wid pretty hair and rub dey hair down, dat child gwine have mustee hair too. A old black 'oman had a baby. She seen somebody wid dat mustee hair (das what we calls black folks wid smooth straight hair) and when her child born, everybody say: 'Look what dis baby got! Long black hair!'"

Asked about persons born with cauls, Nancy grunted:

"Hunh! My mother said it cover my head, shoulders and all! I kin see ghosts. Was a man lived right dere in dat house yonder. His name was Will Beasley but we call 'im Bee. De fus' time he got sick he had a stroke, den he git up. De doctor told him to be careful but he would go out. One night about 8 o'clock I see him go. I stay sittin' here on dis porch, and about 10 o'clock here come Bee out of his house, in his night clothes out de open door and cross de yard. He go behind dat house. I call out: 'Bee, I thought you was gone off?' He didn' notice me no more dan I never spoke. I got worried about him bein' sick and when he come out from behind de house I say: 'Bee, you bes' be gwine indorrs, dress lika-dat. You git sick again.' He walk straight back in de house. Pretty soon here come Bee down de street, all dressed up in his brown pants and white shirt! I grab de bannister just' a-tremblin' and de hair rizzed up on my head. I knowed den he ain' got long for here. He come on by and say: 'Nancy, how you feelin'?' I say: 'Bee, how long you bin out?' He say: 'Why, I bin gone since 8 o'clock.' I didn't say nuttin' but I knowed I seed his spirit and it was his death. He tooken sick two or three weeks later jus' before Labor Day, and died all paralyzed up. A woman come to my house and say: 'Nancy, give dis to Bee.' I didn' want to see him if he dyin' but I went on over. I call: 'Bee! Bee!' He say: 'Who dat, you, Miz' Nancy?' I say: 'Here's a bottle of medicine Miss Minnie sont you.' He say: 'I can't move my right side.' He was: laying wid his leg and arm in the air: stiff as a board. He say: 'Miz Nancy?' I say: 'Hunh?' He say: 'Go down de canal bank and tell my Minnie please come and rub me 'cause she know how. I want my Minnie.' Das de 'oman he bin livin' wid since his wife lef' him. I wait till de King Mill boys come along and call 'em. 'Tell Miz' Minnie dat Will Bee want her to come and rub him.' But she never did come till 12 o'clock and he was dead before she come.

"I did had a niece what died. She was about 20 years old and a good boy. Twas a year in August. I went on so over him, his mother say: 'Don't you know his last words was, 'I'm on my way to heaven and I ain' gwine turn back?' Don't worry, Nancy.' But I did worry. Dat night he come to me in spirit. He stand dere and look at me and smile, and he say: 'Aunt, I am all right. Aunt, I am all right,' over and over. Den it went off. I was jus' as satisfy den, and I never worry no more."

Nancy said she saw ghosts all through her childhood. She did not characterize them as "hants" but spoke of them throughout as ghosts.

"I seed 'em when I was chillun," she said, "me and my sister one night was comin' from spring. Twas in de winter time and jus' as cold, twas dark and I had de light. Sister say: 'Babe, don't let dat light go out.' Jus' den I seed it—a horse's head all spread out in fore! A big ball of fire! I yelled: 'Oh, sister, look at de horse wid a head of fire!' She knock me out for dead! She grab dat light and run home and lef' me in de wood. When I come to I run to my mother crying and she say: 'Now Nancy, you know you kin see 'em but you ought not to tell de other chillun and skeer 'em. You mus' keep it to yourself.' Ever since den, I won't tell nobody what I kin see. Yas'm, I wake up in de nighttime and see 'em standin' all 'bout dis house. I ain' skeered—when you born wid de veil it jus' be natchel to see 'em. Why, I sees 'em on de canal bank when de fog sprangles through de trees and de shape forms on de ground'.

"I hears de death alarm too. One kind of call comes from out de sky, a big howlin' noise, loud like singin'—a regular tune. De other kind goes 'hummmmmmm' like somebody moanin'. I was settin' down and de bull bat come in de house. Me and de chillun done all we could to git him out de house. A woman nex' door was name Rachel. I say: 'Rachel! Dere's a bull bat in here and we can't get him out.' You know what she done? She turn her pocket inside out and dat bat went out de door jus' like it come in! Dat a simple thing to do, ain' it? But it done de work. Dat was on Thursday night. Saturday morning I got de news that my babiest sister was dead. One of my boys was wid her. I was settin' down wid my head bowed, prayin', and a white man dressed in a white robe come in de house and stood before me and say: 'Oh, yeah! I gwine take your sister! Den what your child gwine do?' I sot down and studied and I said: 'Lord, I'll do de bes' I kin.' And Miss you know I had to take dat child back!

"Before I los' my husband ev'y time he go out to work I couldn' hear nuttin' but knockin'—ever he step out de house somebody come to de door and knock four slow knocks. If he go off in de night it wouldn' stop till he git back. I wouldn' tell him 'cause I knowed twould worry him. I say: 'Sam, les' us move.' He say: 'Honey, we ain' long bin move here.' But us 'cided to move anyway. Twas a big show in town. I let all de chillun go to de show. Time I got my things fix up to move and went to cook my dinner come de knockin' four times. I knowed he'd be took sick pretty soon. He didn' 'low me to work. Dat was a good husband! I had six chillun. He say: 'Honey, no! I workin' makin' enough to support you. All I want you to do is keep dis house clean and me and my chillun, and I will pay you de five dollars every week de white lady would pay you.' And he done dat, gimme five dollars ev'ry week for myself.

"A white lady was crazy about my work, jus' her and her husband. I got up soon one mornin', time he left, and runned up dere and washed her clothes and ironed dem. Den I started back home 'bout noon. I heared somethin' walkin' behind me. 'Bip! Bip!' I look round and didn' see nuttin'. I kep' a lookin' back and den I heard a voice moanin' and kind of singing: 'Oh, yeah! I bin here and done took your mother. I bin here and done took your sister! Now I'm a-comin' to take your husband!' Talking to me like-dat in de broad open daytime! I say: 'No, you won't! No, you won't!' I commence a runnin', cryin' inside. When I got home I thow myself on de bed shiverin' and shakin'. Twas no dinner done dat day. When he come home dat night he tooken sick and never got up again. He knock on de head of de bed jus' like de knocks come at de door, when he want me to go to him! He never lived but two weeks and went on to de judgment!

"One night dey was givin' my husband toddy. He drink some and wanted me to finish it. I told him no, I ain' drinkin' after no sick folks 'cause it mean death. His first cousin tooked it and drank it. He was a fine looking man in two months he was gone too!

"My husband come to me in spirit any time I git worried up. When I git in trouble he'll come and stand over me wid his arms folded behind him. He told me one night: 'You must pray, Nancy. You must pray! Um gwine help, and de Lord gwine help you too.' Missy, how you reckon he gwine help me if he dead? I ask de Lord and beg him to take me too, beg him to please carry me home."

Nancy was becoming more and more doleful, and to take her mind from the thought of her dead husband, she was asked about remedies.

"When us had de mumps mother git sardines and take de oil out and rub us jaws and dat cure us good. Sassafax for measles, to run de numor (humor) out de blood. When de fever gone, she would grease us wid grease from skin of meat. Git fat light'ood, make fire, cut de skin off bacon meat, broil it over flame and let grease drip into a pan, den rub us all over for de rash. Couldn' wash us you see, 'cep' under de arms a little 'cause water musn' tech us. For a sty in de eye we nused to say: 'Sty! Lie!' You see dat call 'em a lie and dey go on off. 'Um got a sty! Sty! Lie!' When witches ride me I took a sifter. An old lady told me de nex' time dey come, 'you put de sifter in de bed.' I done dat and dey ain' bother me since. A basin of water under de bed is good too."

Nancy had an experience with a gold digger. He came to board, and had an inconvenient habit of staying up all night. "I nused to have a old man stay here wid me. One night I couldn' lay down it was so cold, so I sit up and wrop in a blanket. He say: 'Nancy, see yonder! In de corner of your yard is a pot of gold.' Now I knows if you go and git de money what de dead done bury, you don't see no peace, so I told him he couldn' dig in my yard. I made him move. A 'oman say he went to stay wid her and when she got up one morning he had dug a hole in de yard big as a well, so she runned him off too. He had all de implee-ments but he wouldn' let nobody see him digging in de night. Well Miss, I knowed dat gold was truly in my yard, because I got up one night and looked out dere, and a white 'oman was standin' right where de old man say twas gold pot. I look at de white lady, a high white lady, and she kep' her eye down in dat corner guardin' de gold what she bury! Den I seed her go on off thoo' de gate and I knowed twas de spirit of de woman what bury it."

Nancy did not remember any stories about witches, booger-men or animals, but she did give a version of the story of the mistress who was buried alive.

"Dat really did happen in Edgefield," she said. "Marster los' his daughter and den his butler went to de cemetery and dugged her up. He was gittin' de jewelries off of her finger when she moan; 'Oh, you hurtin' my finger!' He runned back to de house and she got up out of de coffin and went to de Big House. She knock on de door and her father went, and he fainted. Her mother went, and she fainted. Everyone went to de door fainted. But her father come to himself and he was so happy to have his daughter back, he said God let de man dig her up and git her out alive. He made dat nigger rich. Gin him a whole plantation and two big carriage horses and a great big carriage and I dunno how much gold and silver. Told him he didn' want him to do anything but sit down and live off of what he gin him de res' of his life."

Nancy asked her visitor to write a postcard to her "dear doctor" in Louisville and tell him she was having a hard time. She insisted that the card be signed: "Your Carrie Fryer what used to work for you, with love."

"Come back and see me some more," she begged wistfully, "I bin callin' you in my mind all week."

PLANTATION LIFE

ANDERSON FURR, Age 87
298 W. Broad Street
Athens, Georgia

Written by:
Sadie B. Hornsby [HW: (white)]
Athens

Edited by:
Sarah H. Hall
Athens

Leila Harris
Augusta

and
John N. Booth
District Supervisor
Federal Writers' Project
Residencies 6 & 7

# ANDERSON FURR

Anderson Furr's address led the interviewer to a physician's residence on Broad Street, where she was directed to a small frame house on the rear of the lot. The little three-room cottage has a separate entrance from Pulaski Street. Three stone steps lead from the street to the narrow yard which is enclosed by a low rock coping. Anderson rents only one room and the remainder of the house is occupied by Annie Sims and her husband, George, who works at the Holman Hotel.

Reclining comfortably in a cane-backed chair, with

his walking stick conveniently placed across his knees, Anderson was enjoying the shade of a wide spread oak tree in the tidy yard. His costume consisted of a battered old black felt hat, a dingy white shirt, dark gray pants, and scuffed black shoes. Asked if he remembered the days when the North was fighting the South for his freedom, Anderson replied: "'Member fightin'! Why, Lady! Dey ain't never stopped fightin' yit. Folks has been a-fightin' ever since I come in dis world, and dey will be fightin' long atter I is gone.

"I dis'members what was de name of de town whar I was borned, but it was in Hall County. Lydia and Earl Strickland was my Ma and Pa. All of deir chillun is daid now 'cept me and Bob. De others was: Abe, Bill, Jim, and Sarah. Dere ain't much to tell 'bout what us done dem days, 'cept play and eat. Dem what was big 'nough had to wuk.

"Lordy, Miss! It's lak dis: I is a old Nigger, and I done been here for many years, but dese last few years I sho' has been a sick man, and now I can't git things straight in my mind lak dey was den. I knows us lived in log houses what had great big chimblies made out of sticks and mud. Why, dem fireplaces was 'bout eight feet wide, and you could put a whole stick of cord wood on de fire. Us slept on high-up old timey beds what had big posties and instead of springs, dey had stout cords wove 'cross to hold de mattress. De last time I slept on one of dem sort of beds was when I was a little boy, sleepin' wid my Ma. Pa and Ma was both field hands. Ma's mammy was de onliest one of my grandmas I ever seed. Her name was Ca'line and she lived wid Grandpa Abe on another plantation. Ma's sister, my aunt Ca'line was cook up at our Old Marster's big house.

"Money? Yessum! Dey gimme a little money now and den for totin' water to de field, sweepin' de yards, and a million other things dey used to make me do. De most dey ever gimme was 50 cents. I never spent none of it, but jus' turned it over to my Ma. Chillun warn't 'lowed to spend money den lak dey does now, 'cause dey had evvything dey needed anyhow. Old Marster, he give us plenty somepin t'eat, such as it was. Dere was lots of cornbread, a little meat now and den, collards, whip-poor-will peas and dem unknown peas what was most big as a dime, and black 'lasses—dat was lallyho.

"Us cotch lots of 'possums, but mighty few of 'em us Niggers ever got a chance to eat, or rabbits neither. Dey made Niggers go out and hunt 'em and de white folks et 'em. Our mouths would water for some of dat 'possum but it warn't often dey let us have none. I don't know nothin' 'bout no fishin' bein' done dem days. Yessum, slaves had deir own gyardens, and dey better wuk 'em good if dey wanted any gyarden sass to eat. Cookin' was done in dem big open fireplaces, mostly in pots and thick iron skillets what had lids on 'em.

"Boys wore long blue striped shirts in summer and nothin' else a t'all. Dem shirts was made jus' lak mother hubbards. Us wore de same thing in winter only dem shirts was made new for winter. By summer dey had done wore thin. When de weather got too cold, Marster give us old coats, what grown folks had done most wore out, and us warn't none too warm den wid de wind a-sailin' under our little old shirt tails. Our shoes was rough old brogans what was hard as rocks, and us had to put rags inside 'em to keep 'em from rubbin' de skin off our foots. Us didn't know what socks and stockin's was dem.

"Marse Earl Strickland owned us. Miss Sarah was his old 'oman and dey was sho' mighty good to deir slaves. White folks was heap better folks den dan dey is now anyhow. Now-a-days dey will knock you up right now, and won't be long 'bout it. I can't git up no ricollections 'bout 'em havin' no chillun a t'all. Seems lak I know for sho' dey didn't have none. Dey never had no fine house neither; jus' a plain common house wid a chimbly at both ends.

"Oh, Lord! Marster never had no overseer; no car'iage driver neither; didn't even have no car'iage yit. He did have a surrey what he hitched mules to and driv for hisself. Warn't no hoss on dat plantation, nothin' 'cept mules.

"How big was dat plantation? Good Granny! it was so big I never did git all de way over it, and dere must a been 15 or 20 slaves. Old Marster got us up 'bout sunrise and fetched us in at sundown. He was all time knockin' on his Niggers 'bout somepin. He 'lowed dey didn't do dis, or dat, or somepin else right—he allus had to have some 'scuse to knock 'em 'round."

A little Negro boy, possibly five years old, came up to Anderson with a peach in his hand and said: "Look, Uncle Anderson, C.T. done gimme dis peach what he stole off dat dar wagon." The old man reached out his hand. "Boy, you gimme dat peach," he commanded. "You knows I lak peaches. Give it to me, I say. I do declar', nigger chillun jus' got to steal anyhow. Run git yourself 'nother peach off dat wagon, but don't you let dat man see you git it. Put dat peach under your shirt 'til you gits in dis yard, and if you leave dis yard 'gain I'll buss your haid wide open. Does you hear me, Boy?

"What was dat you was a-axin' 'bout jails, Miss? Yessum, us had 'em. Niggers would git too rowdy-lak, drinkin' liquor and fightin', and dat was when de white folks slapped 'em in de gyardhouse, widout a bite to eat. Gyardhouses is called jails dese days. I'se lak my Ma. I'se a fighter. Ma would jump on anybody what looked at her twice. De onliest time I ever got in de gyardhouse was a long time atter de end of de big War. A man owed me some money, and when I axed him for it, he got mad and knocked me down. I got right up and knocked him out, and right den and dar I was sont to de gyardhouse.

"Good Lord, Miss! Slave folks warn't 'lowed no time for to larn readin' and writin'. Deir time was all tuk up in de field at wuk. Slaves went to de white folks' church, but one thing sho' dey couldn't read de Bible for deirselfs and couldn't write none. Jus' to tell de truth, I didn't take in what dey sung at church, but I ain't forgot dem baptizin's. I'se been to so many of 'em. Evvybody went in dem days. Dere warn't no place in de church houses for to be ducked dem days, so de white folks had a pool dug out by de branch for de baptizin's, and white folks and slaves was ducked in de same pool of water. White folks went in fust and den de Niggers. Evvybody what come dar sung a song 'bout 'My Sins has all been Washed Away, and I is White as Snow.'

"Slave fun'rels was mournful sights, for sho'. Dem home-made coffins was made out of pine planks, and dey warn't painted or lined or nothin'. And slave coffins warn't no diffunt from de ones de white folks used. Our

Marster sot aside a spot in his own buryin' grounds for de slaves' graveyard. When dey was a-buryin' folks dey sung a song what went somepin lak dis: 'Oh, Lord! Us takes 'em to de Graveyard, Never to fetch 'em Back.'

"If slaves did run off to de North, I never heared nothin' 'bout it. Oh, Lord! I jus' can't talk 'bout dem patterollers, for it looked lak all de white folks tried to jine up wid 'em. How dey did beat up us pore Niggers! Us had to git a pass for dis and a pass for dat, and dere jus' warn't nothin' us could do widout dem patterollers a-beatin' us up. Dey beat you wid a cowhide lash what cut a gash in your back evvy time it struck you. Yessum, white folks and Niggers was all time quar'ellin' and fightin'.

"When slaves got in from de fields dey et deir somepin t'eat and went to bed. Dey didn't have to wuk on Saddays atter dinnertime. When our old Marster turned us loose, he turned us loose; and when he wuked us, us sho' was wuked. De young folks had deir big times on Sadday nights. Dey danced and frolicked 'round sort of lak dey does now. Evvybody went to de meetin' house on Sunday, and dere's whar Niggers had a good time a-courtin'.

"Christmas was de time when old Marster let us do pretty much as us pleased. Us had all kinds of good things t'eat, and atter us drunk a lot of liquor it warn't long 'fore dere was a Nigger fight goin' on. Yessum, us had cornshuckin's, cotton pickin's, quiltin's, log rollin's, and all sich as dat. Wid plenty t'eat and good liquor to drink on hand, Niggers would shuck corn or pick cotton all night. It was de big eats and lots of liquor dat made slaves lak dem things.

"Little slave boys played wid sun-baked marbles,

made of mud, and old rag balls, what was sho' a heap diffunt from what chilluns thinks dey has got to have dese days 'fore dey kin have a good time.

"Marster had mighty good keer tuk of his slaves when dey got sick. Dere warn't many doctors dem days. Dey jus' used home-made medicines, mostly teas made out of yarbs (herbs). I jus' can't git up no ricollection of what yarbs dey did put in dem teas. I does 'member dat chillun had to live wid bags of assfiddy (asafetida) 'round deir necks to keep off ailments. Ma give me and Bob, each one, a block of dat assfiddy for good luck. I throwed my block 'way a few years ago, and I ain't had nothin' but bad luck ever since. Dat's why I can't git up de things you wants to know 'bout. My mind jus' don't wuk right no more.

"Dem yankees was on de go all de time. One of 'em come to old Marster's house and axed one of my uncles to go off wid him. Uncle was old and skeered and he thought de yankees might kill him or somepin lak dat. When de War was done over, old Marster told us 'bout how things was. He said us was free and would have to do de best us could for ourselfs. Dem was happy days for Niggers. Dey sho' didn't take no more foolishment off of white folks atter dat, and dey don't pay 'em no mind now. Niggers got so bad atter dey got deir freedom dat de Ku Kluxers come 'round and made 'em be'have deirselfs. One of dem Kluxers come to our house and set down and talked to us 'bout how us ought to act, and how us was goin' to have to do, if us 'spected to live and do well. Us allus thought it was our own old Marster, all dressed up in dem white robes wid his face kivvered up, and a-talkin' in a strange, put-on lak, voice. None of Marster's Niggers never left him for 'bout two or three years. Dere warn't no way for

Niggers to buy no land 'til atter dey could make and save up some money. Marster jus' paid up his Niggers once a year, at de end of crap time. It warn't long atter de War was over 'fore dere was some few schools for Niggers scattered 'round 'bout.

"When did I git married? Lordy, Miss! Such things de giverment do want to know 'bout pore old Niggers! It warn't 'til ten years atter us was freed, dat me and Martha Freeman got married up together. Dat was one sho' 'nough fine weddin' what Miss Sallie Morton and our other white friends give us. Dey give us evvything us had at dat big old feast. Dere was three tables full, one for de white folks, and two for de Niggers, and dem tables was jus' loaded down wid good things. Willie and Ida was de onliest chillun me and Martha had, and dey never lived to git grown. Martha died out and den I married up wid Mamie White. Us didn't have no chillun and Mamie's daid now. Dey's all daid 'cept me.

"I thinks it was a good thing Mr. Lincoln and Mr. Davis did set us free, and I sho hopes de giverment won't never fetch slavery back no more.

"I never will forgit de day I jined up wid Morton's Baptist Church. I had done helped my Pa build it from a brush arbor to a sho' 'nough church house. De reason I jined up was 'cause de Marster had done changed me from nature to Grace. I thinks evvybody ought to jine up in de church 'cause it's de Lord's will.

"Miss, I done told you all I knows and I'se a sick man, so go 'long wid you and let me take my rest."

Slave Narratives

www.ingramcontent.com/pod-product-compliance
Lightning Source LLC
Chambersburg PA
CBHW071649160426
43195CB00012B/1401